D1418628

When I Was Old

When I Was Old

GEORGES SIMENON

TRANSLATED FROM THE FRENCH BY
HELEN EUSTIS

HAMISH HAMILTON
LONDON

First published in Great Britain 1972
by Hamish Hamilton Ltd
90 Great Russell Street London WC1
Copyright © 1970 by Georges Simenon
English translation copyright © 1971 by Georges Simenon

SBN 241 02037 9

Originally published in French under the title
Quand j'étais vieux

Printed in Great Britain by
Lowe & Brydone (Printers) Ltd., London

*"I only did what I could,
no more than I could. . . ."*

CLAUDE BERNARD (1878)

PREFACE

In 1960, 1961, and 1962, for personal reasons, or for reasons I don't know myself, I began feeling old, and I began keeping notebooks.

I was nearing the age of sixty.

Soon I shall be sixty-seven and I have not felt old for a long time. I no longer feel the need to write in notebooks, and those that I did not use I've given to my children.

Epalinges, December 24, 1969

First Notebook

1960

/Saturday, June 25, 1960

It's been four days—from the twenty-first—since I finished a novel, my hundred-eightieth-and-some, which I'd wanted to be easy. But the first day that I began to write it, towards the ninth or tenth page, I had the feeling that it was useless to try to go on to the end, that I wouldn't be able to make it come to life.

As I always am when I'm writing, I was alone in my study, with the curtains drawn. I paced up and down five or six times, and if they hadn't seemed in some way human, I would have torn up those few pages and waited a few days before beginning another book.

That has happened to me two or three times in a year. This time, I began to sob. Then, without too much confidence, I went back to my typewriter. Now I think it's the best of the Maigrets. I will know when I begin the revision. Since the Cannes Festival, I've been wanting to write a novel that would be full of sunshine and tenderness. I had one in mind, with the characters and the background at hand. I only wrote three pages of that one. It wasn't about Maigret, and my principal characters were in their thirties. I suddenly realized that in *Maigret et les Vieillards*, which in a way replaced this abandoned novel, I expressed the same tenderness, put in as much sunshine, but with characters who were all between seventy-two and eighty-five years old. . . .

Well then! That isn't at all the kind of thing I meant to put in this notebook. But I must begin somehow. I have neither any intention of writing my memoirs nor of keeping a journal. Do I

3

want somehow to arrest the flow of life from time to time? Not that either.

I believe that in reality it's much more childish than that, that it stems from a time long ago. From the age of seven or eight, I've been intrigued by paper, pencils, erasers, and a stationery store always fascinated me more than a candy store or a bakery. I loved the smell of it. A special kind of yellow pencil, too hard to be used in school, seemed to me more elegant, more aristocratic than anything I could think of. The same way with certain papers, for instance a drawing paper which was called, I think, Whatman paper and was used by those of my mother's boarders who were studying to be mining engineers at the university. They worked for weeks or months on the same sheet. At the end, when all the tracings were retraced with India ink (the elegance, also, of those little bottles!) they washed the much-used paper like linen.

I suppose my passion for notebooks dates from that same period, not for my school notebooks which seemed childish to me, but for what were called student notebooks, square-ruled, fat, with a red top stain, bound in thick gray or tan canvas. I would slip into the students' rooms to look at these, touch them. Nearly all of them were filled with tiny, scarcely legible writing, and scattered through them were geometric drawings for the science courses, or parts of the human body for medical studies.

I was about eleven years old, I think, when I finally bought my first student notebook, knowing as little as I know today (forty-seven years afterwards) what I was going to put in it. My name on the first page, of course. Then a few lines of verse, several quotations taken from the writers whom I was reading then. I probably filled three or four pages that way, with plenty of blank spaces between.

At fifteen, a new notebook, and this time the poetry in it was my own. Two pages of it at most.

Third notebook at twenty-one. This was the period when I was writing stories for newspapers. I wrote between three and seven a day, to make a living. In the evening, in my notebook, I wrote

4

"for myself." I remember twenty stories which I must have kept in some file, since after they were written I typed them up.

About the typewriter, it seems to me now that I, who so loved beautiful papers, notebooks in hard cover, pencils, penholders, began at the age of sixteen and a half to type because it was expected at the paper where I was a reporter. I got so used to it that for years, even decades, I've been virtually incapable of writing by hand.

In 1940 I bought other notebooks, at Fontenay-le-Comte, where I spent part of the war. By that time it was already impossible to find real student notebooks of the kind that so impressed me in my childhood. No more canvas bindings. No more red top stain.

This time, in '40, I wrote on the first page, in India ink, the word *Pedigree*. Then, on the following page, I drew a sort of genealogical tree of the Simenon family.

This notebook was intended for my son Marc, and I did not hope for any other children, because a radiologist had just told me that I had a year, or two or three at most, to live.

Curiously enough, chance decreed that it should turn out like the other notebooks. I wrote a certain number of pages in which I described my childhood and especially my family for the benefit of my son who, according to the radiologist, would have little chance of getting to know me. (Marc was a year and a half old.) Claude Gallimard came to see me, bringing news of Gide, whom he'd met several times in the Free Zone. (In Nice, I think.) Claude had spoken to Gide of these notebooks. Gide, with whom I corresponded for several years, asked me to send him one. After which he wrote to advise me to abandon the pen and the first person and to type my life story like a novel.

The manuscript pages became *Je me souviens*.

The typed text became *Pedigree*.

Of the three or four notebooks I bought, only one and a half were filled!

(I just mentioned my correspondence with Gide. It is almost the only regular correspondence I have kept up with anyone. And it was always Gide who invited my letters. Actually, I have never written letters unless I had to, and while I do have some friends, I never write to them without some definite reason. As for my wife D., since we have never been apart she hasn't a single letter from me.)

I return to the story of the notebooks. From 1940 to 1960, nothing. Not even trivia. Then, early this year, a telephone call to my friend and publisher Sven Nielsen to ask him to have a dozen made for me. They weren't a total loss, but the shape wasn't long enough. The corners were less rounded. The top stain wasn't red. For three months now these notebooks have been in a drawer in my study and I fear my children's covetousness, for my son Johnny shares my passion for paper, pencils, etc.

Am I trying once again to satisfy a youthful longing? That's a real part of it. It's true that I have long dreamt of being seated in a familiar study, surrounded by objects that I love, and writing by hand. That is how I imagined the life and work of a writer.

Actually, not only have I written most of my novels on the typewriter (except, a few years ago, a sort of daily scribble, in pencil, for non-Maigrets) but I have never lived in my study, I have never known the satisfaction of writing by hand.

Except when I was writing popular novels to learn my trade and earn my living.

Since I first tried my hand at creative writing, it has been a laborious process, hours of anguish rather than euphoria. The more I wrote the more difficult it became, or, more exactly, the more I got stage fright.

Now this anxiety has reached such an intensity that I am physically sick with it on the days that precede the beginning of a novel and on the first morning.

I used to write my novels in three or four days (the popular ones).

Then twelve a year (at the time of the Maigrets).

Then six (for nearly twenty years).

Now it is down to four, because the older I get, the more they exhaust me. It is true that each time I struggle towards greater concentration.

(Gide asked me once how I managed, in the course of a scene, to give simultaneously a sense of the present, the past, and the future. I answered him, truthfully, that this had been my aim from my very first stories on. In fact, one of these stories, *M. Gustave*, written in the notebook of my twenty-first or twenty-second year, bears testimony to my endeavor to make time merge in some way. I have never experimented. I have never tried out new styles as I went along. I have always tried to move forward slowly in the same direction.)

Does all this explain why this morning I began to write in this notebook? Has it a more or less fixed goal? Like the *Pedigree* notebooks? I am thinking mostly of my children. I am addressing them as much as I can. Will they be curious to know more about their father someday? I'm not sure. As for the public . . . Will anyone still be concerned about me and my work in twenty, thirty years? I don't know, of course. At any rate, I don't intend to pose for posterity. On the contrary. I had rather destroy legends, get rid of all the "glamour," all the picturesqueness, to say:

"It's much simpler than that!"

No! Whether I go on with this notebook, these notebooks, or abandon them again; whether they are published one day or whether they remain in one of my children's drawers does not matter to me.

I'm not making a confession. I'm not explaining myself. I'm telling neither my life story nor anecdotes about people I've known. Nor have I any intention of explaining my ideas. If I have any, I suppose they are in my novels, in which case, that's where people should look for them.

To tell the truth, I feel an almost physical desire to be at my desk, without anxiety, without the pressure of creation, of working, of bringing characters to life. But to write just the same. Not to have to reread. Not to have to worry over correcting sentences, their rhythm, their life.

To write for writing's sake, which I once thought was the writer's business, when I was twelve years old. And perhaps it's partly true. Only I'm not a writer. I'm a novelist. And the novelist does not know the joy of writing.

In short, the pleasure I offer myself, at fifty-seven, is, finally, from time to time, to write like a dilettante.

I once knew an old Italian mason who lived in Cannes. In the evening, coming home from his shop, or Sunday after mass, he devoted and still devotes his free hours to building, in his very modest garden, the most outrageously elaborate houses and castles, on a doll's scale, on the scale of the sand castles that children build at the beach. There are bridges joining the miniature houses, windmills, what not. Perhaps someday a cathedral a foot high correct in every detail?

A mason for others during the day, in the evening he relaxes (or takes his revenge) by being a mason for himself, a mason for pleasure, building buildings that serve no purpose.

Perhaps that's what I'm doing. If I see my mason in Cannes, I promise myself I'll ask him how old he was when he began to fill his garden with buildings. It would be odd if he was a little under sixty!

/*Monday, June 27, 1960*

Spent yesterday, a typical Sunday, with a *Match* photographer. He's here for four days, after which he will be joined by a journalist for what they call a feature story. It's the fourth that *Match* has published in seven or eight years about me and my family. These two will be followed by *Good Housekeeping*, then by an Englishman who wants to write I don't know how many articles.

Every three or four months we open our doors to journalists this way, one after another. They are almost always charming intelligent people at first glance, and perhaps they really are. Whether they come from Finland, Germany, or Italy, they appear to be making an effort to understand. They listen, take notes, declare that they will make this one "different," that they will make it "true."

Then, whether it is in Lakeville, in Cannes, or here, the photographers ask us to take the same poses, in the same spots, so much so that the children now know in advance just what they must do.

The journalists always ask the same questions. Haven't they read the articles their colleagues have published? Most of the time they haven't read my books, either, or only a very few.

This has gone on for thirty years, and for thirty years I have wondered if there are really any readers for these articles. I must believe there are, since the editors of newspapers and especially of magazines say they know just what their readers want.

So? Always the glass showcase, where I have never lived, where I have never written a novel, although my friends of long standing, the people who must know, say it's true—and say it to me—that they have seen me inside this cage.

The legend has been established, once and for all, and whatever I do, whatever I say to those who interview me, it is this legend that they publish. It hardly matters what I have told them during those two, four, or eight days. It hardly matters what documents I've shown them. It hardly matters that they have sworn to me to tell the truth, and that they have sneered at their colleagues.

The article will be the same, with the same photographs, and the same mistakes. For they even garble the name of the village, the titles of the novels they mention. And if it's a matter of figures, they multiply by five, by ten, when it's not by a hundred.

Tablets have been just discovered revealing, it seems, that Herodotus did the same thing with history, and so, we already knew, did Pliny.

Won't my children and my grandchildren be tempted to believe this legend too? This irritates me. Wrongly, no doubt, for what importance has it?

Nonetheless I wonder if one reason for these notebooks, for this notebook (for nothing suggests to me that there will be others),

9

may not be to try to re-establish the truth. An approximate truth too, no doubt, since there is no other kind. What discourages me a little is my conviction that it will interest no one.

The photographer just arrived and, of course, takes advantage of my writing by hand to take pictures. So now it will be printed that I always write my novels with a pen, in square-ruled notebooks. One myth supplants another!

/Saturday, July 2, 1960

Last night I was in a great hurry to sit down to this notebook for it seemed to me that I had a lot of things to write in it. Now, this morning, when I have all the time in the world, I find myself confronted with what is nearly a void. My ideas have evaporated, or rather they don't seem important to me any more. To some extent that's the reason I have to write my novels so quickly. After a few days, what I call the state of grace threatens to abandon me, and my characters, whom I believed to be very much alive the day before, suddenly have become strangers.

I have just spent nearly a week with the photographer and editor from *Match*, then with an English journalist.

The superiority of photographers to most journalists. I've often observed them when, at Cannes, for example, they descend in a bunch, almost in a swarm, on their victim. They seem hard, cynical, almost cruel. They often are—aren't "raw" shots demanded of them? They're used to all kinds of dramas and, above all, to all sorts of truths. Actually they do have a good deal of contempt for their victims. A false smile, a studied pose, faked nonchalance, and phony sincerity don't deceive them. Perhaps that's the reason why they can appreciate the truth better than anyone else. So they really seem grateful when you don't try to fool them, to give them a chance not to be tough.

The *Match* photographer, who lived four or five days in the bosom of my family, had not known me before he came but left as an old friend. The writer, theoretically more "cultured," but who managed to ask hundreds of impertinent questions, came to do his work, no more, and add an article, a victim, to his collection.

Why do we receive them and give them our precious time when we might be relaxing? Not for reasons of publicity, for these always inaccurate articles risk wearing the reader out and even, little by little, turning him against an author.

Still less out of vanity. I don't mind explaining myself to a man who is trying to understand, and whose opinion means something to me. But that isn't the case with ninety-nine per cent of those journalists, especially magazine editors.

If it's a beginner, or a free-lance writer for whom this article could be important, I'm sure to remember my own beginnings and give him his chance.

But what about the others, so thoroughly smug, who think they know it all, that they are judges of everything, can solve all questions? They arrive at an author's house having read only a few of his books, some time ago, or even having read only one, on the train or the plane.

Each time, however, I have hope. A hope of finally correcting legends, destroying exasperating myths, getting rid of continuing untruths.

There is none. I always answer the same questions. And I end up feeling sickened.

"How does the idea for a novel come to you? . . . Then what do you do? . . . What time do you begin writing? . . . On the typewriter or by hand? . . . How many hours a day? . . . How many days? . . .

And now I, in turn, must ask myself a very disagreeable question. For thirty years now, since the beginning of the Maigrets, I have given the same answers. For they have to be the same. If I were suddenly to declare (which would be untrue) that I begin to write at midnight, or that I dictate, my old answers would be printed just the same.

. . . Names from the telephone book . . . Index cards . . . Outline on a yellow envelope . . . the coffee I make in the kitchen . . .

I follow this whole routine because I believe it is necessary if I'm to set off the mechanism, so much so that it has become a superstition. . . .

And if, like the readers of magazines, I too am a victim of legend? If I have begun to believe in it by the sheer force of seeing it in print?

What stops me from writing at eight o'clock in the morning instead of at six or six thirty? From not writing a whole chapter at a sitting?

The proof that it's possible is that at Cannes, when I was convalescent and unable to follow my routine, I wrote *Le Fils* entirely by hand, several pages in the morning, several pages in the afternoon, without worrying about the length of the chapters and without making myself recopy them on the typewriter afterwards to give my sentences a sterner rhythm. It wasn't I but my wife who typed *Le Fils*, and this novel is no worse than the rest. It isn't even different from them.

Then why did I go back to my routine right afterwards?

Because of saying over and over that . . .

This bothers me. I'm tempted to escape the rules I have imposed on myself. Isn't it stupid not to dare?

The ritual I've adopted is as strict as the mass, I don't know why, and I've tried to explain it because I've been asked to do so.

I've succeeded so well at it, I've proved so many times that it was necessary to me that now each move has its logic which I finally believe in myself. In spite of the precedent of *Le Fils*. . . .

And this will go on until I begin to write anyhow, anywhere, and on any paper—in ink, in pencil, or on the typewriter, without thinking that for this reason the fire won't ignite.

Then I'll have to explain to the journalists . . .

Why, Lord? What has this to do with them or with those who read them? And above all, why should I concern myself with it?

In three days, just the same, I will repeat the same story—always a true story—to an English journalist who will ask me the everlasting questions for eight or ten days because he has to write thirty columns. It's more exhausting to me than a novel. It gives me no satisfaction. Nothing but irritation when, later, I read the outcome of these interviews.

Why not have the courage to say no, to close the door? Charles Chaplin does it more often than not. Once or twice a year he receives journalists for a very studied photograph, a family group, posed like a royal portrait.

I've wondered if really he is so indifferent to what the public thinks of him. I've envied him. And now he is busy writing his memoirs, in several volumes, without any interference from a journalist.

So it's the opposite of indifference. He wishes to set down his truth or his legend, just like Gide and so many others.

Which reminds me of one of the first questions Gide asked, if not the very first, when, at his suggestion, we met for the first time.

"Tell me, Simenon, at what period did you choose your character?"

Now I'm not sure if he said "choose" or "fix." I didn't understand him immediately.

"My character?"

For a moment I wondered if he weren't speaking of Maigret, and I almost answered that he was not my character, that Maigret was only an accident to whom I attached little importance.

No! He was talking about me. He explained:

"Each of us, at one age or another, creates his character, to which he remains more or less faithful. . . ."

This confused me a good deal. I only understood what he meant when I saw photographs of him at different periods. It was true. From the age of eighteen or twenty, there were the same poses, the same look as at sixty.

Isn't that frightening? I haven't chosen any character. I've changed my attitudes a hundred times. But I wonder now if it isn't, at least in part, because I've read in the papers that I work in such and such a way that I continue to do so.

That depresses me. It seems to me that *I am obliged to* . . .
One of these days I'll have to give myself a shake, not do what is printed in the newspapers.

In that case, it will be best to say nothing about it, so as not to become imprisoned in a new legend.

In fact, I'll have to cheat!

/*Saturday, July 9, 1960*

Revision of my novel *Maigret et les Vieillards* finished.

In five days. By working six or seven hours a day. Otherwise, say seven days at three hours a day, or twenty-one hours of writing. Add to that more than thirty hours to revise. The first Maigrets were revised in one day! I daren't reread them.

All of yesterday, an English journalist who is here for several days, and, during the afternoon and evening, often two of them at once, Roger Stéphane, who wants to write a book on me. I talked nonstop. I tried to explain, to convince, and I didn't even convince myself. I should have the courage to refuse these interviews. From hearing the same questions asked, from hearing myself talk as if about a "case," I end by not believing in myself.

I always stress the role of intuition. In good faith. It's what I believe in. But by talking about it periodically for hours or days, I run the risk of becoming too conscious of it, or losing that very intuition.

On the other hand, should I, instead of answering them, let them write all their nonsense which irritates *me* so?

I would like to be able to be silent. I am, for months of each year, at least nine tenths of the time; then I allow myself to be tempted by contacts. I have nothing to gain by it. I have everything to lose.

Although I drank nothing but water and Coca-Cola all day yesterday I find myself this morning with a hangover and a bad conscience, that sort of near-physical depression and anxiety of the drunkard.

A moving letter from Miller in the mail. He believes in my stability. He envies me. He's probably right. But, by continually furnishing reasons for this rather precarious balance, by analyzing it, by dissecting oneself for the benefit of others, doesn't one risk going completely off the track?

To be silent, yes! But then one seems pretentious. And this silence would require a good bit of arrogance, like Montherlant's, and I don't have that.

Quiet! I promised myself not to talk about these things any more. And here I am, after more than a week of interviews, and ten minutes before starting in again, with the need to explain myself in writing! . . .

Explain what? There is nothing to explain.

/*Sunday, July 10, 1960*

In a few minutes, as I do every Sunday morning, I'll be going with the children to get the papers at the Lausanne station, and then for a few minutes' walk on the shore of the lake at Ouchy. Tradition. The house is full of small traditions. I think I'm the one who unintentionally inculcates them in the children. Isn't that a bit like a guardrail or the banisters on a stairway?

It's possible that I'm repeating myself—I hate to reread. Even, and above all, my novels. Revising them is torture. And when a film is made from one of my books, if the producer or director wants my advice, I hardly can recognize the story he's talking about. I have to ask my wife to reread the book for me and then to remind me of this or that detail.

That's not at all what I wanted to jot down before going out. It was only a sentence that struck me in my bath and which will probably come back to me at the last moment. Yesterday, three people to question me, each one following his own notion, which I'm unaware of. For example, the English journalist (a former lawyer) observed me and asked questions for two or three days and will continue for an indeterminate number of days without my being able to guess what she has in mind, the point of view she's taking. It's a little like stretching out on an operating table without knowing what operation the surgeon is going to perform. An unpleasant thought.

S., himself a novelist, a biographer, has come with a definite idea, a character he has already decided on, and I sense that he is determined for me to be this character. He scales down reality to a point where it coincides with his point of view. He could just as well write his book or his essay (?) in Paris without having met me.

Stranger still was the one sandwiched between these two sessions of questioning. A criminologist, a professor in the Law Faculty of Poitiers, a graphologist to boot, he came to interview me for . . . *L'Echo de la Mode*. Each time I say something he declares:

"That's not for our audience. . . ."

What is for his audience? A few picturesque touches, carefully arranged, a few anecdotes, also arranged.

But he announces that he will be *also* writing for a law or criminology review.

All this is a bit confused and reminds me of the Festival at Cannes, where from morning to night I shook hands, answered questions, without knowing any more who was who or what he was doing there.

There are those, I know it from friends who have been in my position, whom this reassures, to whom this idea gives a sense of their importance. Not I. On the contrary. If I had complexes, and I can't be sure I don't, this would give me an inferiority complex.

Good! I'm getting to my little idea from the bathtub. Last night, showing pictures to the Englishwoman (this gives me a subject, a connection, instead of talking in a void), I stumbled on a pile of photos I took in Africa, while passing through the Belgian Congo, from the Sudan to Brazzaville, around 1932 or 1933. Different races, different tribes, at different levels of evolution. At the time, I wrote several articles entitled "The Negro's Hour" (published in the magazine *Voilà*, which no longer exists).

I got them out of the files. But will I have the courage to re-read them? At that period, Paris was covered with posters for a film, *Africa Speaks*. It was made by the French government to encourage enlistments in colonial troops.

(Yesterday I observed to my Englishwoman that Kipling, on a literary level, is a victim of political evolution. The English are distressed when you mention him. It reminds them of their pride in the Victorian era, a state of mind for which they have both nostalgia and a sense of sin.)

This morning the radio announces serious trouble in the Congo. The blacks are disarming white officers and throwing them in prison. The Belgians who live there are fleeing. . . .

Troubles in Cuba, also in Italy . . . Not to mention Algeria. . . .

I have a horror of wars, of cruelty in all forms. . . . Horror of the use of force, of violence.

But, listening to the radio this morning, I wondered if war really is the result of ambition, of nationalism, etc.

Or if it was not quite simply a necessity, not just of biological selection, but, for man, for survival? If wars, since the earliest times, had not served, without man's knowing it, to produce types who are capable of endurance?

Certain American schools no longer begin teaching History with the Egyptians, nor with the Sumerians, but with paleontology, if not amoebas. One's perspective is changed by this. Our revolutions and our wars diminish, are only a little ripple.

The white of today is only the result of many cross-breedings of races.

And if it were necessary, for the man of tomorrow, how many other cross-breedings . . .

This gives me or permits me a somewhat caustic serenity.

I had to glance at the last sentences written, otherwise I'd have gone on about the same subject. I was no longer sure of whether I'd spoken of it here or to one of the journalists whom I saw afterwards. I'm surprised to realize how small is the number of more or less original ideas—or ideas we believe to be original—that we carry with us through the years and which are sometimes enough to furnish a whole lifetime.

We shouldn't even discuss them for we get nothing in return but a certain ridicule. The mandarins have raised barriers between different domains of the mind which it's better not to cross because the response is only shrugged shoulders. Doctors, for example, are the most susceptible to this. If there is anyone who tries everything, it is they. They paint (annual salon of doctor-painters in Paris) or are art critics, often very poor ones. They discuss the theater, literature, music. In a single year I've received four or five novels from doctors, novels whose themes have nothing to do with medicine. The suggestion that literature is at least as complicated as medicine would be poorly received by them. But just dare to put forth an idea on a medical subject . . . In the Anglo-Saxon countries they have invented, or rather adopted, the word "layman," previously used by priests, if I'm not mistaken.

However, the history of medicine is easier to study than that of literature. Most of them don't know it very well. Many of them don't keep up with their colleagues' work, and French doctors, for example, almost purposefully ignore American discoveries except for those that have reached a point of general and universal acceptance.

Isn't it the same with all specialists?

But why the devil don't they admit that a novel, a sonata, a picture, are also the work of specialists who have given years to research as arduous as the research of the laboratory?

If a Faulkner, a Picasso, a Buffet, a Prokofiev judged a new serum, a biological theory, with a phrase, condemned a certain tendency in psychiatry with a word, how ridiculous!

Any small-town doctor, anyone at all, in fact, can judge a work of art *ex cathedra*.

And I shouldn't go outside my specialty either. Each time I allow myself to express an opinion—and I can't resist—no matter how timidly, with how much humility I do so, I still feel I have diminished myself and that I invite sarcasm.

And if I promise myself not to talk about myself!

But whom should I talk about, for God's sake?

And why not have the good sense to be quiet?

A man doing his work all his life without saying anything about it, without anyone knowing anything about him. There must have been some. I only need to open a few works that are not five feet away from me to assure myself of that, but I haven't the courage. And I'm afraid it would humiliate me.

Same day, 10 o'clock in the evening

Two friends in the drawing room, whom I'm separated from only by an open door. Sat them down in front of the television; *Hamlet* at Carcassonne. Am tired of talking, a little sickened. I find pamphlets on the Algerian war in the last mail.

In the television news, three stories, three massacres: Cuba, the Congo, and the plane shot down in Russian waters.

I have a horror of violence in any form, of brute force. I want to be indignant. I am indignant. Yesterday I saw young Belgians, in their twenties, who sang as they climbed into the plane taking them to the Congo. Proud to have guns. Proud of going to fight.

And basically, I know, they aren't really soldiers, these are little boys who are making noise so as not to feel frightened.

Horror of political discussions, articles, newspapers that speak of greatness (meaning force, always), horror of politics.

Then I wonder if I'm not wrong, if all this isn't normal, if it isn't the biological law of natural selection. I sometimes reach the point of wondering if it isn't out of a sort of cowardice that I condemn all show of power in my innermost soul, and I hesitate to talk as openly with my sons about it as I've been doing here.

I am certainly bringing them up like young anarchists. Johnny already hates uniforms, war.

Am I right? Am I wrong? An idea came to me just now that should be developed at length and better than I could do it, and this idea reassures me.

Not altogether. Not too much. It is too tempting to believe what suits one's temperament and mind.

The history of the entire world, what is written, sculptured, painted, digested in encyclopedias, could actually be concentrated in a few hundred men (who could be further reduced to a few dozen), philosophers, scholars, artists, who are the landmarks of our evolution and who are enough to give us a little pride in our humanity, a little hope.

Power has always been against them, whether it was serving religious ideas, political, or patriotic. Almost all those to whom we have erected statues were to some extent, at some period of their lives, victims of force, of brutality, and the ideas which incite these.

So why should it be otherwise today? For three years I have refused, even in more or less official ceremonies, to wear decorations. Don't these indicate that the powers consider you a good servant? A good servant of force?

Trite, of course. But behind these clumsy sentences I feel something that I haven't managed to express. Nor is it in any of my novels. I avoid even alluding to it there, touching on any idea of this kind. Not for fear of displeasing, but out of modesty, for fear, too, of seeming committed. In fact I'm not, neither on one side nor on the other.

The committed man, whatever he is, makes me afraid, makes me bristle. I wonder if he is sincere. And, if he appears to me to be so, I wonder if he is intelligent.

I only speak of this to my ten-year-old son. It doesn't interest my eldest. So much the better? Maybe.

I love man. His history, above all his first stammerings, moves me more than all the dramas about passion. I love to see him in search of himself, century after century, failing each time, forcing himself to go on again.

How heartbreaking it is to watch him, no longer alone, but in a crowd, and to hear those who call themselves his leaders and who are so because they have been chosen.

These notebooks are definitely not destined for publication, and I believe, if I go on, that I will ask my heirs to destroy them after having read them.

They only serve to rid me of what gnaws at my brain. When I have to answer an important letter, I do it at once so as not to have it nag me for days. I do the same thing here, I bury what is bothering me so as not to think about it any more.

This morning, as every day recently, I was feeling in top form physically. None of my usual and also, I suppose, unimportant little troubles. So my morale is excellent. (Trotsky, whom I met once in his exile at Prinkipo, wrote some astonishing and moving lines on man's aging. Fifty-five years old. I'm fifty-seven.) After luncheon, slight argument with my wife. Not even disagreement. Misunderstanding, for no reason. That was enough. A little afterwards, in town, vertigo, pain in my shoulder, etc. And, if I let myself go it would have been total collapse. Everything takes on another color.

The slightest touch is enough. The body follows.

In spite of the work of psychotherapy, medicine is no less largely technique, occupying itself with the disease more than with the patient (except for a few old family doctors who most often don't keep up with medical progress).

And justice treats men as if they were constantly the same, whether fasting or well fed, at rest, euphoric, overworked, or after a conjugal dispute.

Not only is each one a special case, but each should be studied at each hour, at each minute of each day.

It's impressive to think that one is only an instant in the history of the world, only a portion of that instant, and that this portion, which has no present, is imperceptible.

Trite, to be sure. Not to be written down. But it passes the evening.

Still, I had a bad afternoon because of a word ill understood, an intonation that changed my mood and, as a result, my physical equilibrium.

Another word, perhaps, a look, a pressure of the hand, would restore my well-being.

Is it wrong to be so involved in the inner man, to want to understand him, cure him, with such tenacity? Have we come to a sort of sentimentality and was health, on the contrary, rather in the untroubled brutality of what once was called the hero?

Every day my pediatrician friends see the birth of infant idiots, of Mongoloids, of monsters of all sorts who will remain monsters and whom charitable institutions will pass back and forth from one to another.

Others display prodigies of skill, of devotion, create a science almost, out of pure kindness to keep alive (?) impotent old men who are a burden for family and for society.

Criminology, in its way . . .

I believe in it. I'm one of those. I feel that I am of the family of those who devote their time to trying to better man's life, no matter what man, no matter what human embryo, no matter what offal.

Is this really a good? Doesn't one risk creating an anxious, self-pitying humanity, incapable of facing realities?

Will there be enough men to take care of others, to be responsible for them? Enough strong ones for all the weak?

Will there be any strong ones left at all?

All this, again, because of a small cloud in the conjugal sky! What would it be after a real argument?

Actually, I know the answer, because at least once I took my pistol out of its case.

/*Sunday, July 17, 1960*

Lots of people in the living room with the door open. This has gone on for three days. Good friends, however. Talk. Listen. Talk. My not drinking is no help; it goes to my head all the same. And later I'm ashamed of what I've said, of positions I've taken or seemed to take. I have had enough of talking . . . maybe also of listening. I would have liked to write at length this morning, about Brisson, about Gide, about sincerity, about small ideas of no importance that have plagued me since yesterday. Maybe I'll do it tomorrow. I hope so. Talk to myself, in fact. That way I have fewer complexes. A rotten word which I detest.

/*Monday, July 18, 1960*

A short respite before my guests come up and the Nielsens arrive. The latter don't tire me because with them I don't have to make any effort at conversation. Yesterday, Pierre Benoit. That's a different matter, for he is devilishly sly and at the same time very sensitive. I'm always afraid of hurting him, and I have the feeling of talking on tiptoe. In any case that has little to do with what I wanted to write.

I wrote four pages that I crossed out because there were too many names, too many people who are still alive and whom I wouldn't want to hurt.

In spite of the discrepancy between their public and private lives, I still question myself on their sincerity.

The question bothers me. Others, much younger than I and

who have lived less, don't have such scruples and readily talk about hypocrisy and cynicism.

Put them in the presence of a human being and they flee him after a short contact.

Not only have I scruples, but I don't understand. For I don't believe in force, physical or moral, nor in cynicism, nor in calculation, at least not in the sense intended by these people of whom I've been talking.

I try to understand and I see that it's very hard. Financiers? Celebrities from Paris or London? Stars of Europe or California? Fame, money, power, life . . .

All this doesn't exist, doesn't exist in a state of nature. After all, they are only men, as vulnerable as the rest, if not more so.

From this point of view I wonder how, why . . . How do they manage to write what they write, to believe, or seem to believe, in what they would have us believe . . . ?

I would like to call them decent men. As decent as the average laborer, as the conventional and often generous white-collar worker.

However, they react to the Congolese crisis only in terms of their shareholdings in Katanga, or the Cuban crisis in terms of their instinctive revulsion against Communism.

They falsify everything, the Algerian war and internal politics. Do they really see only what they want to see? Is it a strain for them, and have they moments of doubt, when they know that they shirk the truth?

Don't their interests force them into convictions which seem incompatible with everything they know to be true?

They meet great doctors, biologists, lawyers who daily deal with men as they really are.

How can they go on seeing man as he is not, seeing him as he ought to be in the interest of their interests, so that their own image may stay untarnished?

It's too easy to see these people as all of a piece. I know they are weak, riddled with complexes, that they are often afraid, ashamed, that they seek reassurance.

But my intelligence, because once more I must use terms that everybody uses, furnishes me no satisfactory answer.

For myself, the only possible approach is to write a novel, to become, for the time being, the character, to feel as he feels. I have the impression, perhaps the illusion, that this gives me more of the truth.

I could have cited other names, other men whom I know as well or as slightly. It happens that these, here, have come in contact with me in one of the rare periods when I haven't put up a fence around my life as a working novelist, and around our family life.

The parade has gone on for two weeks. I have a hangover from it. It's possible that I repeat myself—repeat myself often. Indeed I have always been astounded at the small number of ideas—and can one even call them ideas—that a man collects in fifty-seven years of life. I'm not speaking of ideas one can get from books, of course. I'm speaking of those that have been digested, of what is left, of what has finally become part of ourselves.

Is there really anything left?

A certain attitude, perhaps, with me a curiosity which is never satisfied, a desire to understand and not explain, to feel the real man beneath men's appearance.

I often have the impression that it would only take a little extra effort to discover that I am like them, that they are like me, that it is only habits, attitudes, words in which we differ.

Even if they upset and infuriate me, I love them, perhaps because I feel they are weak.

But why the devil do these people censure, and why do others, in turn, censure them?

/*Tuesday, July 19, 1960*

The last ones have left and I'm a little ashamed of the relief my wife and I feel. For I really like them, these people who came to share a moment in our life. Some of them are friends. I have a deep affection for Sven Nielsen because I believe I understand him. Even the journalists, when they've gone, leave me with a pleasant memory.

Still, it is more and more disagreeable to see our house invaded, its rhythm broken, people sitting in my chair (the one in my living room where I watch television) and in my wife's.

The obligation to speak, to listen, becomes almost unbearable to me and perhaps it's so I won't have to listen that I talk so much.

Is it age? Once I liked to be close to people, and the days without visitors seemed empty and dull to me. I would chase around, to Montparnasse, to the Coupole, or what have you. That was the great era of Montparnasse. I even had a bar in my own house on the Place des Vosges (1925 or 1926) where I officiated with professional flourish. No doubt I had a reason. No children. Just my wife.

Perhaps there was another reason too. I was young, just arrived in Paris. I had everything to learn. I had discovered, or believed I had discovered, that men reveal more of themselves when they are having a good time than when they are at their work. I spent evenings and nights at dance halls, at cabarets, looking, listening. The later it grew, the more people who must have been impressive in their offices became accessible, often pitiable.

In my bar on the Place des Vosges, I forced cocktails on my guests in order to produce more quickly the release that would permit me to see them naked.

But the evenings when I drank myself? Wasn't it just an alibi then? And if, during the small hours of the morning, I arranged it so that several women were naked, was that just to study the behavior of the other males, or for my own satisfaction?

I must speak of this sexual question, for others have spoken of it (like P. in the book he dedicated to me), and in my opinion they have been completely mistaken.

I don't intend to write a confession on this subject but to express certain very simple truths.

For the moment, what concerns me (not much, really, but enough to get it off my chest) is this sort of instinctive withdrawal, more into myself than into my family, into my house, into certain rooms of that house; my irritation when my routine is interrupted. If it is age, too bad. But I'm not sure that's it. I was greedy for contacts up until . . . until I met D. in New York in 1945. And I've become more and more miserly with our intimacy. The children enlarged the circle. Echandens * is arranged around us, according to the functions of each and all of us. I feel comfortable here. I establish habits here. Going into my study in the morning (not to work there, I'm not speaking of the times of the novels), my eyes seek a certain reflection on a piece of furniture, and a pencil out of place bothers me. I am with the children, in thought, in the house. I know where each one is, what he's doing.

Don't strangers have anything to teach me any more? Have I no more curiosity? I have no idea, but isn't it odd that I feel disturbed even by the children (and by the staff) if they burst in when I'm alone with my wife, if for instance they come into my room when we're having coffee after lunch?

D. and I aren't even talking; we're looking through the papers. We pass them back and forth and it's a half hour of what at fifteen I called perfect happiness. At that time too it went with coffee and reading and additionally the eating of a wartime pudding that I had concocted myself, since rationing kept us hungry.

I continue to love people, to be curious about them, to become passionately involved in their behavior, in their "motives," but at the same time I have a passion for our little family universe.

The respite will be short. The nurse has left for a few days of vacation. One of the maids has had an operation. My wife is without a secretary until August. This means that I will not see her except on the run, busy with her different functions. On the weekend she will begin to pack, since we have promised Johnny and Marie-Jo to take them to Venice for ten days.

This trip will no doubt be pleasant. I'm looking forward to it as

* At the time of writing, Simenon lived in the Château of Echandens, near Lausanne.

they are. Nevertheless I feel a certain uneasiness about leaving the house.

I've spent my life traveling, moving, changing my ambiance, my habits (except the ones that are connected with my work). But now I hesitate to leave my shell. It was the same way in Lakeville, in Carmel, in Tucson, in Florida.

I make my nest. I settle down with my family and I hate to leave until one day, without knowing why, I don't feel at home any more and I take my little world elsewhere to start all over again.

I wonder if when I take off that way it isn't because of people, neighbors, intimates, all those whom you are forced to become acquainted with when you live somewhere. You spend a certain amount of time meeting them. When I know them all, when I can no longer step outside without being spoken to, I leave.

Is that the real reason? Are there others? The fact that reality doesn't last long, for example? I mean the time during which one regards as real, as important, as personal, certain walls, certain furniture, the color of the curtains, the road to town . . .

There must be something to that, because each time I move I get rid of my furniture and most of the objects so as to start again almost new, from scratch.

To start one's life over each time from scratch!

That's almost the same miracle that each child brings us: reliving the first years with him.

There, perhaps (Pierre is thirteen months old), lies the explanation I seek at random.

People who come steal a moment of life from me, leave a hole.

/ Wednesday, July 20, 1960

I've thought for a long time, in fact since I began to observe people, that I learn more about them when I talk than when I listen.

If they speak, they generally repeat dicta which are always the same and which reflect the truth as they wish it were. When I speak to them, when I try out different ideas on them, their reactions are much more revealing.

I just took this notebook to write that single paragraph, which had been more pithy when I first thought of it and which I wished to turn better. Now, there is sun in my study this morning, for the first time in ten days. This delights me. I am also delighted by rain, and I delight in a spring that is unlike any I have known since 1940.

I could swear that for the two months of the invasion it didn't rain once. As I wrote in my last novel, it was the kind of spring one remembers from childhood. May and June of that year were tragic. The invasion, the defeat, the retreat, fear, and, no doubt, also a certain shame (why?), refugees on the roads, air raids, the uncertainty of tomorrow. Now, what remains the most vivid in my memory is the sun, the color of the sky and the sea at La Rochelle, the smell of spring and of the terraces. I could swear, too, that I'm not the only one, that for thousands of soldiers and of refugees the tragic has been obliterated, leaving only this impression of radiant life.

For example, lying in a field to escape strafing from a plane which passed so low that my eyes met those of the pilot (he didn't fire), I discovered some wild plants that I had not seen during years of life in the country, plants that I used to see as a child when I went to play on the parade ground at Liège or on the bank of the canal, plantain for example, others I don't know the name of which grew beside the railroad tracks, beside rivers and roads.

For three months I have wanted to write a novel about this period, about a refugee from Jeumont separated from his daughter and his pregnant wife by the bombardment of a train (it is cut in half, each half going its own way afterwards). Not concerning himself with his family but with a warm female lying near him in a cattle car. He is having an unexpected holiday, in fact.

———

One might say that the collective is quickly forgotten to allow only the individual to survive. Which explains why history is necessarily false.

My son Pierre, at thirteen months, amazes me by his capacity for wonder. This would seem to confirm my theory of little joys which is no doubt infantile, though I have continued to maintain it since I discovered it at twelve or thirteen. A hundred times a day he points to a picture, a flower, a piece of furniture, the design in a carpet, a bedspread, and, as if in ecstasy, gives an "Oh . . . !" of delight. Everything is beautiful. Everything is a source of pleasure.

It was the first feeling he expressed, months ago. Will it last? I hope so. Johnny, at ten and a half, still has the same enthusiasm, with the difference that if there is a shadow in a picture, a little fault in an object, a delay in expected joy, he suddenly falls into despair.

Pierre doesn't see the shadows yet.

I myself adjust to them.

Same day, afternoon

Certain works can be written only by the young. I wonder if this is because they demand more energy—creative energy. In the long run, I think it is because they are affirmative works. Later, one no longer affirms. One asks questions. But are one's works less good? They are different.

If I think this way, is it because I am reaching the age when others have stopped writing novels? Are we inclined to believe —in perfectly good faith—what reassures us?

This brings me back to people's good or bad faith. I don't willingly believe in intrinsic bad faith. This would demand, like true evil, true vulgarity, more strength of character than I see in man.

Man needs a certain amount of self-respect. You might say that he comes to terms with what is called his conscience.

Later, if someone should read these lines, it is possible that he will be amazed that at this moment I have preoccupations which do not appear to be proportionate to reality.

The Belgian Congo—Cuba—Algeria. A heightened awareness almost everywhere, in students (this delights me), threats of war . . . if the event were to take place tomorrow, which is not impossible, one would be tempted to say:

"At the edge of cataclysm, a man asked questions about . . ."

About very small things of a more or less personal order, I confess.

I'm not the only one. It has always been that way.

History happens every day and the importance of events only becomes evident after the fact.

One doesn't live with History, or rather one doesn't live History. One lives his little personal life, or that of a group, or of an instant of humanity, of an instant in the life of the world.

Besides, all these little questions which plague me have a relation to what one calls the great questions of reality.

In rereading the history of the scientific discoveries of the last three or four centuries, especially all those in the field of medicine and biology, I have been amazed to observe that they almost all grew out of the patient observations of naturalists, scholars depicted in popular illustrations as beings with wild hair and armed with magnifying glasses, dedicating their lives to a single species, almost always a very lowly one, a fly, a mold, an oyster, a frog. . . .

These scholars are the only ones whom I envy. True, just like other men, they only rarely arrive at certainties. The further they advance, the more their questions lead only to other questions. However, they do succeed in contributing one solid little stone, one pebble of truth from which others will build edifices of hypothesis. I think of the researchers at the University of Leiden, of the correspondence they exchanged for two or three centuries,

31

from country to country (often in wartime), a few resolute men bent on enlarging their knowledge of the nature of our species. In spite of battles and blockades, the Royal Academy of London corresponded with scholars in Paris and neither one nor the other were considered traitors.

Like the great naturalists, I would like to focus on certain human mechanisms. Not on grand passions. Not on questions of ethics or morality.

Only to study the minor machinery which may appear secondary. That is what I try to do in my books. For this reason I choose characters who are ordinary rather than exceptional men. The too-intelligent man, the too-sophisticated, has a tendency to watch himself living, to analyze himself, and, by that very process, his behavior is falsified.

I devote myself, in short, to the least common denominator.

If I were capable of understanding snails or earthworms, I would be happy to write a novel about snails or worms, and I would no doubt learn more about life and about man this way than in drawing my characters from contemporary men.

In interviews, I often speak of the naked man in contrast to the clothed man.

What a dream to go back, if it were possible, like the biologist, to the unicellular organisms!

Pierre woke up and we went to do errands in town. With the three children. Three and not four because Marc is married. Next there will be two left with us, then one, then . . . It's true that Pierre is only a little over a year old. My mother will be eighty next week. I don't know her well, and she knows me still less.

Isn't this inevitable since I left her when I was nineteen? We lived nineteen years together, during which I was first a baby, then a little boy barely aware of the world, then a student more interested in his teachers and comrades than in his family, and finally, at fourteen, fifteen years old, a secretive boy.

Isn't it always this way? Marc too left at twenty. Do I know him any better than my mother knows me, although for those twenty years I observed him as passionately as I observe his brothers and his sister?

Of our children too, all we know is a moment, a fraction of their development. They, for their part, only know of us the person we are at a given period.

On that we judge each other.

How not to be mistaken? Marc's friends in Paris know a man whom I can only guess at, and his wife too knows him better than my wife and I, who raised him.

The naturalist is luckier: he can study within a species a certain number, a great number, even generations.

As for us, we only know the second half of the generation that precedes us and the first half of the one that follows us.

As for our own generation, is it possible for us to see it with a clear eye? One has only to look at old classmates or fellow members of a regiment who meet and warm to each other when their only shared point is having been born in the same year in the same town, or of having passed eighteen months in the same camp.

A man who had seen four or five generations born and dead, for example, would be interesting to listen to. On condition, of course, of being able to understand him. Wouldn't he risk having himself locked up?

P.S. Perhaps it will be objected that we have the lessons of history at our disposal. But history has only been lived and written by men who can draw on a maximum of eighty or ninety years. Same for philosophers. No, in the understanding of man (the opposite of the so-called sciences) the experiences of one and another cannot be placed end to end. They are superimposed. Perhaps each erases the preceding one. To put it another way, men cannot be added up. They replace each other. So that isolation appears to be a miracle—or an accident, in the least agreeable sense of the word.

Enough, poor Jo! It's time to go take a walk with the children, who still think you have answers for all their questions.

Sun in my study. Going to go into town with Johnny and Marie-Jo. I've always loved the city in the morning, especially on a nice morning, when the shops are tidying up. It's a little like a stage being set. I remember pubs in Liège, on the Rue de la Cathédrale, for example. Sun on the sidewalk. Inside, a bluish shadow, and the waiter, not yet dressed for the day, sweeping up the sawdust or spreading it afresh. Smell of beer. Barrels of beer rolled on the sidewalk, and enormous brewery horses which wait, sometimes striking the pavement with their hooves. Their conspicuously enormous stallion's member hanging almost to the ground.

I'm beginning to understand why so many writers have kept a notebook, a journal. You write freely, without thinking of the reader. It's chatting with yourself.

You can allow yourself to be ridiculous. Yesterday, for example, I was thinking of Rembrandt. I was reviewing in my mind some of his pictures. And it wasn't accident that these images came to me. I had just been recalling those men who, in a very few centuries, had created biology, given new dimensions to the world. The father of Cartesianism foreshadowing Darwin and Freud. Perhaps Einstein too.

Suddenly it seemed to me that these discoveries existed seminally in the pictorial world of Rembrandt. His chiaroscuro is already a critique of pure reason. Man no longer has definite outlines. For the first time the figure is not the essential element. It is part of a whole. Space has more value than man.

Are painters precursors? I have only to take a few steps, to open a few works to find, on pages which I know, references that would give some weight to this embryo idea. Parallel, with dates to support it, between certain works of art and certain discoveries.

I'm almost sure that it is the works of art that came first. Corot, van Gogh, Gauguin, then the Impressionists . . . The Impressionists most of all, who placed man in a new context. The real (I mean what up to then passed for real) is closely mixed with what yesterday was still unreal.

Didn't Dostoevsky precede Freud? Freud himself said he had read him and one may wonder if, without the Russian writer, he would have created his new image of man.

If that's the way it is, I'm behind the times. Abstract art would itself be a sort of precursor and it is a fact that it confirms scientific theories that are coming to light. Now, outside of a few exceptions (why?) abstract painting irritates me or leaves me cold. So I shall only be able, like so many others, to go a little way down that road. And, if it's the rule, a man living in two hundred years, according to my hypothesis of yesterday, would teach us nothing since he would stop after having accompanied human evolution on his own bit of the way.

I say evolution. I never dare pronounce the word "progress," for the same reason that I mistrust the word "happiness" and its opposite. It seems to me that in the end everything is compensatory.

Is a middle-class American who earns four hundred dollars a month happier than the peasant of the Middle Ages? With the monthly bills to meet, the necessity of buying what advertising imposes on him, is he any less a slave?

Another embryo idea too, which is funny, or rather which places me among the laymen, the dilettantes who adventure into forbidden territory. Four or five years at the university, a few books—which are, after all, within anyone's reach—a few courses which are only lectures, without contact, most often, between the professor and the student, several hasty visits, for future doctors, to hospital rooms, are enough to establish a barrier that none can breach without being ridiculed.

Too bad! I won't pay attention to it, at least in these notebooks. And what does it matter if someone says later that I was riding my hobbyhorse? Is it any better to play cards or with an iron-ended stick and a hard little white ball, as in golf?

Bacteriology, and especially virology, fascinate me. Even here, to be taken seriously (?), I would have to look at one of the books I've made notes in, cite names, references. I don't want to clutter up my mind or my memory with what I know is at my disposal in my library.

Well then, I have the impression that there is a tendency (oh, barely perceptible!) towards the simplification of diseases, or, more exactly, that some researchers are more or less consciously moving towards a unity of disease.

The Greeks (it was not Hippocrates but, if I'm not mistaken, his successors) have already said that there are no diseases but only sick men.

Then a number of diseases, more and more serious, were discovered and classified. After the bacteria and Rickettsia, the virus was arrived at. Eight-hundred-and-fifty-some at the last census. Now, seen through the electronic microscope, they are all the same and one cannot distinguish one from another.

Forty-eight viruses just for influenza.

And all evolve. New forms develop from cultures.

By dividing, does one not move towards simplification, to arrive, perhaps, one day at that unity which some foresaw and sought?

Hasn't this unity almost been attained in physics?

To arrive finally at one disease, *Le Mal*, Evil, or the destructive principle, but as many forms of this illness as there are invalids.

For a number of years we knew only of four types of blood—O, A, B, and AB. Then the Rhesus factor was discovered. By now, seventeen or eighteen new subdivisions have been found, and a hematologist told me recently that it is not impossible that each person has a different type of blood.

At the same time, about forty per cent of specialists tend to consider virus as a chemical composition rather than as living matter.

From there to thinking that the reactions of different types of blood in the presence of an element which is unique in principle but which is transformed by each new contact, that these reactions, say I, constitute *the* multiform disease, rather than diseases . . .

There is nothing scientific about this, obviously. But weren't the theories of a Paracelsus often even more literary?

It would be curious, intriguing. The mystic foresees science as Confucius foresaw the composition of the atom.

Man first envisages unity.

Then, forcing himself to divide, to partition, to multiply the elements . . .

And, by dint of dividing thus, returns to unity.

It is unimportant whether this is true or not. It delights me. And it gives me an impression of complicity with the world that surrounds me. I should say of solidarity, but I prefer complicity.

It bothers me to belong to a human group, a nation, a race, a society. I feel more at ease in thinking that I am part of a vaster whole in which I am side by side with amoebas, on a level if not of equality, at least of . . . I can't find the word and I won't stop for it.

A difference in time. The happenstance of arriving at this or that point on the curve. I am a man but I could have been an amoeba. Difference of degree, then, in evolution.

It will be said that I haven't sufficiently digested reading I wasn't prepared for. It's very possible. So much the worse and so much the better. I say so much the better because I find it to my profit.

Noon. I'm back from a short walk in town—and purchases, of course!—with the children. Each time I open this notebook it's with the intention of writing a sentence or two. Then I stretch it out.

Medicine and social work, during these past years, have more or less suppressed natural selection. A new law has been added to the famous Rights of Man: the Right to Life. The right of the embryo to become a complete so-called being, at any cost. And already one glimpses the Right to Health. Free medicine, free care foreshadow it, as free studies foreshadow the Right to Knowledge.

By dint of claiming or receiving rights, won't man come to lose them all? What will be left of him, what will the human being be after several generations of no selection?

And, as for the Right to Health, what will happen on the day, which seems near at hand, when worn-out organs, deficient glands, will be replaced by other human organs?

Yesterday, at a medical convention that was held in London, an expert from the United States (I don't like the word "expert" which the newspapers and consequently the public today apply to anyone with a diploma who enunciates any hypothesis whatsoever), an American expert, that is, could say, without rousing any protest, that by about 1980 or 1990 medicine will be able to practice prenatal selection of the individual, in the embryonic state, that it will be possible to produce human beings of superior intelligence (by what criterion?) and human beings who, totally fearless, will make ideal soldiers, all muscle, and others . . .

So many centuries of effort to arrive at the ant!

Is this science's answer, its solution, to the problem of natural selection? The word "natural" no longer applies since it is a matter of a human, in some sense abstract, solution.

This frightens me as much as planned teaching, the schoolboy's report book which, beginning with his twelfth year, accompanies the future man, comments from teachers and physicians who, at various stages, decide first the fate of the child, then that of the young man, then that of the adult. Custom-made competencies to fit the needs of the community, taking natural aptitudes into account.

This revolution—for it is one, and very much more important, I think, than the French or the Russian Revolution—is being accomplished under our eyes without arousing a single protest.

Social security is no less a revolution since it assumes that man is neither free nor responsible for his own future. The community takes him in charge. And, taking him in charge, takes on, in all logic, rights over him. Yesterday, in the French Chamber, for the first time the principle of the suppression of home distilleries was discussed.

This means in general that drunkenness in the provinces is costing the State too much. It also means that the apples from his apple trees no longer completely belong to the farmer since he may not turn them into alcohol *for his personal use.*

Aspirin also is dangerous for some people. And so are fried potatoes. These are far-reaching things. I wonder if those who decide these measures realize what they imply.

(I am always the first to deplore drunkenness, but isn't it an illness, both individual and social, which, has only the vaguest relationship with apples, plums, and the wastes that these home distillers transform? What frightens me—or makes me laugh—or enrages me, I'm not quite sure—is the erosion of certain basic principles that were in use for so long and their replacement by principles that are not yet written, nor formulated, but which spring no less from measures which, at first glance, appear to be only measures of a practical order.)

/July 22, 1960

The other day I spoke of evenings spent in dance halls and cabarets, then of nights on the Place des Vosges. This was my first contact with a world other than the one that was open to me in Liège. At that time I did not really know either the country or the sea. The country only by having gone three or four years for several weeks at a time to Embourg, where one arrived by trolley, and which is now a suburb. The sea by having seen it twice from the Belgian coast. I was a real city boy then, used to pavements, houses touching one another, small gardens separated by walls.

I think it was in 1924 that I went to Bénouville, then to Etretat, and that I spent three or four months there. In 1925, at Porquerolles, I discovered the life of the sea, of fish, of crabs, of algae, and I remember that it made me dizzy and frightened me. It was a little like wine that was too strong. Above all, what I discovered was the incessant struggle for life, how fish were always on the defensive or on the offensive; innate, indispensable cruelty.

The next year, I wanted to discover France, and I didn't do it by highways or railroads. I wanted, as I've since tried to do in all things, to look behind the scenes. It wasn't as a sporting event (it wasn't one at that period) that I chose to follow rivers and canals from the North to the South and from the East to the West.

A little town, a village, are not the same seen from the river or from the canal as they are seen from the road. One sees their true face, their most ancient one, this way.

My first boat was the *Ginette*.

A year later, I had my second boat built at Fécamp, the *Ostrogoth*. I brought it first to Paris, where I had it christened (on a whim) by the priest of Notre Dame when we were anchored at the Vert-Galant.* Then Belgium, Holland, Germany.

At Delfzijl, on the bank of the River Ems, I wrote my first Maigret; there and at some other places, among them Stavoren, where I spent the winter on board, two or three other novels in the same series were written.

But I didn't intend to tell here about my life at that period, at least not today. Again I only meant to put down a few sentences.

After my return to Paris, there followed a succession of trips almost right up to the war. Norway and Lapland in winter, then a long tour of Europe, Africa, in particular a route from East to West, at the time a very difficult and complicated undertaking, the United States, Panama, the Equator, Tahiti, New Zealand, Australia, India, etc. Also Russia, Turkey, Egypt . . .

Now I'm at the point I was aiming at. I was not in search of the picturesque. There's little of that in my novels. You can count on your fingers my novels which I would call exotic: *Les Clients d'Avrenos* set in Turkey, *Quartier Nègre* in Panama, *Coup de Lune* in Gabon, *Quarante-Cinq Degrés à l'Ombre* covering the

* A famous restaurant on the Ile de la Cité, on the Seine.

route from Matadi to Bordeaux, *L'Aîné des Ferchaux* in the Congo, *Le Cercle de la Soif* in the Galápagos. I may have forgotten some but not many. *Touriste de Bananes* in Tahiti, *Long Cours* a little bit of everywhere. Still the exotic element did not play any great part.

I maintain that when one lives in a place, a tree is a tree, whether it's called a kapok tree, a flame tree, or an oak.

Local color exists only for people who are passing through. And I hate being a tourist.

I'm not seeking the sense of being abroad. On the contrary. I am looking for what is similar everywhere in man, for the constant, as a scientist would say.

Above all I'm trying to see from afar, from a different point of view, the little world where I live, to acquire points of comparison, of distance.

I traveled at my own expense. But since I knew several newspaper or magazine editors, before I left I proposed to one of them a series of six, eight, or twelve articles to be written under contract, which would cover my expenses. I did the same when I traveled for nearly a year in the Mediterranean, on my third boat, the *Araldo*.

Since, in the past week, the Congo has figured so large in the news (what style!)—it still does—I felt a curiosity, which I've never had before, to read over the articles I wrote. I was surprised at first to see that my style then was so full of sparkle, much more brilliant than my style of today; and that fascinated me, because for years my chief effort has been to simplify, to suppress, to make my style as neutral as possible in order to make it fit as closely as possible the thoughts of my characters.

What struck me most was that these hastily written articles, with no philosophical or political intent, foresaw everything that has since happened in Africa. The very title could be used today: "The Hour of the Negro."

And the conclusion: A film at that time was called *Africa Speaks*. I took this title and added: "It Tells You: Shit!"

On Sunday, my publisher Nielsen and I debated whether to republish these articles, which would no doubt help people to understand the African situation today. Sven had decided for it. Finally, I said no.

I am a novelist and want to be only a novelist. Above all I don't want to give prominence to manuscripts I've dug out of a drawer. The title of another series, on Eastern Europe, in 1933, is no less curious to read today: "Hungry People." Then it was audacious, almost a taboo subject.

Another series, "Europe 33," was a panoramic view of Europe during a moment of its history.

"Mare Nostrum," a consideration of Latin–Anglo-Saxon antagonism. Even then I was sometimes pulled to one side, and again to the other, which explains how I was able to feel myself American during ten years in the United States and return to being more or less Latin in Europe.

Eventually, in these articles and in others, I rid myself, in advance, of what I didn't want to put in my novels, the picturesque, and also of some more or less philosophical or political cogitations.

I didn't do it on purpose. I instinctively adopted this hygienic practice which I've consciously discovered only today.

There is another series that I must reread, in spite of my horror of rereading myself. It is called, I believe, "Police-Secours," a study of crime in Paris, taken by districts and written for a daily with a large circulation.

Now once more I find studies of the same kind in the very professional *Journal of Criminal Law, Criminology and Police Science,* published by the Northwestern University School of Law in the United States.

I'm not foolish enough to take myself for a prophet or a phenomenon. What I note, with satisfaction, I admit, is that unconsciously I've steered my life in such a fashion that it has served my function as a novelist, little by little ridding myself, in the form of articles, of what could not serve me and which threatened to weight me down.

If I've just gone on at such length about it, it's because it explains my need of these notebooks. I no longer write articles (nor stories, nor novellas). I'm incapable of it. I no longer think that my feeling on this or that subject has any value whatsoever. I would not dare make statements, as in "The Hour of the Negro," and finally my style has been "neutralized," "toned down," to such an extent that outside of a novel it seems dull. I need to advance "step by step," slowly, by little touches, with backward glances, regrets, to wed the simplest states of mind of my character with the simplest possible words. The story, the novella, demand plots, telescoping, and finally what is called ideas, things that have become foreign to me.

With these notebooks I have found the means of releasing the overflow; in any case, that's what I hope. Whether the formula works (the term "formula" is not correct here, since I did it without conscious purpose and anyway all this is only a hypothesis), I will only know after I've written several novels.

It's taken me four pages to say such a simple thing!

/*Saturday, July 23rd*

I was right not to get too excited over the Congolese affair. Last night we learned that everything was settled, not so much by the offices of the UN as between the Congolese government and an international financial group that is largely American.

For eight days now the papers—even those of the right—have been revealing financial combinations influencing the attitudes of Belgium, of Kantanga, etc. A few years ago, they would not have mentioned them. This backstage activity was then known only to some initiates. In France and in many other countries this sort of thing is still kept secret from the general public (in France, the affairs of the Sahara, Algeria, etc.; in England, "scandalous" stories about the Court).

With regard to the Congo, one might say that an ingenuous people suddenly refused to follow the rules of the game and spilled the beans. Naïveté or trickery, it makes little difference.

Previously, only a few people in the know. Then, in what is called democracy, a few hundred.

Suddenly the general public.

This last has largely become uninterested in (or mistrustful of) religions. Now also of politics . . .

I'm delighted. A little worried at the same time. Who will replace the Oracles?

The same people who applauded the implausible de Gaulle were willing, for the space of three days, to risk a war in order to defend the poor white victims of the wicked blacks.

That reminds me, I don't know why, of a comment I made as I was reading medical reviews and medical works, French as well as American or English. There is no immediate connection between the two subjects. However, I think there is a hidden connection.

Some physicians—the majority—and some professors use the most technical language possible, as if this were the only one that is scientific. To the point where a doctor who is not himself a specialist does not understand half of the communications from this or that specialist.

I follow all this patiently, as best I can, because it fascinates me. And I have come to observe that it is the best, the most assured of the learned inquirers who use the simplest language.

I do not speak here of journals or popularizations, or even semi-popularizations, but of texts addressed to professionals.

Men who have made important discoveries, who have shown intuition, genius, have been able to express themselves in terms that their little brothers the pseudo scholars consider vulgar.

Will we ever be through, or nearly through, with taboos, with "initiates," with the phony mysteries and phony science, the phony good breeding an example of which was touted by the magazines of this week with their articles and photos of the marriage of one of the daughters of the "pretender to the crown of France" with some Württemberger prince.

I've always thought that what is needed in schools is a chair of "demystification" or demythification (neither of these two words is in the dictionary but the second is in the process of becoming popular, which worries me) which would teach how to recognize accepted false values, "self-evident" false truths, etc., the whole jumble of conventions in which pitiable humanity flounders.

Last evening I find, in the *Presse Médicale*, the most staid and serious French medical review, the following caption: "World Hunger." The article deals with the production of vegetables, fruits, and vines throughout the world, and the needs of populations.

It's not just the pun which is a sign of the times.° In 1933 I wrote "Hungry People" and not a specialist in Europe took my articles seriously.

I wish I liked the work of my friends who write. I try to make myself. I try to pretend, for it's rarely true. Perhaps that is why I have few writer friends. I have them only by chance. Then I like them as men, while regretting that I cannot admire them professionally.

If I invented subtitles to go at the head of each of these notes, I see that it would make a sort of dictionary: childhood, blacks, travel, inspiration, doctors, friends . . . etc.

And if I started at *a* to get to *z*, I'd be sure of forgetting nothing.

I see too, with annoyance, that I use words here that I never use in my novels because I don't trust them: abstract words, vague or overfamiliar words, fashionable words. Put another way, because I am trying to give voice to a few minor ideas, I adopt unintentionally the vocabulary of after-dinner talk.

I even think I wrote "concept" and "distinguished" . . . and "important" in speaking of a doctor . . . This morning I had in mind a dozen words that figure in these notes which I defy anyone to find in my novels. I've forgotten them. "Distinguished,"

° Translator's note: in French, "La Faim du Monde," "World Hunger," sounds like "La Fin du Monde," "The End of the World."

probably . . . and "exquisite!" . . . tired words, which help give shape to hollow ideas. If that is the case—and I'm very much afraid it is—I'm wrong to play with keeping this notebook.

I want to tell it simply, without comment. Yesterday, D. and I had an apéritif. We don't do this often. For several weeks she has been on edge, because of the secretary, then because of one of the maids, etc. She is capable of enormous energy and she can keep going for a certain length of time with two or three hours of sleep a night.

Yesterday was the last straw, on the eve, almost, of leaving for vacation.

I suggested to her that we go out in the evening, which is even rarer for us than having an apéritif.

"Go where?"

There is only one night club in Lausanne.

"No, I only go out to go to someone's house."

But we never go to anyone's house unless we have to. She named two names. They were hardly what one would call friends.

And, for the first time, she said what I knew, or rather what I suspected:

"I need to talk to someone besides you."

She explained:

"You know everything I have to say before I can get my second sentence out. And you don't talk to me about things that . . ."

She needed to be with other people in order to reassure herself.

With me, no matter what I do, she somehow has the impression of inferiority.

Fifteen years of inferiority . . . She needs to be heard by others. . . .

She telephoned to the two families in question; both were out, as I had foreseen, on a Saturday evening.

We stayed home.

It was the children, finally, who made her relax, and we had an agreeable hour or two of talk together (at least from my point of view).

I love her. D., you are touching. But happy is what I want you to be.

Last evening my wife told me something I didn't know. My eldest son, Marc, was married last April, on his twenty-first birthday (with my consent). Johnny, who was then ten and a half years old, said to his mother:

"I don't understand why Marc is getting married and going to live in Paris when he still has the chance to live X years with Daddy. . . ."

I don't know if he gave a number. If he did, D. didn't tell me. In Johnny's mind, it wasn't so much the pleasure of living with me as the opportunity of knowing me and learning something from me.

This explains to me why he dogs my footsteps, continually asks permission to come into my study, follows me to town when I do errands, finally, an almost sacred moment, sits beside me in the evening in front of the television. It has become an obsession and he is unhappy when, for one reason or another, one of these tête-à-têtes he has promised himself does not take place.

He asks me questions about everything and I feel that he takes in the answers, that he attaches a great deal of importance to them. He has become a sort of disciple, which is disturbing. It's a relation I'm not used to, and when I'm conscious of it it bothers me.

Another X years . . .

He brings to this a kind of eagerness to build my image little by little in his mind, against the time when I shall no longer be here.

No doubt this image which is forming now will be more living in the end. It is through it that I shall live on. In turn, he will try to communicate it to his children.

I didn't think that a boy of less than eleven years could have this kind of idea. This explains to me certain secret glances, certain sudden outbursts. He sees me living, and he sees me already dead.

I don't like drinking—or the mornings after—because it makes me either sentimental or aggressive, two attitudes I hate. It humiliates me to an incredible degree.

/Saturday, July 30th

I had to look at the date in a newspaper. We're on vacation at the Lido, long familiar to me, but I feel more off the beaten track than I did in a hut in the Congo on my first trip to Africa.

It's not Venice that makes me feel so, nor even the tourists. It's living the holiday life, everybody's holiday. When I wrote stories for the biweeklies, shortly after my arrival in Paris (1924–1925), two or three months ahead we had to write on "seasonal" subjects. In October, it was Christmas and New Year's. Then winter sports, spring, Easter, summer vacation . . .

Papers continue to do it and it always seems to consist of the same caricatures of households or families at the beach or in the mountains.

But now, here, I feel like one of those ridiculous characters. I go through the same acts, at the same hours, with the same impatience and the same bad temper.

In short, it's the first time in fifty-seven years that I've taken the holiday train, that I've stayed, with my wife and two of my children, in a hotel catering to the holiday crowd.

As a child I used to go to Embourg in the suburbs of Liège with my mother—I've already written about that—and sometimes she would leave us there alone in a boardinghouse, my brother and me. Not at a hotel. With a good woman who kept a tavern and where we were the only boarders.

Never, either with my mother or father, or with one of the two, did I sleep in a hotel, or take a meal in a real restaurant. If we took a trip we took along our "snack."

The first year that I spent as secretary to the Marquis de Tracy, I accompanied him to Aix-les-Bains in August. But I worked from morning to night. That wasn't a vacation.

The following summer at Bénouville, near Etretat, where I lived three or four months on a farm, I was writing several stories a day.

Afterwards, at Porquerolles, I typed my forty pages of popular novel each morning.

I examine my memory in vain for traditional holidays.

On board the *Ginette,* then the *Ostrogoth,* I never stopped in the crowded places and I worked almost every day.

I spent one winter in a villa in Antibes. But I was working with Jean Tarride on the scenario of *Chien Jaune,* then with Jean Renoir on that of *Nuit du Carrefour* while writing several Maigrets, among them *L'Ombre Chinoise.*

Again at Porquerolles, later, sometimes in summer, often in winter, and more novels.

At Les Sables-d'Olonne, at the end of the war, I was in bed. Still not a vacation.

At Sainte-Marguerite-du-Lac-Masson in Canada in 1955 we went skiing, D. and I. But I was writing *Three Rooms in Manhattan, Maigret à New York,* etc.

Same thing six months later on a beach in New Brunswick, where we never spent so much as an hour on the sand.

Still the same in Florida, where I was writing *Lettre à mon Juge* among other things, then in Arizona, in California.

Finally in Cannes, we still weren't vacationing.

It had to wait until we were living in Switzerland and the children wanted a change.

And here we are, like the caricatures, following the schedule decreed by . . . By nobody, probably. We follow the crowd. And, in Venice, among thousands of tourists, we buy stacks of useless things that we'll throw away when we get back.

This creates a mild degradation. One loses all personality, all individuality.

I was forgetting that two years ago we spent a month on the canals and lakes of Holland, also with the children. But it was aboard a boat we rented and we followed no rule.

The preceding year, I believe, we spent two weeks at Villars-sur-Ollon. That was a holiday hotel. I only remember it because it rained without letup and because we spent the whole time playing bridge.

Actually this is my first vacation, and I scarcely glance at the newspapers for which I have such a passion and the daily reading of which seems to me as necessary as my coffee.

This won't last more than ten days in all. But if it lasted a month? A year? Or more, as for the prisoners of war in the camps, or the regular prisoners in prison?

What would be left of me? What desires? What reactions?

Would I revolt after a certain length of time?

I wonder. It frightens me a bit. It seems to prove that by carefully organizing men's use of time, what happens is that . . .

And I certainly have the same look of happy stupidity as the two or three hundred other people who are staying in this hotel.

In the end would we begin to look alike?

I wanted to write about something entirely different, about the sincerity or rather what I consider the impossibility of a total lack of sincerity even in those who pass for cynical. I've already talked about that here. But it plagues me. Perhaps I'll come back to it. I think of the Congolese, of the Russians, of the Americans, statesmen or journalists. Is it possible that they act out of a complete, an absolute, I was about to write, out of *pure* bad faith? I can't believe it. But then, to what extent our interest or our passions can falsify our judgment!

To be compared, when I come back to it, with a simple argument between husband and wife. Perhaps that will give me an answer.

Four journalists, on the day of our arrival here. This comes back to my mind because I am thinking of the news (still the Congo, American elections, de Gaulle-Adenauer, etc.) and of public opinion, of the way it is formed. Or the reverse. I mean that political personalities one speaks of are perhaps locked into their legend, and because of that, obliged to . . . but that's too long a story.

The first journalist was a good all-round reporter (hotels, stations, airports, police stations, clinics, hospitals) with his photographer.

Two or three questions, the most commonplace. Maigret on vacation. A child? Two here? Names. Ages. Thank you. And the others? Names. Ages. Thank you.

He will get the names and ages mixed up. Not that it matters. He will caption it "Maigret in Venice."

"Are you writing at the moment?"

"No."

"Do you expect to write a novel about Venice?"

"No."

That shocks them, in whatever country, in whatever city. So, in order not to hurt their feelings, I explain that I can only use settings where I've lived a long time. Several years as a resident, not as a tourist, which is true.

As my daughter comes in at this moment, the reporter has her pose with me and the photographer asks her to hug me. Very natural!

Second journalist. Important Milan paper. Fifty to sixty years old. Sophisticated man of the world type. He asked me for an evening meeting. At the appointed hour, he takes a paper from his pocket with typed questions and blanks for answers, like the questionnaires papers send out at vacationtime.

This is no simple reporter. He observes me, with a malicious glint in his eyes.

"Have you been in swimming?"

"Yes."

"For how long?"

"A half hour."

"Do you always go swimming for half an hour?"

What to say? I say Yes, and he writes Yes, gravely.

He pauses a moment, slier than ever.

"Meat or fish?"

This must mean: Are you a fish or a meat eater?

"Fish."

He gloats:

"I was sure of it!"

And to him it really seems important.

"Work in the morning? At night?"

"Morning."

"Blood pressure?"

"Medium. 12½-7½."

He notes it down, delighted with himself and with me.

Two or three questions of the same kind which I've forgotten and he thanks me and leaves, his duty done.

The third is from a big Rome daily where, he tells me at once, he only writes for the literary page. An intellectual. A real one. He speaks only Italian and is accompanied by a blonde Viennese of twenty, a painter, who is to act as interpreter. She repeats the question to me in French first, but since I feel that this French is very labored and approximate, she moves to English.

I understand enough Italian to realize that she translates only a third of the questions and a quarter of the answers and we, the journalist and I, end by speaking to each other directly in a mixture of three languages.

He isn't interested in Maigret. Durrell, Faulkner, Hemingway, Sartre, the younger generation . . .

Above all this younger generation which worries him, they suddenly are arriving too fast, like a train that is going to knock down the station.

He tells me about his concern. He hasn't come to listen to me, but to have his worries confirmed.

"You are a pessimist, aren't you?"

"Not at all. I'm a born optimist."

"Even with things going the way they are?"

"How are they going?"

"Atomic war, crime, population explosion, girls . . ."

I play at being contrary, to prove to him that juvenile crime has not increased in the last hundred years, that at fifteen, his ancestors, if they were nobles (they must have been), already had at least one death on their record, since a young man had to prove himself by fighting in a duel.

He held that the world was in turmoil; he desperately wanted me to paint it black and my optimism only reinforced his feelings, of course.

"But you're interested in men!"

"In man. And if one looks at his history not just in terms of a few centuries, but since the beginning of time . . ."

I improvise. I'm not entirely serious. He sinks deeper into depression.

"A history that will end in an atomic cataclysm."

"You think so?"

Suddenly I tell him a story, very intense.

"Take staphylococci aurei instead. They lived in peace and prospered, because we hadn't found a defense against them. You see! Suddenly a gentleman invents penicillin and generations of staphylococci are exterminated. . . . Those that escape mutate, God knows how, and penicillin no longer destroys them. . . ."

Next a new antibiotic, streptomycin or the like. A new extermination. A new mutation.

Aureomycin . . . I go on . . .

"Twenty times . . . Twenty-eight times, I think . . . And now these devils of staphylococci aurei anticipate future attacks, prepare for them so well that the new strains are often impervious to the new antibiotics. They confound science!

"And with all this," I say, "do you despair of man, who is so much further evolved than the staphylococcus aureus?"

He left deeply disturbed, I'd swear. Because of noise too.

This "modern plague" of noise, this bustle that no longer allows man . . .

I remind him that in seventeenth-century memoirs, for instance, Parisians were already complaining of the noise, of the traffic, of the vehicles that scraped against the walls, of the cracking of whips, the cries of street vendors, etc.

Imagine a post station relay . . .

I know. Parisian doctors have just demanded larger apartments in public housing, attributing a great number of nervous ailments to lack of privacy. Three rooms for a household with two or three children . . .

The peasants of earlier times had one room for themselves and their nineteen or twenty children. And often it opened on the stable! I cite the narrow streets of Naples, of Rome, even of Venice, the houses there where there was a whole family to a room, too.

The truth is that in those times one didn't worry about the common people.

And Versailles? What a beehive! Every cell was occupied and there wasn't a square yard of free space, so to speak.

Papers only print ready-made ideas. Psychologists, sociologists, seem never to have read any history outside their manuals.

What will this journalist's article be like? It probably won't contain a word of what I've said. Perhaps, in our three-language dialogue, neither of us has understood the thoughts of the other.

I'm waiting for the fourth, who will be here for two weeks; he has already interviewed me once in Cannes. A first-rate man. We met on the beach where he was with his children, I with mine, and we postponed a serious interview until later.

Serious? About what? Why? I have nothing to tell him he doesn't already know.

But he is a journalist, I am a novelist. So, an interview.

He must wonder, as he stares at the sea, what new question to ask me.

What happens to all my words that people print?

Previously I used to answer:

"Nothing."

And I would say whatever came into my mind.

Later I saw that all those words thrown out like confetti did not disappear. They finally were formed into a whole that became a legend, and this legend in turn took on a character of its own.

Hitler must have spoken of the Jews as I spoke Tuesday of the staphylococci aurei because someone asked him to speak and this appeared to him as a good subject. I'm beginning to believe that he didn't know that he would be forced to return to it and finally to kill I don't know how many millions of Israelites.

De Gaulle spoke of the greatness of France because the Frenchman loves to hear his greatness talked about. Where will this lead him? He doesn't know himself. Now it is his legend that takes over and rules him.

I'm not interested in politics. But still I'm intrigued by a problem posed by politics: that of sincerity and insincerity.

That of politicians as well as that of the crowd which follows or attacks them.

If all of them are irresponsible? If . . .

That's enough for today. I've mixed everything up. As I do when I'm falling alseep. Just as last night when I was trying to sleep and all this—and many other things which I have fortunately forgotten—passed through my head.

Then I took an Imménoctal.

/Monday, August 1st

I would be curious to leaf through an anthology (which may exist, for someone must have thought of it before me): a collection of all the national songs of the world, present and, preferably, past.

The comparison between them would be revealing, it seems to me.

First, the changes in the course of time, which would give an indication, or rather illuminate the evolution of the sentiments of human groups.

Villages, then provinces, then nations. Each village is persuaded that it is more intelligent and above all stronger than its neighbor.

I believe that one would find almost the same thing in the national songs, the same words, the same phrases: we're the strongest, the bravest. We are calm, peaceful, but our arms are ready, prepared to defend our rights, our liberties. . . .

At the discovery of America, it was found that each Indian tribe had its motto. The same for each black tribe in Africa. No doubt in Asia too.

Peaceful and strong. Fearless. No one is afraid.

Approximately the same attitude is found in children.

Check also how many times the word "God" recurs. Each tribe, each nation, is protected by its god, who is often, and increasingly so, the same as its neighbors'.

I would like to compare all these songs, sentence by sentence, word by word.

Huge scholarly volumes are written on the style of this or that writer, on his use of adverbs or commas, etc.

Wouldn't it be at least as interesting, if not more so . . . But, once more, no doubt it's been done, just as the little ideas, the embryo ideas that I put in these notebooks must have been expressed many times more fully and knowledgeably. That's why I only touch on them, out of a sort of modesty, sure I'm repeating myself, and continually tempted to put a final period to these notes which would make a laughingstock of me if they ever saw the light.

What I just said about national songs is connected with what I was writing yesterday. The need of peoples to believe in something, in themselves. The need to create heroes for themselves. They believe that they decide and that they are free. But they are slaves.

Who really decides for the masses? One often speaks of financiers, of great private interest groups, in copper, in oil, etc.

And if they themselves are only pawns?

Who decides? No one, I think. The cohesion of History is not apparent because it is visible (?) only after the fact.

So there would not be any great men among those who seem to rule the people, and the others, scholars, artists, really capture only a moment in the evolution of the world, explain only the small truth of an instant. Rather, they are mediums, what were once called prophets. One out of a hundred thousand or out of a million sees aright, expresses a truth that is found to coincide with the truth of their period or of the next.

They are all only human beings. And no one yet has given a definition of the human being.

Isn't it remarkable that we continue to seek one?

Along the way, we find everything, gunpowder, the compass, the infinitely small, and the laws that rule the infinitely large, atomic and electronic energy.

We do the best we can.

/*Wednesday, August 3rd*

This question of sincerity or of insincerity is only, after all, the question of good and evil. (I wrote *only* as if that simplified the problem.) But I've ceased to believe in evil. Only in illness. And that's questionable, too.

On the subject of the "menders of destinies" whom I believe I've already mentioned, a detail comes back to me which I'd forgotten. When very young, I used to dream of being one, or, on the other hand, of benefiting from their advice.

But now I'm sure of one thing: towards the age of twenty,

when I was beginning to write popular novels and stories to earn a living, writing in the evening, for myself, pages that remained unpublished, it occurred to me to want to work in peace, without material ambition. I would have liked to be given so much a month for life, regulating my time, taking care of my health, etc., and I would have written with no worry. I would have been ready, at that period, to give up my literary rights for such an arrangement. And I wouldn't have asked for luxury. A decent life with a modicum of comfort in a modest neighborhood. So I wasn't materially ambitious. Did I become so later on? I suspect so. A house mouse and a field mouse at the same time.

Same day, afternoon

Still on the subject of cynicism. I think that a king believes, or rather used to believe, he was king by divine right, used to believe in his mission; in the necessity, in the name of his country or dynasty, to fight his enemies, indeed even members of his family. The Pope ends by believing himself Pope. The general believes in the necessity of sacrificing a hundred thousand men in a battle. Truman believed in his right to drop an atomic bomb on Nagasaki.

I once knew a gentleman farmer, a young thirty-year-old count, who owned a huge manor and several farms. He had just married a girl who was not an aristocrat but who brought him twenty-five or twenty-eight farms as dowry. He bought his clothes at bargain stores and they lived penuriously in a château crammed with treasures. I remember some details. Next to a telephone which might be used by the rare guests, there was a saucer and a sign: "Please deposit X francs for each call." This was during the war. One could not make long-distance calls. So a call was very cheap.

One day we were talking about marrying for love, and he expressed himself frankly.

"This is something forbidden to us. We have received a heritage from our ancestors. We are only trustees during our lifetime. We must pass it on intact, and if possible increased, to our heirs."

He was sincere; he ate little even when he was hungry. Though he was a young man, and this was not in the last century, but in 1942.

He did the marketing himself; after having ordered fish for his wife and himself, he asked for fish that was less fresh for the servants.

He saw no harm in it.

We speak of conscience which alerts us to distinguish between good and evil. How can it vary from place to place and period to period?

My count had an easy conscience. So did Truman. Also the cannibals whom I've met in equatorial forests. It's only the sense of sin that creates the sin, the taboos of the place and the period.

Once written down that way, it looks idiotic. Nevertheless my idea, confused enough, it's true, is that in the last analysis each one believes in the necessity of what he does, or in its usefulness. . . .

One kills one's enemies in war. The Pope blesses cannons and armies. But if an individual murderer, let us say, is a schizophrenic, aren't all men his enemies?

This has been said so much better, so often!

Why does one persist in living and in thinking, in teaching others to think "as if"?

But who is "one," since those who invent morals, who teach them, who define them or impose them, believe or end by believing in them?

Nixon really believes himself the champion of the United States, de Gaulle the rebuilder of France. Nobody locks them up. If they were not their own dupes at the beginning, I would swear they have become so.

Like my count, with his collection plate by the telephone and his spoiled fish for the servants.

In short, no tyrant and no victim. Only victims. This is almost what I wanted to say. Only almost.

(The rest, and, I hope, the end of this subject, which is beginning to sound more and more like vacation homework. In fact it is, since we're still in Venice. We're leaving Saturday morning, and I will go back to my usual thoughts again in my study.)

The first man who declared himself king by divine right was no doubt neither a swindler nor even a man of ambition in the usual sense of the word. He believed himself king by divine right. Many around him believed that he was, some, most probably, pretended to believe it out of self-interest. And they then discovered that it was their duty to continue to pretend. Their duty to serve.

Jesus must also have believed that he was the son of God. But he did come to doubt it.

Perhaps this is the real tragedy. They all came to doubt. Their followers, their "faithful," prevented them from reversing their stand.

After that, many men believed themselves kings, emperors, or gods. Most of them were shut up in psychiatric hospitals. They came too late. They were imitators.

The use the Russians have made of Pavlov's theory is much discussed, including its use in surgery, in which they use conditioned reflexes to replace anesthesia.

For centuries the Catholic Church, and before it other religions (less systematically, less well), used the same principle.

If you don't believe, or if you doubt, pray. Recite sentences to a prescribed rhythm. Music. On your knees. Stand. On your knees. Bow your head. . . .

People talk about their brainwashing, too.

In religion, it begins with baptism, catechism, first communion, etc. On waking, at table, before and after meals, at noon, at night. . . .

"I am guilty."

By my birth as a human being, I am guilty, each day, at each hour. According to the day, the Gospel, the time of the year, I am torn between hope and despair, between paradise and hell, between evil and good.

The child, the young man, the young woman, the father, the mother, the old man, the dying, all are guilty, and ceremonies absolve them, stage by stage.

Bear children in pain. . . . Earn one's bread by the sweat of one's brow. . . . The eternal flames of hell after suffering the death throes. . . .

A mechanism admirably designed to leave the faithful no time for recollection and barely time to live.

Whatever you do, you're guilty, and you must confess.

If this mechanism had been set in motion cynically by a man or a group of men to ensure profit and power, it would show admirable intelligence and, as we say today, efficiency.

But no! I don't think so. That posits supermen.

At each stage someone really believed it. . . . And the edifice was erected little by little.

The same goes for kingship, and also for the economic system.

The day when de Gaulle no longer believes he is de Gaulle, he will be locked up.

Napoleon at Saint Helena continued to believe he was Napoleon. He pestered his guards with ridiculous demands, subjected his entourage to idiotic protocol, dictated a Memorial which defied good sense. As a result the English consider him one of the greatest men in History, and in Paris he occupies the insane mausoleum which he prepared for himself while still living.

What would have happened if he had had second thoughts, or rather if he had allowed his doubt to show?

He would have shared Hitler's fate, no doubt. And I'm not sure that Hitler will not one day be apotheosized.

It was Clérambault, I believe (I read Romain Rolland's book thirty years ago), who, when war was declared in 1914, read the mobilization posters without emotional reaction. He was "against." Then a military band went by and he noticed that he was falling in step with the soldiers.

I've often had to resist. It's the easy solution. There are moments when noncommitment passes for treason and when all the world is against one.

Every "ideal" ends in a more or less fierce struggle against those who do not share it. Even religions have inspired massacres.

I feel myself nearer to the Cro-Magnon man than the man of the Renaissance, for whom life (the life of others, of course) counted so little. And even the Cro-Magnon man is too close. The cave paintings show us that man was already proud of killing— animals, to be sure, but still killing. One must go even further back.

A family of gorillas in a film gave me the deepest thrill, and I was not thinking of Darwin, I was struck by a sort of grave nobility.

No animal called wild has yet gone hunting in order to line up a large number of "trophies" *for pleasure.*

Does one see a lion proudly aligning thirty or forty antelopes which it will not eat?

I know all this is trite, confused. The basic truths have been formulated time and again, and excellently. So well, indeed, that I mistrust them. All proverbs contradict each other. So do the Gospels, and the Church is so well aware of it that voluminous tomes try to prove that these contradictions aren't contradictions.

La Bruyère's *Les Caractères*, which are so admired, seem to me false because they try to condense the truth.

Intelligence explains all. Falsely. As if it were arithmetic.

I prefer to grope around a little idea until I *feel* some answer. But, if that more or less succeeds in my novels, I have the feeling here that I'm getting nowhere. More serious, I continue to seek for something without ever feeling satisfied.

No doubt I was wrong to begin this notebook, which risks infecting me with a passion for reflection. This would be catastrophic. It reassured me a bit that these pages are without importance and that I have the option of burning them.

It amuses me, though, to blacken them and to see them accumulate.

/*Echandens, Sunday, August 7th*

In my study again. It's the first time in my life that I've stayed in my study (I should say the first study where . . .) outside working hours. Is it age? Is it the study itself that seems really "mine"?

Yesterday, by train, Venice-Lausanne, with my wife, Johnny, Marie-Jo, and a young neighbor who has been nurse for the two children during our vacation. Five people. I had reserved the six seats of a first-class compartment. But the train was jammed as the ones in cartoons, and as only Italian trains are. The corridors filled with travelers and luggage, trunks, bags, parcels of all kinds, with old men, with children. There seemed to be several layers, and it was impossible to get to the washrooms, which were blocked off by passengers and full of luggage besides.

There was an empty seat in our compartment. Children were standing in the corridor. I knew that Marie-Jo would be train-sick during the trip and would have to lie down. But, even without that, we still wouldn't have offered the seat to anyone. All the time I had a bad conscience. At the same time I was furious that I was forced to travel under such bad conditions.

I'm no longer able to stay in a hotel where I haven't a private bath and perfect service; I can't even eat in a bistrot.

Why? As a child, I didn't have running water in my room, or any toilet except down in the courtyard. I suffered from the odor of chamber pots and pails. We washed "down there" only once a week, on Saturday, in the kitchen, in a wash tub. A shirt and a pair of socks a week.

In those days, miners left work without having taken a shower, with black faces and white eyes. They called themselves Black Mugs.

Today they have showers, and often own their own homes.

An English M.P. said recently on television:

"What weakens the Labour Party is the worker's acquisition of property. He has no more wants and he becomes conservative. . . ."

Not only have the people become conservative, but they have adopted bourgeois morals and taboos.

At one time, it seems to me, the two extremes of society, the little man and the great landowners or the aristocrats, more or less escaped the narrow morality of the middle classes. Then the lower rose, the higher descended. The middle class expanded on both sides and, with it, bourgeois taboos.

Everyone owns something, a bank account, a house, a car. . . . So everyone has something to defend.

Against whom?

I don't know any more where I was heading. Probably nowhere. It's unclear. This is connected with everything I've written up to now, but the connections are vague.

For example, a decree is issued (not a law, a decree, because France has gone back to decrees) limiting the freedom of the press. Virtually no newspaper protests.

The whole world knows that it is a financial cartel, the Union of Mines, which this very morning stands in the way of peace in the Congo and creates a dangerous situation. The deception is obvious. It has been exposed in the papers, or at least in some of them. The Belgians, when forced to do so, gave freedom to the Congo. But one of their straw men, named Tshombe, declared that Katanga too was free.

France claims that it is vital for her to keep Algeria.

However, without Katanga, the Congo isn't viable.

It's been almost a week since everyone agreed on this point and the UN was supposed to enter Katanga yesterday.

It didn't.

You don't risk a "holy war" with the blacks in Africa.

What happened? To what propaganda or blackmail do we owe this reversal?

This also is connected with my Black Mugs from the coal mines of Liège at the beginning of the century, and with my travel experience yesterday.

"It is harder for the rich man to enter into the kingdom of heaven than for a camel to pass through the eye of a needle."

I have often thought of that Gospel saying. I am often ashamed, as I was yesterday. I wonder if I don't act dishonorably by raising my children in what is called luxury.

If I were alone, wouldn't I renounce it? I've been tempted to; I often still am. I live with my convictions and my instinct at odds. It is possible that this causes me twinges of conscience. Anyway it makes me uneasy. I make peace with my conscience, like the rest of the world, telling myself that otherwise I couldn't work, that I'm not harming anyone, that at this stage of the evolution of the world, it's natural that . . .

It isn't true. And it's just because others make the same compromises that . . .

On the other hand I know that equality does not exist, that a semblance of equality is possible only by leveling inequalities. I recognize the biological necessity of a natural solution which this equality is about to abolish.

However, this is not enough to set me at ease. I write this in a manor house built for a seventeenth-century family, for an almost all-powerful bailiff, since there are three prisons at the far end of the courtyard. And, for three years now, I have gone to the greatest trouble to make each room perfect, each wall beautiful to the eye, each piece of furniture a little marvel.

It's still allowed. By whom?

Perhaps this too is connected with what goes before. Lying down for a short nap, a flash of the kind of place for which I have most nostalgia came to me. There aren't many left in the world. Thirty years ago in Equatorial Africa, in the South Seas, it was called a general store. I know they have changed since. One still finds a few, under the name of Trading Posts, in some obscure corners of the United States and Canada.

There men who live more or less in isolation within a ten to a hundred kilometers' perimeter come once a week, once a month, or twice a year to buy whatever is needed in their life. Matches, for example. Gasoline or carbide, storm lamps, soap, fishhooks or cartridges, wool blankets, rough clothing, leather or rubber boots, thread, needles . . .

Merchandise is piled up in casks, in barrels, in cases. It hangs from the ceiling. There is liquor to be had there too, of course.

Necessities. Not things you're made to buy because someone needs to sell them. Today, a French minister announced that each Frenchman should eat three more kilos of tomatoes this year than in previous years to prevent a slump. (Thirteen kilos instead of ten!)

Two wars, more precisely two occupations, have taught me the true value of provisions, the satisfaction of possessing them when it is almost a question of survival. Sugar, for example. Sugar with a capital *s*. During the last war, afraid of a shortage, especially for my son (I had only one at that time), I bought beehives. I sweetened my coffee with honey. The tricks for getting a few liters of gasoline because you couldn't count on the electricity. Carbide too. Rice, pastry. And, since I had three cows, the search for barbed wire.

Thick shoes to protect against cold and mud. An overcoat of thick wool or one lined with sheepskin.

Things took on their real value again. Their real beauty, too. The beauty—and also the odor—of a barrel of black soap, for example, and of beginning the winter knowing that we wouldn't be cold, caressing the woodpile with our eyes.

This atmosphere of "stores" I already knew as a child, in a city, however, at my Aunt Maria's house beside the canal at Coronmeuse. I've often written of it in my novels and in *Pedigree*. She used to supply the boatmen whose barges were moored above the locks. Boatmen bought what they needed there and my aunt had to stock what they wanted, from Norwegian tar to starch, along with anything else simple, rough people might need.

The *real*. This defines as nearly as I can the word "real" for me: that which relates directly to the life of human beings. That which makes it possible.

The real is never ugly. But as soon as one gets near the realm of the superfluous . . . See the bazaars, the shops with many counters, etc.

The place where I would like to live, if I had the courage, or if I had no responsibilities, would be a house, a cabin, as real as those stores: essential furniture of pine, partitions of fir, a stove, a pump in a corner, maybe a shelf for books . . .

This environment is artificially manufactured today, and those for whom these places, called camps, are built, in the United States, in Canada, in Kenya, in Polynesia, are the people who have the most money, the most responsibilities, those who are called billionaires and who relax by fishing, cooking their own meals, and making their own beds.

On a more modest scale, the ordinary camper does very nearly the same thing.

Hence this must be a virtually general need, this return to the real, but a prefabricated real. Why does the word "lard" suddenly make my mouth water? I haven't eaten it since the war of '14–'18. I see it again, spread on black bread. It meant a fatty substance. We no longer need fatty substances. Eating it, we had the sense of protecting ourselves.

Compared with this, how artificial and joyless gastronomy seems!

Another memory of war, of the second, this time, 1939–1945. At La Rochelle I directed the Belgian refugee service and I had the right to requisition—among other things—unoccupied apartments or insufficiently occupied ones. Women with children, babies, the sick, the old were sleeping on straw.

A woman whom I knew well, a so-called friend (I use this word too, but it has no meaning for me), urged me:

"Be sure to send me *nice* people!"

Someday I must take the time to explain myself on the question of money which preoccupies so many journalists who interview me. My position is rather complicated. I've often thought of it. I would like to get as close to the truth as possible and it is for fear of not being precise enough that I always hesitate. It will come.

I've been reunited with my son Pierre and already I find it hard to believe that he has walked only for a month. Soon I will find it improbable that there was a time when he was unable to talk.

God! How fast it goes. And how one worries over useless concerns.

The man seated on the threshold of his cabin who watches the sun set and does not think.

And the gorilla, surrounded by his family, on the watch in the forest.

He is already one step above the man in the cabin, isn't he? He doesn't need matches.

/*Monday, August 8th*

No doubt I'm going to write some more nonsense. But won't this whole notebook seem childish? That's what it's for, after all, to get rid of all the silly ideas that pass through my head. And I'm trying to forget all philosophical works, and avoid their vocabulary on purpose.

We tend to be sentimental; at any rate we look—at least most of us—on little children and the dying with compassion.

Between these two poles, for the being that is no longer a child and not yet dying, we have a tendency to be strict, even to be aggressive.

And yet they are the same beings, only at different stages.

Is it because at these two stages they do not compete with us, if I may put it this way?

There is another explanation. The child and the person in the process of dying are, as it were, beings in their natural state, undisguised.

As adolescents or adults, other factors will be added to their natural state: education, instruction, profession, environment, nationality, etc.

To put it another way, they are: Man + . . . + . . . + . . .

Each of these "pluses" brings mannerisms and taboos with it.

Suppose it were only those +s that we hate in our neighbors?

Suppose, under that little crust of +s, we were to discover that man is no different from the baby or the dying?

Suppose it were only the *acquired* factors that separate us?

Curiously enough, as one sees in times of catastrophe, war, earthquakes, floods, shipwrecks, etc., whenever a powerful external event momentarily attentuates or destroys these acquired characteristics, there is sympathy, compassion, a sort of love between men who hated each other the day before.

The difference between what I call the naked man and the clothed one.

Are we really moving towards the naked man? It seems possible, since today, for the first time in history as far as I know, the undernourished peoples are talked about and the overfed people have bad consciences.

Is this healthy? Was it healthier for each one to defend his place in the sun, to subject the weak to slavery and to kill for a yes or a no?

We begin to respect human life to a point of extremity. We almost make a religion of it. It's true of me. But I sometimes wonder if this is not sentimentality, if we are not going against natural law.

The events in Africa worry us.

What is most troubling of all is to consider the same events, in turn, from the historical point of view, the biological, the sentimental, and the political.

In the past, we must have had instinct, which guided us to where we are now. Is it still with us? Where is it? When does it speak?

And if we have lost it, when and why did we lose it?

Same day, afternoon

A mass-circulation paper, hence a paper that caters to public opinion and is careful not to shock it, yesterday or the day before carried an article by a lawyer not noted for his revolutionary opinions. It was concerned with the archaic quality of the Penal Code, both here and elsewhere, with laws that take no heed of our medical knowledge, particularly in the matter of the degree of responsibility of the criminal. He envisaged for the future a jury of specialists—not specialists in jurisprudence, but in medicine and psychology—and the conversion of prisons into asylums.

This is a familiar theme in specialized journals almost everywhere in the world and particularly in the United States. The idea began by seeming revolutionary. Even today, among the doctors whom I meet, many are skeptical, and lawyers continue to believe in exemplary punishment and Society's revenge.

My very first Maigrets were imbued with the sense, which has always been with me, of man's irresponsibility. This is never stated openly in my writings. But Maigret's attitude towards the criminal makes it quite clear.

I don't write this in order to demonstrate that I was ahead of my time. I invented nothing. Even at that period these ideas had certainly been formulated by others. But it is still a fairly recent movement. It began with articles in the criminology reviews.

Now it is reaching the general public. I'm delighted. Now that the idea has reached this point, it is bound to lead to reforms.

Does anyone realize what these will imply? Certainly not the public, for it would not feel reassured.

The whole basis of society is changing, with a new concept of man. A concept already apparent in unemployment insurance, social security, old-age pensions and more or less free medical care, including cures at therapeutic spas and dental prosthesis.

I'm delighted, as I said above. That's true. But I'm a little worried too. In fact, I wonder if our "humanity" will not someday be called sentimentality and if it will not be recognized fearfully that we have transgressed natural laws. Certain methods of agriculture have killed the soil for hundreds of years. By destroying insects with DDT we have diminished fertility. The English have to import bees to save their fruit trees. When, for a while, the rabbits disappeared from France, the rangers were concerned because the balance of the forests was disturbed.

How curious is man's fate! He is determined to know, discovers fragments of truth, draws conclusions, acts on them only to see afterwards that he has transgressed some still unknown rule and unintentionally unleashed catastrophes.

He struggles to readjust his knowledge, makes new discoveries which, in their turn, on application prove to be just as dangerous.

What admirable and moving perseverance!

The Eucharist—another concept affected by science, by scientific vulgarization, or our false—or fleeting—discoveries in human behavior.

The Host, the body of God, which the faithful incorporates by swallowing, was no doubt one of the most poetic and *real* flashes of genius of the Church. Primitive tribes ate the brain, the heart, the sex, some part of the human being, to reinforce in themselves that part and its function (an idea which, though in a very different way, is pursued by certain bypaths of present-day science). The mother may say to her child, in a burst of tenderness:

"I could eat you up!"

The lover and his mistress . . . The *absorption* of one part of the beloved being answers a sort of need for fusion.

71

The idea of incorporating God in man was thus admirable psychology.

Then, after the public became familiar with the details of digestion, with the chemistry of the stomach and the intestine, this poetic idea began to seem almost repulsive or profane.

The Church wanted communion to be taken fasting, in the morning, in order to obviate any image of this material process.

Today communion and Mass can take place at any hour, under certain conditions, which are very nearly those of surgical operations.

Communion, because of our knowledge of the digestive tract and what follows, has lost its beauty, like the tribal chief his right to eat the brain of his enemy.

All this is linked, related. A new way of looking at man himself, and, consequently, at his relationship with other men, is on the march.

One of these days it will shape into a new religion, or a state religion, which amounts to the same thing.

Surely, in the name of this religion, we will kill those who . . .

Is there any change?

6 o'clock in the evening

I just happened to try out on someone the story of the baby, the dying man, and the man between these two ages or between these two states. The result was catastrophic.

It seems to me that people would rather confess to the worst crimes than admit that they have not received the very best education (?), that their manners are not the only acceptable ones, that their taste in all things is not good taste, etc., etc., all these characteristics furthermore affected by the city, the neighborhood, the social position, the family, the street . . .

Perhaps it is the heritage of the clan, and the tribes of Equatorial Africa may attach the same importance to tattoos.

What surprises me is to find these survivals so deep-rooted, and such violent reactions among educated and—on other subjects—open-minded people.

Heard an American in Florence saying to his wife:

"These people don't think or live the way we do."

There was astonishment and perhaps some pity in his reaction.

This is a reaction I never had during the ten years I lived in America, any more than I had it in London, in Italy, in Turkey, in Russia, or in Switzerland.

It's true that I don't belong to any clan, to any human unit, and in moments of discouragement it occurs to me to regret it.

It must be reassuring to belong to a race, a country, a superior class.

Alone, one is superior to nothing.

I begin to feel a novel coming on. Tomorrow, Dr. R., one of the ones writing a book about me. On the 15th, another, for another book, the fourth this year. This last, Bernard de Fallois, is the most intelligent of the four, I think, a critic I've never met. What questions will he ask me? What will he make me think of this time?

I'm in a hurry for this to be over, in a hurry to be plunged into a book again, and to be writing nothing in this notebook because I'll be writing a book. Provided the stage fright is not too long or too painful this time. I would like to show, bring to life, a strong man, or fairly strong, anyway. But this is not necessarily what will come out. I grope. I avoid pinning myself down. I am waiting for the spark and it's a very uncomfortable period during which I suffer because I can't help being irritable.

What a crazy profession! Balzac complained all the time about his slavery, and Dostoevsky, in his correspondence, used the term, very romantic for him, "prisoner of the pen."

I don't like big words. Let's just say that it's a bad moment to get through. As for knowing why one imposes the job on oneself. . .

Still a little sickened. As always. Dr. R. brought me his book, which he told me was almost finished. He insisted on reading me two or three short passages. Asked me a series of questions. Made me promise to read the manuscript and tell him what I think of it when he is finished, about a month from now.

Have no desire to read it. No curiosity. As for him, he has read a hundred of my works. What surfeit! And above all what obsession. He is a pediatrician but he has been a neurologist. He informed me that the basis of his work about me will be, to some extent—no, this sentence leads nowhere. I wind up talking the way these people do. He is studying me, it appears (?), from the viewpoint of a work by C. von Monakow and Monyne, written twenty years ago and called *Biological Introduction to Neurology and Psychotherapy*.

I'll read that book. But not for the same reasons. I've always the same discomfort in reading what is written about me. All right if it's about my work, although I rarely have the impression that the critic has understood. Gide's praises never really gave me pleasure because I felt he was studying a case. Next, *Le Cas Simenon* by Narcejac . . . then that first volume of P.'s, full of fake Freudianism. One after another they come to peer at me under the magnifying glass.

It ends up giving me stage fright. I'm afraid of writing now. They interpret everything in their own way. And when they talk to me about my novels, which I never reread and of which I retain only a vague memory, I no longer recognize them.

The hundred-and-ninetieth will be next. Provided this won't be another disappointment, that once all this is over I can clean myself out with a good novel.

They have managed to disgust me also with this notebook; among the passages from *my* books which they've read me because they are quoting them, there were sentences almost identical to what I set down here. Am I just repeating myself? Saying over, only worse, what I have already said?

And I don't like the photographs they have made of me any better—especially the ones which the others consider good. I don't recognize myself.

Last year, for the third or fourth time, we took up with Sven Nielsen (it had already been done with my other two publishers, getting the three together one day in my apartment in the Georges V) the question of my complete works, illustrated perhaps, in a semi-deluxe edition, putting several titles in each volume, of course. Even so, because of the number of titles, this poses such complex problems, both technical and financial, that we put the project off until later. What was mainly lacking was a suitable person to see such a long project through.

Commercially speaking, not more than two or three high-priced volumes could be published annually. At that rate it would take almost ten years and if, during those ten years, I kept writing at the same pace . . .

In short, the project was postponed. However, I've received some beautiful dummies, big books with white pages in solid bindings. It's tempted me, I've chosen the most beautiful, and I've begun to make notes in them from time to time.

Now that I've begun this notebook, I'm going to see if there's anything in those notes I'd like to copy here.

I noticed immediately that here and there I wrote a word as caption to the day's notes, like a dictionary, which I'm almost tempted to do here too. As here too, I'm mostly asking questions.

So, on page 1:

"Is there a possibility of establishing (by intensive research on fossils) a numerical proportion between men (including hominoids and prehominoids) on the one hand and the different species of animals on the other in the successive periods of history and prehistory?

"(Cf. the considerable number of fossils of mammoths in Asia as compared to the number—alas—of human skeletons—though these are less fragile than those of the small mammals, which are very numerous.)

"Number of men and of bison, for example, at the time of the discovery of America by Europeans.

"Same for Africa (elephants, predators, antelopes).

"Same for Australia.

"Etc.

"Rise, fall, or disappearance of different species.

"Same for insects. (Probably impossible.)

"Period of the organization of ants, bees, termites . . .

"Increase or decrease of species?

"*Rats:* does their rising curve (?) follow that of the human race?

"Diseases of prehistoric animals.

"Then of those that succeeded them.

"Of prehominoids . . . hominoids . . .

"Does the number of diseases follow that of the growth of populations and the life of societies?

"Comparisons between:

"Biological struggle against disease.

"Intellectual struggle against disease.

"Have mutations coincided with the periods of more or less radiation?

"Is there a connection with the changes in the mineral kingdom?"

End of this note. I looked for the answers in a good number of specialized books and reviews. There was only scattered information. Nowhere did I find a systematic study of these questions. Perhaps I wasn't thorough enough in my search?

Second note (they aren't dated).

"Relationship insects-fermentation.

"Is there a shrinking of the number of insects? Of the number of species?

"If so, does this affect the number of birds?
"Then on . . ."

The relation of men to rats seems to me important. Parallel evolution? Coinciding numerical growth?
Reason for the adaptability of the rat.

Third note: "*Intelligence and Instinct* (all right, that's my hobbyhorse and no doubt that is why all those who write about me question me when all I do is question myself).

"Comparison between animals, hominoids, men, living in families or in small groups, and those living in large herds. Bison and lizard, for example. Primates and dog-faced baboons. Same for insects.
"Is organization lessening or killing intelligence little by little, or individual instinct?
"Experiment: what would become of highly organized insects, ants or bees, if one transplanted the individuals strictly indispensable to fecundity? Would they start the process of organization all over again?
"This must have been tried. What was the outcome?
"*Idem* for man. (The Australian experiment? New Guinea?)
"Group instinct or intelligence, where each individual is specialized, as against individual instinct or intelligence.
"Evolution of each genus. Rise or decline as specialization is accomplished?
"Influence of this specialization on defense against disease.
"Same in psychiatry."

"Comparison between animals, hominoids, and men living in society and those in isolation *from childhood*.
"At what age, in each group, does self-defense develop?
"Influence of society or group on precocity.
"*Idem* for number of offspring in the litter, among mammals.
"Number of offspring among hominoids and prehominoids."

"Triplets, quadruplets, quintuplets, which are a rarity in our times: are they an accident or a kind of throwback to earlier stages?

"(Twins seem to be a hereditary characteristic. Was there a time when they were the rule or the majority?)

"What is the frequency of twins, triplets, etc., among primates?"

End of quote. Since then I've looked for some answers without finding them. But not in a very systematic way. Perhaps future reading will permit me to fill in the blanks.

No doubt the rest will come much later, when we discover new ways of investigating the past, as we have just discovered the process of determining the age of a fossil by radiation (which is not quite exact, I'm summing it up in a word).

Same day, 5 P.M.

Intermission. Photographer for two hours. English this time. Study. Pencil. Children. Garden, library, etc.

I'm continuing copying my notes. They date from barely six months back. However, I'm transcribing them rather uneasily.

The same discomfort I feel when I am obliged to reread a passage from a novel only a year or two old. Or when I think of such and such a year in my life. Or when I see old photos again.

It always seems so incomplete to me! (*It* means me.) Tomorrow it will be the same for the present. Isn't this true of man in general? 1900 seems ridiculous to us, childish. Yesterday's science makes us smile. Today's will make us smile in its turn. At what moment will I be satisfied with myself? I'd rather not answer.

Nevertheless I am copying, without conviction, like a lesson, knowing that it all is leading nowhere and probably will diminish me in the eyes of those who read me.

Another caption: "*The rat.*"

———

"At what period did the rat appear? Before or after man or the hominoid? Was it a sort of parasite of man from the beginning? Before that was it the parasite of another animal? Has it always lived on the 'remains' or the offal of another creature?

"(The word 'creature' leads to nothing or rather to too precise a meaning. All words, basically, are tendentious.)"

Another title: "*Isolated territories.*"

"Why have certain animal forms ceased to evolve in certain territories that have suddenly (or progressively) been isolated from others?

"The Galápagos, for example. There one finds species that are no longer found elsewhere except in fossil form. This can be explained. But why did evolution stop at a certain stage?

"*Idem* for New Zealand (kiwi—moa—tuatara).

"*Idem* in part for Australia (kangaroo, etc.).

"Did certain animals cease to evolve because they had no enemies that forced them to?

"Why, when, with the appearance of man, such enemies appeared, none of the earlier species began to evolve?

"In other places one finds only a certain percentage, more or less high, of extinct species.

"Here, they *all* seem to die out, save domestic exceptions like the ostrich.

"Is there a moment when evolution becomes impossible?

"In the Galápagos, up to recently, no apparent struggle between the species.

"The struggle seems to begin with the arrival of domestic animals which return to the wild state in very little time (another tendentious word!).

"Aren't the human races that are called primitive (Pygmies, Hottentots, Guineans) on the contrary degenerate branches, returned to their wild state like the asses, cattle, and pigs of the Galápagos?

"Instead of a rise with plateaus haven't there rather been rises and descents, with only certain races representing the rises?

"Why, for example, in Africa, are one, two, or three generations, sometimes only one, enough for an evolution which, without contact with the white race, would never have taken place or would have taken centuries to produce?

"Personal experience: in one month one can teach an illiterate black who has never seen whites before to drive a car.

"Facility in absorbing mechanical concepts for the first time.

"But in four centuries, in Martinique, it has been impossible to teach blacks philosophical concepts. The Bible and the Gospels were transformed into the Voodoo cult.

"For an African or an Asiatic the bases of nuclear physics are easier to digest than elementary philosophical concepts (ours, of course!).

"Ethics is more strongly incorporated into man and more difficult to replace by a foreign ethic.

"The exact sciences, on the other hand, do not take the place occupied by something else.

"Vacuum propitious to exact sciences?

"In the United States, statistics indicate that mathematics is more easily accessible to less philosophically developed classes, and it is the middle classes (and below) from which future students of the great schools like M.I.T. are recruited and cadres of engineers are formed.

"In France, blacks had been studying at the Polytechnic for a long time, while there were still cannibals in their native lands.

"Does this only indicate a certain laziness, a resistance to certain disciplines, on the part of the children of rich or advantaged classes? Are the sciences of interpretation or of synthesis more attractive?"

"Apathy, and, in some respects, resigned and *sad* refusal of evolution by the large primates like the gorilla. They make no effort to slow or avoid extinction.

"Antithesis of the rat, which adapts to all conditions and all climates.

"Doesn't adaptation go with the philosophical mind?

"Are there, in fact, resigned races and aggressive races?"

"In man: aggression in primitives—nonaggression in the evolved?

"Does evolution regularly stop at a certain stage?

"Would this explain why each people, in turn, arrives at a certain degree of civilization, stops, gives up, and leaves to others the exertion of going first?

"*Idem* for families of individuals?

"*Idem* for molds?

"Will there be an age of aggression and an age of philosophic resignation?"

"Possibility of a relationship of zoology and anthropology to psychology."

"Everything seems to me to have been born out of the sea. So one finds the first men at the seashore. First food shellfish, then fish, then small mammals.

The weakest races, thereby more or less doomed, are always hunted further inland by stronger races, into the forests, then into the mountains. Higher and higher as the competition becomes more intense.

"So the doomed species, the last examples of the doomed species, would be found in the high mountains.

"*Idem* for men? (Examples of the Indies, of Borneo, the Andes, etc.)

"In seashore civilizations, then on the plains, one finds a certain exuberance, a certain gaiety.

"The higher one climbs . . . (Muteness and sadness of the people in the high mountains.)

"Comparison or parallel between animals and species that are too weak and retreat before disappearing.

"It would be interesting to compare religions, legends, traditions, songs, dances, etc., of the seaside peoples, then those of the plains, the hills, and finally those of the mountains from this point of view.

"Aggressiveness of races which have a future and passivity of the races which no longer have one?

"(This could be applied to human types and even to professions that are disappearing.)"

"Few animals in large flocks on the peaks, even among birds. Life becomes more and more individual. Solitary and hunted down, in contrast with the socialized life of the seashore (recalling the swarming of schools of fish)."

"A geography of aggressiveness and resignation could be established.

"Doomed races which climb into the mountains like the old men who climb coconut palms?"

(Another parenthesis. Basically, I'm not sorry to have gone back to these notes from last winter. Not that they have any value. But they reassure me. If, at that time, I was asking myself so many questions about myself, at least rather personal questions, it is because first at Cannes, then here, journalists and those writing books about me made me submit to their questioning, uncovering many anxieties. In my normal state, it seems to me, if I ask myself questions, they're of a more general order, which does not mean they are any more pertinent. Good!) (The next page begins badly with a word underlined.)

"*Need* for superiority. Does this explain the famous 'age of anxiety'? The individual is doomed to be the center of his world. As a result he needs to feel he is an important part of this world.

"Some kind of superiority is indispensable to him. In primitive society, in Africa or elsewhere, one finds the same thing: the best hunter of a certain animal, the best fisherman, jumper, runner, warrior, healer, singer, dancer, etc., etc. In short, each member of the tribe is the best something or other. And each is the bravest.

"In Greece, the adolescent had to spend a year alone in the mountains, feeding himself by his own efforts, before he had the right to the title of man. In Africa one finds the same thing, among the American Indians or elsewhere similar tests (including the girl alone in the forest at the time of puberty).

"The great schools today, Saint-Cyr, the Polytechnic, Cambridge, West Point, have their tests which the newcomer must undergo.

"And each village in France or elsewhere has its best craftsman in this or that specialty, the best horseman, etc.

"There is the woman who makes the best soups, the one who bakes the best cakes, the best dancer, and so on and so forth."

"Industrialization has almost leveled professional superiorities. Substitutes have been tried: in Russia Stakhanovism, in the U.S.A. the best salesman, beauty contests, the most beautiful legs, or the most beautiful hair. Miss Orange or Miss Whatever.

"This is artificial and everyone knows it. Each one seeks another superiority deep within himself, and finds it only rarely.

"Curious parallel: the sons of Roman emperors of their own free will tested themselves to establish personal superiority; saying nothing to their fathers, they tested their strength against wild beasts in the arena.

"Today, the children of important or rich people often race cars or airplanes, etc."

"In America doctors recommend that everyone have a 'hobby,' an interest outside his profession, if it is only collecting matchbooks. It is less for relaxation than to establish a feeling of superiority in some easy little domain."

"Christian society itself speaks of the *most* pious, the *most* humble, the *most* charitable, the *most* worthy. . . ."

"It is more and more difficult for the masses. Superiority as a workman, as a bus driver? Nevertheless each year in France someone is chosen the *best* truck driver. And the oldest worker in France, the one who has worked longest in the same plant! Isn't this enough to explain why many people welcome a declaration of war with relief? Don't some men discover their natural superiority in a catastrophe?

"The American experiment is frightening. Superiority of money, of one's automobile, of one's club, of 'status' miscarries. The man at the top pretends to believe in it and to be satisfied. But at bottom he is not convinced. The number of psychoanalysts proves it."

"At school, in the street, between kids, there is superiority too. The best marble player, the best runner, ball player . . .

"At sixteen, the identical need!

"And, at the summit of the hierarchy: the most powerful, the one who uses others best, who imposes his ideas, his products, or his will.

"Always the *most*.

"The nostalgia of veterans, former noncoms, officers, generals, decorated with this or that, members of the Resistance who were nearly shot, who were prisoners, escapees . . . Creation of societies . . . Parades, flags, flowers . . ."

"No matter at what price, one day each must have his superiority. . . ."

"Above all the man, the male. No matter how low he was on the social scale, once at home he became all-powerful. No one argued the superiority of the Head of the Family. (And the woman, the mother, also had her different superiority.)

"Today, government, schools, etc., have been substituted for the father; also propaganda, newspapers, radio, the movies, television.

"He is no longer the one who knows best, the one who imposes his will. Coming home from the factory or office, where he is nothing, he finds a family where he still is nothing.

"What is left between the two, on the way home, is the bar, where he can still have his little personal success—the best drinker of pastis, or of red wine, the best pelota player . . . or the funniest . . .

"But not the most gullible.

"His power has been taken from him. He refuses the responsibility illogically expected of him."

(Here I hesitate. I'm a little ashamed. However, I'm transcribing, out of honesty (the most honest?), a definition which defines nothing.)

"*Education:* conscious or unconscious manipulation by one generation through material, intellectual, and moral pressure to model the following generation according to the rules and principles which, most often, the educators haven't themselves followed, and of which they have sometimes recognized the inanity, if not even the danger."

(That's exactly the kind of sentence I hate. Too bad. I'll put it down without elaborating on it because I'm waiting for the surgeon who will tell me if I should have my appendix out or not. At fifty-seven, this would be my first operation and I admit that, having been raised in a period when the operating table still inspired awe by its very name, it's not without some anxiety that I'll lay myself down on one. I don't like the idea of being put to sleep.)

E-N-D, or nearly. Soon. Just a few words. Our adventure, my poor notebook, hasn't been a long one, and the eleven other brand-new notebooks will go to my children.

Last night we went out, D., Aitken, her secretary, and I. We drank a bottle of champagne in a cabaret. The only one in Lausanne. An enjoyable evening.

Then, at three o'clock in the morning, in our room, D. had the courage to tell me what I already sensed and which has occurred to me to write in these pages.

For example, that I have always said that I ought not to deal in abstract ideas, however simple.

That the novel is my only tool, my only medium.

That perhaps the trouble I had in writing the last one was caused by my preoccupations—the ones I've tried to get rid of here.

That . . . My God, that perhaps I was beginning to take myself seriously. . . .

All that, I'd already thought it myself.

I'm stopping now.

"You've got to the point of copying notes. . . ."

True!

But since there are a few pages left, I'm not copying them, only collecting them here in order that this monument to naïveté and pretension (even the word "monument"!) will to some extent be complete.

D. will read them.

———

"A man's ambition for his children.

"Need to make them climb a ladder . . .

"Most of the time, however, it isn't in terms of money. Rarely the ambition to make a merchant, a financier, etc., of them (unless that is already the family profession—and even then!).

"Nor ambition for power. A peasant will rarely say:

"'He will be a deputy, or a minister. . . .'

"Deeper. *Unconsciously* an ambition for usefulness, for *greatness*."

"The reproach critics most often make is that I choose my characters from people who are not civilized, and, as a result, they seem to say, incapable of resisting their instinct and passions. Aren't these critics the ones who think of themselves as civilized because they have digested a few historical dates, won some diplomas, also the ones who take our fleeting civilization for definitive and our youthful morals for humanism?

"Don't biologists, for the most part, begin with the simplest forms for their study of life? And, today when the doctor and the psychologist have new ways of looking at man, don't they too study the most limited forms?

"I have observed, besides knowing it by my own experience, that intellectuals, civilized or cultivated men, react to deep instincts and passions in the same way that others do. The only difference is that they feel it necessary to justify their attitudes.

"Little difference between the behavior of a Napoleon and any ambitious small-town man. A matter of scale, of proportion. The fundamental elements are the same. Balzac behaved as naïvely in private life as the simplest, the most elementary of his characters.

"Rages, resentments, ridiculous petty intrigues in a Hugo, even a Pasteur. I have seen the greatest doctors plotting shabbily to win a medal, a decoration, a chair at the Academy of Medicine.

"No difference between basic behavior, reactions to passions, among primitive and cultivated man except that the mechanism is complicated by more or less specious reasonings, by rationalizations (Memorial at Saint Helena) and by so-called problems of conscience.

"Mauriac acts exactly like his concierge or his wine merchant, with the single difference that he gets a book or an article out of what he considers his unworthiness. *Idem* for Graham Greene and the others. Freud in his private life is the prototype of those he describes. Same for Dostoevsky.

"The Greek tragedians, Shakespeare, and all the other playwrights have done nothing but take passions in their natural state —the passions of the man in the street—and for the purpose of highlighting, dramatizing, and amplifying them have attributed them to kings, emperors, and other great personages.

"If I have chosen the limited man (not always. See *Le Président, Le Fils,* and other novels) it is just to avoid theatrical explanations, artificial reactions created by education or culture.

"Behavior is less falsified, more visible, purer, in the simple.

"Persistence in using words that no longer correspond to concepts or scientific theories of the moment—or to the beliefs of those who use them.

"In particular, words borrowed from the religions—including the most ancient and the most foreign.

"Haven't we kept mainly the words that express a curse, guilt, a prohibition, a punishment, etc.?

"A whole heritage of terrors, from the most distant times, maintained by a hundred religions, which we preserve, which we transmit through words, to our children at the same time that— ironically—we try to give them the most rational and scientific idea of the world.

"So we extend thousands of years of terror!"

There! I've finished my *collage*. Without rereading it. That's wiser.

D. is a courageous woman. Operation with slight anesthesia: a bottle of champagne.

I don't want to end at the bottom of the page.

"Have you nothing to add?"
What's the use?
"No, Your Honor."
All that's left is to open the window.
Adios, notebook!

Second Notebook

1 9 6 0

I promised myself there wouldn't be a second notebook. This morning writing in this one, without writing any number on the cover, I tell myself again that there won't be another perhaps, but perhaps I'm not entirely sincere.

To tell the truth, I missed it. And yet I've passed a part of the time since Venice first in a clinic for a simple operation for appendicitis, then in bed after I got home (a few hours later, when I thought I had recovered) because of some virus.

Then Bernard de Fallois, who has been working on his book on me, without asking me stupid questions.

But once back in my study, I missed writing. The study seemed more empty to me. This need to write here, no matter what, may only come during those hours of the day when I'm waiting for D. to finish working so that we can go out, or simply waiting to be with her. Will this be better next month when she will have two secretaries instead of one? Man is not made to live alone.

Anyway, I promise not to put down the slightest abstract idea. What I shall write—if I continue—I don't know at all. No abstract ideas, anyway. Otherwise, in the long run I would have to think before I write, which goes against my principles. (Have I principles? They are attributed to me. People remind me of pronouncements I made twenty or thirty years ago.)

Today, I'm giving in, really, to a kind of anger, a certain resentment. I believe I've spoken of all the journalists and critics who have streamed through Echandens during the past months.

The first was a woman, L., a friend who is editor of a big magazine. She had telephoned asking permission to send one of her writers to interview D. immediately. This was three days before our departure for the Cannes Festival. We didn't want to refuse, and while we were getting ready for this departure, fittings, luggage, instructions to the household staff, children, etc., we had this charming woman and her photographer at our heels from morning to night.

On our return from Cannes, three weeks later, it was a certain C., from another important weekly. C. stayed four or five days—with his photographer. To both, I repeated that I refused to talk about money, that I would not answer—nor would my wife—any question on this subject.

Before leaving, C. read us his article, in which, in fact, there was nothing about money. I warned him against his editor, who, I know, loves to raise such questions. He made us every promise imaginable.

The two articles waited in type until the news (Brigitte Bardot, Vadim, Distel, Yves Montand . . .) left space for them and as it happened this week both periodicals published their interviews at the same time.

In one: "The man who pumps billions from his inkwell." In the other: "The man who sold the television rights to Maigret for a billion three hundred thousand francs." And my wife handles millions (daily, according to them). A thirty-six-room château!

I don't want to get up to copy the exact texts. And in one, our love becomes the panting romance of a popular novel.

Result: begging letters begin to arrive. There will be more next week. It is as regular as clockwork. If an article appears in an English magazine, England "begs" for two weeks. Professionals. Sometimes, a year later, I get exactly the same letter from people who forget that they have already written. Then it's Sweden, Denmark, Italy . . .

Some readers are indignant at our boasting, sure that we are the ones who talked complacently about our income.

However, the figures are wrong. C. told me that they estimated the amount of our B.B.C. contract, which no one knows, according to averages calculated as exactly as possible. But since this contract is a partnership contract, no one, not even ourselves, can foresee what it will yield.

What infuriates me is the rank prejudice shown by the owners of the big newspapers and magazines. It's a matter of policy, the same in every country. These people are almost all great captains of industry. They handle billions, not every year, but every week. They have five, six estates, country places, town houses, yachts.

For the most part they have inherited their fortunes, all they had to do was to increase them.

But each week they publicize the hugeness of the fees, or income, of this star, that painter, that writer.

It's a sort of alibi for them, an excuse. We act as lightning rods. No one speaks about them, about what they earn, what they spend, but everyone knows the falsely astronomical figures of artists' earnings.

I think that if I were to read the two articles about us with different names I would hate the people they were written about.

Is that the purpose? One begins to wonder. Upper-middle-class jealousy?

When Buffet, by a miracle, after starving—I've starved too, like Chaplin, like so many others, and I'm very glad of it—when Buffet, at thirty, sells his canvases for two million bad francs and buys a château that is in fact quite dilapidated—the papers positively organize campaigns against him.

Because he earns money, he can't be a real painter. His prices will go down. He's just about finished. His downfall is at hand.

The public reads all this and passes on! This week, in the eyes of thousands of people I pass for a lucky dog who piles up royalties—a good thing I didn't steal them—caring nothing for the distress of so many homes, for the ill-housed, ill-fed, the sick children and the old who are dying for want of care.

Not a word about forty years of efforts which were sometimes almost desperate. I am just a juggler. I've won in the literary lottery. I'm a clever fellow or, at best, I've known how to take advantage of human stupidity.

Raimu once spoke to me of his bitterness on this subject, and I wrote a short article about it.

It's not the first time it's happened to me. Probably it's not the last. Must I close my door to journalists? That would be useless. Three years ago, the representative of a big English daily said to me:

"I've been particularly commissioned to ask you a question about your income. My editor insists. If you don't give me an answer, I'll invent one and you can always sue me."

I answered him:

"I'm so little involved in money matters that I would have a hard time telling you what I earn. I'm sorry for the people who are so concerned."

Which he translated in his article into something like:

"Simenon told us that money is coming in so fast that he can't keep track of it. . . ."

Disgusting, isn't it? It is, however, what literary history is made up of, and we are judged by it.

An excellent lesson in humility, if I needed one, and which should be enough to remove all desire to set down opinions in these notebooks. I finally had a limited edition (two thousand copies, I think) printed of a pamphlet: "Le Roman de l'Homme" (lecture at the Brussels Exhibition). I sent it, as a token of friendship, to thirty friends and to those people who, I know, follow my writing assiduously. I didn't receive more than five acknowledgements.

My wife and I take pains to answer all letters. I go through all the manuscripts and books that are sent me. Often I read them thoroughly. And I write personally to the author.

Nielsen did the publicity, less than usual, I suppose, because of the small number of copies printed and also because the edition was sold out. For my novels, I receive a great number of press clippings. For this little book, there was only one review, or rather a single mention, in *Paris-Presse*. And even that only quoted an anecdote about Charlie Chaplin. It is now going the rounds of papers, especially the English ones. About the rest of it, nothing. Yes: *Paris-Presse* says that this book, in spite of its small number of pages, is packed with intelligence. Thanks.

I was quite wrong in publishing it. I didn't want to do it. I gave in when people wrote me about it from all over.

Serves me right!

I had noted on a bit of paper:

> Tepid fruit dish
> Marsilly statue
> Place des Vosges
> First move
> The hundred days in Tucson

Nothing important. Memories. It will come back, no doubt. For the moment, we've finished packing. D. and I are going to take a rest in Versailles for six days. She's the one who needs it most. As for me, after the operation, and especially after the antibiotics, I would like to get back in shape for work. In a hurry to plunge into a novel. Now, all I can do is hope. We'll be back around the 10th. End of the month, the 29th, is Johnny's birthday and I can't be working on a book then. Will I have time between the 10th and the 26th or 27th? It's unlikely.

We have the best-organized house there is. But the better organized we are, the less leisure we have because we become slaves to routine. We have to eat at an exact hour (give or take five minutes) as in an army camp. The least slip-up, the least whim, spoils everybody's schedule.

But to write a novel I need almost a month of peace without any disturbances (seven to eight days of writing, it is true, but to get into the mood and identify with my characters it takes me longer and longer. I don't believe it is age, weakness, drying up, but that it has more to do with my becoming harder and harder to please. There was a time—twenty-five years ago!—when I used to˙say to myself: "It's good enough for the public." Now, it's no longer the public I'm preoccupied with. Perhaps I'm wrong).

So, we'll just hope. No journalists, friends, obligations. And not even world events must trouble me!

Each time I think I am ready, something makes me put it off three days, then eight, and I end up letting my characters evaporate.

D. struggles with the mail, the house, organizes, smooths out difficulties. She exhausts herself so that nothing may bother me, and seeing her struggle this way distresses me.

Besides, I am more and more the paterfamilias. I'm not sorry. On the contrary. I would like—like D.—to be with the children all the time. And it's the nurse and the staff who see the most of them!

Well then! Plane at three o'clock. Versailles at about five thirty. Bringing a maid so that both of us will be free of cares. D. is bringing her typewriter.

This shouldn't be taken for bitterness. I was feeling low when I thought I was writing less because I was beginning to be impotent. This must be the thing that haunts all creative people. (I don't like the word "artist," which, like the word "poet," seems pretentious, quaint to me, and the term "creative person" even more so. How to put it? How designate a profession which basically doesn't exist?)

Summing up, I've decided, after a good deal of worry, that it's my external life, more complicated all the time, that keeps me from writing as much as I used to do. And maybe the fact that my books are both shorter and simpler.

Pierre is playing under my windows. I just went to look at him.

I want to go down to be with him. D. is in her boudoir and I want to go up to see her. Then to look for Marie-Jo, whom I've barely seen today, then to go get Johnny from school. So I feel guilty about spending a few minutes on these lines which have no interest, no importance, except, perhaps, later for the children.

And this gets me to my note "The hundred days in Tucson." But this morning, that would take me too far afield. Maybe at Versailles, where we'll be on holiday? Holiday? In any case, we'll both be there and I'll be able to talk to D. at any hour of the day without someone—other than the telephone—interrupting, which rarely happens here. To have a ten-minute conversation we have to take the car and drive someplace!

/Saturday, September 3rd

In Versailles since Wednesday for a conventional rest in a conventional hotel where, as in Venice, I find people doing exactly the same thing I am.

I'm amazed to observe again what has struck me so often. The lack of cleanliness, of real comfort in what are called luxury hotels. How can so many people be satisifed with this? Some spend virtually their entire lives in such places. Served by strangers who come and go in your privacy by relays, appear and disappear without your knowing their names. Is this a personnel crisis, as the management claims? It's possible.

For a number of years already, in France, in England, in the United States and elsewhere, I have been appalled at certain specimens of fauna in these places: valets, floor waiters, chambermaids, especially the ones on night duty. Where do they come from? One guesses at dreadful secrets. They answer you with surly or scornful indifference.

What is there under these uniforms of questionable cleanliness, questionable as the armchairs, the draperies, the pantries on each floor where our coffee or tea is prepared, among the brooms and God knows what?

The public dreams of this luxury life, which few housewives would find acceptable in their own homes, with the negligence, the lick-and-a-promise cleanliness.

I looked back at entries. They don't seem interesting any more. I'll explain the last. When we were in Tucson waiting for Johnny's birth, we had to be separated from Marc for the first time, who went ahead to Carmel-by-the-Sea in California. Marc was ten years old. He didn't read French. My English was still poor. And he would have had trouble making out my handwriting.

During the hundred and some days of this separation I wrote him a letter in English every morning on the typewriter, racking my brains to interest him, each time trying to think of a "joke." Although I was sure he never read these letters to the end. Did he even open them?

I wonder if these notebooks will have the same fate. I'm probably wrong, since Johnny seems curious about everything I do and write. Perhaps in the end they all will be interested in my chatter?

Why do I want them to be? It won't teach them anything, except that I am much pettier than they may have imagined.

In fact, that's just what I'd like to happen. To be known in my natural stature, not as a father, not as a writer, but as a man with all that the word implies. Isn't that the best way to help them if they need help someday?

"My father was . . ."

No halo.

"My father was like me."

A little less good. I hope so.

And now for those hundred days, which had nothing Napoleonic about them. It was very hot in Tucson. Those hundred and some letters in a foreign language probably gave me more trouble than the hardest novel. Not to mention the pain of separation.

I'm coming to the lukewarm fruit dish, which no longer has any importance and which came back to my mind, I don't know why. That will be for tomorrow or another day. I'm getting lazy and above all I see no reason—today, anyway—to tell these tales with no beginning or end and giving the impression, wrongly, of attaching importance to them.

D*

Recently one of the greatest French cancerologists died of cancer, and up to the end his colleagues managed to hide the nature of his illness from him. This doesn't seem extraordinary to me. I've seen other doctors in similar situations. And probably it's the same for everyone. We are lucid, sometimes perspicacious, even clairvoyant about what concerns others. But the nearer people are to us, the more our judgment is likely to be distorted. I don't think a healer has power over his own.

D., last evening, reread my first notebook. We talked about it this morning. I believe that I understand her better, or rather that in the future it will happen less and less often that I misunderstand her for short periods. It's more difficult because she lives not outside but inside me. Thank you, D.

Paradoxical. I think that conventions, basically, if one traces them far enough, come from a need to be singular.

Example. My grandfather was named Christian. He was no more Catholic than any other person. Average. This name was given him because in Belgium it is unusual, and his parents must not have known that it meant Christian.*

My father, through a kind of family piety, gave this name to his two boys, my brother and me.

In turn, I gave this same name, also three times, to my three male children, who will no doubt do the same thing with theirs.

Did my uncles do the same thing? I think so. So that one day there will be dozens, perhaps hundreds of Simenons with Christian as their given names.

Not by choice. By tradition. And if they are asked why, they will think that once upon a time it was a profession of faith.

Idem. In my parents' house, each person's birthday was celebrated the day before the actual day. In order to avoid having friends, acquaintances, congratulate before the family did.

I've continued the custom. My children will adopt it in turn.

* Translator's note: Simenon's grandfather's name was Christian, while the French word meaning Christian is *Chrétien.*

Then their grandchildren, but they will no longer know why.

Families invent traditions, transmit them. Nations too.

How can one not deceive oneself when, centuries later, one tries to explain them "logically"?

We create—create for others—obligations, rules which finally no one dares to break.

Or even obligations which in turn threaten to become a matter of morals. In any case, a form of slavery.

One man's singularity becomes, at a given moment, decades or hundreds of years later, an inexplicable rite. Or an affectation. Only a few wore Eton ties at first. It was a countersign. Then hundreds wore them, thousands, hundreds of thousands.

The fruit dish will come later. It seems too long to explain. I would like to note here only items of a few lines. And things as badly written as possible so as to stay away from literature. As I sometimes write my friends; the style of my letters is in inverse proportion to my friendship. With strangers, I am careful. With acquaintances, a little less so. With those whom I really love, not at all. Watching one's language, whatever one may say, distorts thought. I prefer the approximate word, the ordinary, the first at hand to the precise word which has slowed down thought for even a few seconds and by that fact has robbed it of spontaneity.

I have some of the same feeling about my novels. That's why it is so laborious for me to correct them. One of the reasons. The principal reason being that once written they are alien to me.

/*Monday, September 5, 1960*

I must get to it, just to be done with it, even though it now seems to me without interest. I ask myself even why I made a note here that I ought to talk about it.

I must have been a little over seventeen when I wrote two pages under the title "Le Compotier Tiède." Not a story, nor altogether a prose poem. One of those things one writes at that age and gets published in little magazines. The "Compotier" was also published in a fairly important review in Brussels, *La Revue Sincère*, and I was recently surprised to see in Scharbaeck, I believe, a Rue Léon Debatty, named after its editor. So I too, against all I really thought I believed, I almost went the way of the little reviews.

It doesn't matter. This worthless piece of writing still ought to be (?) in my file. It would be easier just to insert it here but I hate the thought of digging up this sort of thing. What is important (in my eyes and actually more than it seemed a few days ago) is the theme, the sunny courtyard of our house on the Rue de l'Enseignement, in the morning, at around ten o'clock, with my mother, in the kitchen, making preserves. On the table, in a shaft of sunshine, a dish of tepid stewed prunes. The smell all over the house.

I knew I was leaving, that all these things, including my mother, were already part of my past. It was a sort of good-bye to my childhood. But my mother did not suspect it. She thought I would be there for a long time. Only I myself knew that the cords were cut.

To some extent that is the theme of all my novels. Reality which trembles on the brink of unreality, making way for new reality. Severed cords.

Now I would prefer to say severed umbilical cord. A feeling I have again with every new departure. Because there is no more substance to be drawn out. It has all been used up and one must look for new substance elsewhere.

In psychology, the boy who stays with his mother is treated as a neurotic. In a lifetime, is there only *one* umbilical cord to cut? To linger in a street, in a city, in a group, isn't that neurotic too, and a weakness?

Someone searched for the reasons for my perpetual departures in *Pedigree*: hatred of my background, neuroses, etc. It's so much more simple! Need of new nourishment, even if, at certain moments, I've appeared to hate, or I've believed that I hated, the environment I was leaving.

I begin to regret having written *Pedigree,* where everyone is always finding wrong reasons for my behavior. Behavior that they believe exceptional, even neurotic, when in my eyes it is quite natural.

Each time I have settled down, I have thought it would be for life. Fortunately, my instincts have been too strong for me.

In Marsilly, when I moved into a small country house called La Richardière, my first home after the Maigrets, I was so convinced that it was final that when I bought an enormous stone statue from an antique dealer in La Rochelle (three blocks on top of each other), an eighteenth- or nineteenth-century virgin and child with the head missing; when I'd had it set up in the woods a hundred yards from my window, I decided it would be my tombstone.

I left La Richardière three years later, without having lived there more than three or four months a year, for that was the period of my trips to Africa and around Europe.

Nevertheless I had electricity, running water, heating, etc., etc., put in, planted trees, including walnut trees which would take twenty years to produce their first crop.

There too I cut the cord. The umbilical cord.

What was it I wanted to say about the Place des Vosges, which was, before Marsilly, my first household? I've forgotten. There I had a bar built in. The furniture was ultra-modern, that is, *Exposition des Arts Décoratifs 1925*. What originality! . . . And every evening I used to go to Montparnasse as young people went to Saint-Germain-des-Prés later. I wore elephant-leg pants in *bois de rose* color, as people later flaunted dirt and wore their hair long. No originality either then or now.

Like measles—or "mange" for dogs. It was nothing to be proud of. Should one be ashamed of it?

Mankind changes so little. And there is so little difference between one man and another, between an adolescent and an old man.

We are scarcely able to tell one Chinese from another. In the United States, they find it hard to distinguish the French from Italians or Germans. They are all Europeans.

And we are all men.

If only one could remember that each time one meets with another near-self.

Still at Versailles. Life together, pleasant and gentle. Hours in which nothing much happens, or nothing happens at all and which one remembers later nevertheless as one's happiest hours. You will see, D. You are still too young to know.

/*Versailles, Wednesday, September 7, 1960*

My dear Sigaux:

First because of your letters and also because of your considerate friendship, and also because of my trust in you, I have just decided to do something that I always find unpleasant. When it is a matter of a book, a study in a review, or a critical piece about myself, it is a bit like going to see a film taken from one of my novels. I've seen only five or six of these films, because it upsets me to see my characters changed by the director, the adapters, and the actors into beings who are strangers to me.

I react all the more so, nine times out of ten, when it concerns my own person, my intentions, the mechanics of creativity, etc. . . . Things that seem simple to me suddenly become complicated, and to tell the truth I hardly ever recognize myself. So I am a poor judge, as must be the case for every writer. Moreover, as I said to Dr. R. when he came to see me for the first time, it is not my business. He very considerately asked my permission to write the book. I stressed that my authorization was not needed, that anyone had the right to write such a book, with the single condition of not putting words in my mouth that I had not said. I also told him, at that time, that I would not read his manuscript. I have done so. I told you why. And it matters very little that I was somewhat hurt, this does not constitute a judgment on my part.

However, to you who know me well, who have written what I

consider the best pages about me, I would like to give a few impressions. Please understand that I am not asking Dr. R. to change anything in his text. I am going to give it back to Nielsen at lunch, without comment, leaving it up to him to decide if he wants to publish it or not. So the notes in the margin are only a commentary that has no other purpose than to give you some very personal impressions.

First, it appears that Dr. R. has taken a conventional point of view, I mean morally conventional, throughout. This is apparent particularly when he speaks of good and evil, of sexuality, specifically of the wish or of the temptation to murder.

Nowhere do I feel any of the biological understanding I would have expected from a doctor. And he read "Roman de l'Homme," which does not appear to have enlightened him as to my intention, the intention which is the basis of all my writings. In fact, from the beginning, from childhood, I have never been revolted by poverty, by mediocrity, etc. . . (or very little), but only by such morality, and if I have, from the beginning, tended to show man totally naked, it has been just because of this feeling. Each stage is marked, it seems to me, by a greater detachment from this morality, a more direct approach to man as he is and not as he would like to be, or as he believes he is.

Beyond this, R. has confused religious (cosmic) sense with Catholicism, which is something quite different.

In my opinion, he has committed another basic error. Though he recognizes that I only trust instinct, and accordingly devotes his most important chapter to this, he gives an explanation that misconceives the place of instinct in my development. For example, he speaks of my Balzac period, in some way allowing it to be understood that in the *Testament Donadieu* I was trying to imitate Balzac. Actually, I was talking only about what I was discovering by living at La Rochelle, and by being the friend of the big shipowners of that city. As to the length of that novel, it was decided (not that I attach any importance to it) by the fact that this book was an assignment from the *Petit Parisien,* which requires very long novels.

Also, all the novels of that period are characterized not by my desire to create "suspense" but by the fact that they all were intended to be published as serials.

My Conrad period? That would seem intentional—entirely opposite to instinct. Not a single Conrad character, not a Conrad theme in my novels which he calls exotic. I was traveling a great deal at that period. And, quite simply, I told about what I was seeing as, in the first Maigrets, written on a boat, I talked about canals, about the North, about the ports, etc.

Do you understand my position? It is the direction of my development that is falsified by his commentary. There was nothing intentional about it, except to escape from literary and moral convention, and also to escape from the demands of newspapers and publishers.

I knew where I was going—from the very beginning—but I did not know how I would get there. And I did not know what I would discover when I was free from all that I had overcome without meaning to.

Where I expected R. to be most original—because of his profession—he went back to *Pedigree*, like P., and drew almost the same easy conclusions from this book. He also borrows a good deal from his predecessors, P., N., among others, and the best is from you.

I won't quarrel with his division into three periods. But he does not give their true meaning to these periods. Still less to my intentions. But perhaps that indicates that my novels do not clearly say what I wanted them to say.

He did not understand one of the most important in my eyes: *Lettre à Mon Juge*. Still less did he understand *Dimanche*, where, like a Catholic *petit-bourgeois*, he sees the praying mantis in the poor primitive child! Strictly speaking that is his right, but it makes me gnash my teeth. Have I made myself so little clear on this point?

When, at my home, he asked me:

"Could it be said that perhaps it all leads to God?"

I answered:

"I wouldn't say yes or no."

This he translated as:

"I wouldn't say no."

And what God? We didn't discuss that. He places his own, *ex officio*, as the goal of my preoccupations, as if a hundred others didn't exist.

The man who interests me, the man who forever fascinates me, is turned into just the conventional man I've always taken such pains to escape.

Do you understand what I mean, dear Sigaux? I don't doubt that he examined my work honestly. But he wasn't looking for me. Without wishing to, without knowing it, he was looking for himself.

I don't blame him. Once more, it's not my business. And perhaps, after all, I'm the one who is wrong. I have been given an impression of myself and my work, and it is probably inevitable that I do not recognize myself.

But a few comments are still to the point. There are too many scientific terms for my taste. I too have studied the works he refers to and this can all be said much more simply.

This is a first impression. I haven't been lint-picking. I read it quickly. This kind of thing is always difficult for me, as I told you, which probably explains my severity. You would have written differently, wouldn't you? And you would have written something different?

All the same, the work will probably have its uses, its readers. All opinions are worth having. And, I repeat, I am the worst judge. Once Anatole France indignantly sent back the portrait that the painter van Dongen had made of him. I won't be so ridiculous. And when I'm back on my feet I'll return to my novels. It isn't healthy for a novelist to analyze himself, still less so for him to discuss the opinions others have of him.

Nielsen, however, will decide. I am persuaded that he will publish the work, not at the *Presses*, no doubt, which would risk making the book look like a puff, but in one of his other houses. That's up to him. And, for myself, I continue to respect Dr. R.

without bitterness. Isn't it also one of my themes that no one knows his neighbor, or even those who are dearest to him?

All that for your ears, my dear Sigaux, because I am fond of you and because I know you understand me. I'll be at Versailles with D. until Monday morning. We are "incommunicado," the two of us, doing nothing at all, seeing no one at all, and if I don't see R., it's nothing personal. I need to rest, and if I once open my door . . . But I'll see you soon. I hope so.

My affectionate best wishes, and my wife's.

Yours,

Georges Simenon

I won't reread, otherwise I probably wouldn't send you this letter, which I wanted to be spontaneous and totally frank.

/Friday, September 9th

Out of laziness, instead of copying two or three passages I've pasted in a photostat of my letter to Gilbert Sigaux on the subject of Dr. R.'s book about me. Does this mean that I attach much importance to these details? It would be a mistake to think so.

For more than thirty years—more than forty—people have written all that they wanted to about me in various publications, true and false, much more false than true. And they go on.

I have never made use of my right to answer. I haven't sent any corrections. Moreover, I have not, afterwards, discussed their opinions with journalists, critics, etc. I have said nothing of N., nothing of P. Others are now putting in their oar. All of them pretend to know me, decide *ex cathedra* on my most intimate feelings, on my instincts, on my opinions (which I have never expressed).

Is it really surprising that I feel the urge to correct all this? There is something to respect in every opinion. Perhaps there is truth in what these people write. But isn't there some chance that some of my ideas—about myself—are true too? I've only raised a few minor points in my letter to Sigaux. This may help to fix the truth somewhere, insofar as a truth exists in what concerns the individual. Enough on this subject, this time, and I hope for a long time to come.

Yesterday we went to the Vlamincks', at La Tourrilière, for the first time since Vlaminck's death. The house has not been made into a shrine. One isn't forcibly reminded of the absent one. The mother and daughters continue their quiet life. It is comforting, not sad, and I am grateful to Berthe for her attitude. There exist, then, also undemanding widows.

/Saturday the 10th

Went to — restaurant just now, alone, since when we're traveling D. doesn't eat lunch. Pale sun. The restaurant bright, gay, welcoming, with a pretty terrace facing the fence of the château of Versailles. Made you want to stop there, to eat there. At just 12:30, buses filed past, some of them stopped, from Belgium, Germany, England, even from Canada. Each one disgorged its cargo. The tables were ready, and the meals, arranged several months ago by agencies, planned meals.

I'm not one of those who groan about the times. Actually, I don't think they're much different from any other. As with countries, the differences are mostly on the surface. The Romans knew about spas, the villas, and the traffic jams at the city gates.

Day before yesterday, in an interview televised in France, Kennedy, candidate for the U.S. presidency, finished by saying:

"We sent you millions of tourists. In return, you must send us some French ones."

Not so that they may get to know the country. Not in order to make contacts. Tourism has become a question of commercial balance.

Once, there was Baden-Baden. Other spas had their day. Then

there were jokes about Switzerland, where a guide waited for foreigners at the foot of each glacier.

Yesterday, in the French papers, it was announced that the government was going to campaign for an increase in the consumption of ice cream, in order to absorb the overproduction of milk.

The arduous drive to get people to drink apple juice has begun.

Man is made to travel for financial reasons. He is forced, or almost, to buy a house or an apartment even if he is a nomad. He is forced to consume this or that. Gas must be burned and automobiles must be sold.

It is even announced, always officially:

"Next weekend there will be ninety deaths on the roads."

And the forecast is accurate within two or three.

The Bible was concerned with the behavior of each person, with his food, his hygiene. And in earlier times, there were great priests and sorcerers who performed the same role.

Does the public realize it? Today, people cannot be unaware that their individualism is being scientifically hunted, that if his means are increased, it is in order to make him consume more, and, in the last analysis, to consume only what he is intended to consume.

This happens no longer in the name of religion, barely in the name of hygiene. It's an economic question. And it is cynically admitted as such.

Man doesn't revolt. Nine times out of ten, he submits.

One sheep . . . two sheep . . . three sheep . . .

He jumps.

And, looking at the faces of the people whom the buses disgorge on Versailles, there is no reason to believe he isn't happy. So?

Too bad about the tenth. He must jump too, and he can still grumble, which is not yet wholly forbidden.

Today is a beautiful day and on television I watch the end of the Olympic Games in Rome where tens of thousands of people —as centuries ago—are seated on the tiers.

/Sunday the 11th

This morning, at Versailles, a Sunday morning like those I recall in childhood memories. From a distance of fifty years in spite of all the discoveries, inventions, styles, etc., very little difference in the atmosphere of a small-town Sunday morning.

/Next day

Back home. Versailles closed on an idiotic note. And we would have it that our passions and our acts depend on personality alone!—when we don't call it intelligence—when the least change in outward atmosphere influences us. The moon madness that the blacks in Gabon talk about may not be so stupid after all.

/September 20, 1960

Changed the furniture in my study (English now, except for a table, which I'm looking for), books in place. Threw out (or rather sent to a hospital) a good third of my old books. Leaving for Paris tomorrow. I read this passage from a piece in *Newsweek* of the 19th of September on Sydney Smith, Professor of Forensic Medicine at Edinburgh University—one of the founders of modern forensic medicine—at the end of his career:

"After a lifetime spent in the study of murder and murderers, does Sir Sydney have a theory about the kind of person who kills? 'In my recollection,' he writes, 'they have been devoid of the characteristics they are commonly credited with, and [are] *quite ordinary individuals such as you and me.*'"

For thirty years I have tried to make it understood that there are no criminals.

Want to write a novel as soon as possible. If Professor A. will get rid of my dizziness for me.

/September 25th

Arrived at the house yesterday—once more—with the same joy, the same sense of well-being, and a new regime. The four children are under the same roof all at once for several days, the youngest not recognizing the oldest. D. perfect. Indeed, she made a gesture that touched me (her gift, to Marc, of her car, which she loves). But it's something else, I don't know what, which gives me pleasure, which makes her closer to me.

About that, I don't want to write. Nor about anything else, which means, I think, that a new novel isn't far off. Providing my head cold and dizziness f . . . off. Have rarely felt so clearly as during this brief trip to Paris—a dress rehearsal, supper afterwards, visit to the doctor, dinner at the Elysée Club with friends —what a stranger I am to all that, only interested in our little family unit. And, when I have a desire to escape it, it is for an even more limited unit: to be anywhere at all, in a hotel apartment, or on the sidewalks, with D. The essential unit: the couple. After which one gathers one's chicks under one's wings.

An amusing (?) idea came to me just now. At last report, Professor A. *dixit*, and he seems to me right, that the cause of my recent troubles, minor dizziness, etc., could be an infection of the inner ear called Ménière's syndrome.

Now it so happens that among the recurring motifs which are found in my novels, and which some people have tried to explain

112

by hook or crook, is a sudden sensation of unreality of the environment, of people, of the outside world, which one of my characters experiences.

If, someday, the critics learn that I was more or less subject to attacks of Ménière's disease, they would discover that this sometimes causes such sensations.

From there, to conclude that . . . It's utterly idiotic. And I'm aware that one could thus go on infinitely to make diagnoses of books and authors.

I had this sensation of unreality even as a child. I'm sure that every one of us has had it at one time or another in his life. I would swear that it is inherent in the human condition.

But the critics wouldn't believe that. Didn't I react as they do with regard to Balzac and to Cushing's disease? So much the worse for me. Not to mention the fact that it hasn't the slightest importance.

/September 27th

Regret I wrote the preceding. Seems to me both pretentious and forced. But I promised myself neither to cross out nor to tear out pages. On the subject of A., I'm struck by his assurance, and that of other top medical men.

Is he, are they, really sure of themselves? Isn't this a professional attitude which they find necessary to use with certain patients? Do they come to believe it themselves? I suspect so, and this fits in with what I've said about statesmen, politicians, etc. They speak, make gestures, go and come as if . . . But in reality? A very small detail struck me. At a certain moment, A. gave me his latest book, a big treatise which, I think, is considered important by people in his field. Apparently it was to have me read a quotation of Ménière.

"You see that I too write my novels!" he then said to me in a voice in which I sensed some bitterness.

There was no doubt he would have traded his big treatise for a few novels. His colleague, Professor D., spends half his day at literary tasks, the other half only at his scientific works.

What does that prove? That they are not so easy in their skins as they would like to appear. They do not believe in themselves, or at least they don't believe in themselves all the time.

The more I know people the more I mistrust self-assurance. I would like to ask the Pope a few questions, eyeball to eyeball.

Tomorrow Johnny's birthday. I see Tumacacori, Tucson, twelve years ago, D. and me eleven years ago. It's so much more important than anything else. But that has no place here, nor anywhere. Basically, I'm talking about everything except what I really have in my heart, because one cannot speak of certain things without falsifying them.

Happy birthday, my dear old Johnny! And Marc, and Marie-Jo, and little Pierre. And D., who wants so much to make us all happy.

One doesn't find any of that in my novels, either.

/September 28th

I know, like all men of my age, no doubt, how old a novelist is by the meaning he gives to the word "old," or to the age of someone he calls "old man." In my first books, old men were often scarcely more than forty-nine or fifty years old.

But what young men cannot understand is that at fifty-seven, or sixty, or seventy (I don't yet know) one has just the same hopes that they have.

Today, for example. I had a twinge of the heart about Marc and his wife leaving in a car for Paris with a little suitcase on the baggage rack of the MG. We too, D. and I, used to take off that way, without preparation, for anywhere at all, or sometimes quite at random.

Now, the slightest whim, sometimes just to take a walk in town, demands complete preparation, orders to give to everybody in the household. You would imagine—I used to imagine it too at one time—that after a certain age one settles down, is almost without wishes, dislikes whims and the unforeseen. How indignant one feels at the idea that a mother and father at the age of forty still make love!

They imagine that we no longer have other satisfactions, other desires than to enjoy a big house, have a comfortable life, buy furniture and pictures. But all this is only imposed on us. We submit to it. The kids will realize one day all the desires held back because of them, without bitterness, only, sometimes, with some sadness, a remembering of the time when it was possible to make love any time, I was going to say any place, without wondering if . . . and if . . .

It's no use having an enormous house—and for work and relative freedom of each it is indispensable that it should be so—D. and I still have to make a great effort in order to be alone together for a moment. I regret none of it, on the contrary. Each time I meet a bachelor of a certain age, a couple without children, aging or aged Bohemians, I can't help feeling sorry for them.

And I know very well that one day, when all the children have flown the nest, we will think nostalgically of our house when it was so full. It is true that I will be really old then. But will I think myself old? I am beginning to wonder. My carcass will have shrunk, surely. But will the rest change? For the better? For the worse? If I live long enough I will know the answer one day. But it is not impossible that I will keep putting it off until later, until so late that no one will be able to give it, which would explain why we never have enough satisfactory answers to these questions. So why ask it?

I often say I'm apolitical, and I think it's true. However, at this moment if I were a French national, it is probable that I'd yield to the temptation to sign the manifesto of the 121 or 125, the number doesn't matter, which demands the right of desertion for the soldier sent to Algeria and more or less forced to commit acts against his conscience. I envy a little those who have risked it and who are now suffering for it. I hope that all actors, authors, etc., will go on some sort of strike in solidarity with their colleagues who have been barred from television, films, subsidized theaters—and worse, the teachers, who have been hit even harder. All these things upset me, make me indignant.

I do nothing. Not only, I'm sure, because I am not French, but because, as always, I feel that there is exploitation for murky ends on both sides. This is neither egoism nor, I'm sure, concern for my peace of mind nor that of my family. Nor is it wisdom. It is more an uneasiness that I feel in the face of a certain kind of use of ideas, no matter how pure they are.

At the same time I am aware of a feeling I am ashamed of but which I can do nothing against. From the beginning of the de Gaulle experiment, I was revolted by his conceit, by his scorn of the opinion of others, by what he and his entourage represent (theoreticians from the great schools who are obliged to reduce social problems to equations—all more or less tools of the great banks and business groups), I have been revolted, I say, and also convinced that the experiment will inevitably end in failure. That must have been two years ago.

This failure, for a time at least, for a short time I hope, is a failure for France. It can be seen today, it will be seen even more tomorrow in the United Nations if nothing unforeseen happens.

I love France. Of all countries, it is the one nearest to me, although I do not belong to it and I don't go there regularly.

So, I am surprised by myself, watching television, for example, when I hope for a new failure of French policy, because it is de Gaulle's policy.

Is it because I hope, in a more distant future, after God knows what revolution, for a return to the past, a real success for France? Isn't it so that I'll be proven right? Or because I rejoice at the failure of a man who is antipathetic to me, for whom, however, I begin to feel pity now that he is almost alone?

I would like to be sure that these last hypotheses are not the true ones.

/*Sunday, October 2, 1960*

D. and I, in the company of Pierre, have just made our traditional trip to the Lausanne station for the papers. This morning I want to tell a story, not because I attach importance to it, but because it came to my mind just now while I was shaving, and also because it's a beautiful autumn Sunday, sweetly familial, and then perhaps because I hope to begin a novel on Tuesday or Wednesday, which I'm getting into little by little, because I don't want to go too fast, because the birth of the characters must never be too thought out, or willed. I'm giving myself a short respite. An intermission.

The story has been told in the papers several times, but never, if I remember correctly, in an exact way. And sometimes an attempt was made to connect it with the character of Maigret, who must have been born ten years later.

I was a beginner, a reporter of the Liège *Gazette*. Every morning I used to write one of those daily columns like the ones one sees published in italics in most of the provincial papers. Maybe it was the Lausanne *Tribune* that refreshed my memory today. These little columns most often focus on local life, with a bit of poetry, some facile and affected philosophy, some irony, etc.

To indicate clearly that my little corner in the *Gazette* was separate, my editor had proposed to call it "Outside the Henhouse" and to sign it "M. le Coq."

I admit that at first I did not understand either the title or the

117

signature, which I changed later into Georges Sim, because one of my colleagues told me that Le Coq was a collective pseudonym for the editors.

All this takes a long time to tell. It seems to me that in a novel it would be given only a sentence or two. It must have been in 1920, hence a little more than a year after the Armistice of 1919 and the liberation of Belgium. About the war as it had developed in France or elsewhere, those of us who lived under the occupation more than four years knew only what the Germans allowed us to know, plus a few gleanings from the rare Dutch papers that got across the border from time to time.

At that period I liked to roam around City Hall, which, at Liège more than any place else, is the real center of the life of the countryside. I wandered, sniffing the wind, eating cherries in spring, later candy or biscuits that I kept in my pocket, because I was always hungry. I loved the noise, the bustle, the colors, music. . . . I loved the little cafés of the neighborhood which smelled of gin and were frequented by Walloon poets and actors from the local theaters.

Professionally, I was obliged to be at police headquarters behind City Hall every morning at eleven o'clock, where my four colleagues and I would be given the daily reports.

Opposite, to the left of the staircase of City Hall, was another station, and one day, by chance, I saw three monumental and very heavy cases in the corridor which seemed to me mysterious. Who told me about them? I forget. Still, I learned that these cases had been sent to the city of Liège by a Belgian violinist living in Paris, and that they contained a complete collection of *L'Illustration* (the big magazine of that time) of the time of the war, along with other reviews and journals.

The sender offered this documentation to his fellow citizens and asked that it be placed in the public library.

The cases sat there, unopened, for more than a year. Wasn't it important, for us who knew so little about the war, to be able to consult these collections?

Soon, I was at the home of my editor-in-chief, Joseph Demarteau, and I told him my plan. He approved of it with a certain amount of hesitation, and he warned me that if anything went wrong I could not make use of his name.

The next day, on a beautiful sunny morning like today, I left the paper in the company of a linotypist who is still alive and continues to give me news of himself from time to time, he pushing a handcart, I looking unconcerned. A big wedding was taking place, so there was much activity in the court of City Hall.

In a few minutes, my linotypist, who was stronger than average, put the three cases on the handcart without anyone's questioning him. A half hour later they were in the hands of the head librarian of Chiroux, the kind Walloon poet Joseph Vrienst, who had sent me his first books when I was a boy of ten.

Two hours later the *Gazette* appeared with an enormous headline across an entire page:

INDIFFERENT ADMINISTRATION
POORLY GUARDED CITY HALL

The story was told in detail. At five o'clock, I was called to the office of the police chief, who told me there would be legal proceedings, at the request of the alderman of Public Instruction and Fine Arts.

The next day, for fear of ridicule, the alderman withdrew his complaint. He held it against me for a long time. Later, when he was a very old gentleman, I saw him during one of my trips to Liège, and we talked, laughing about the famous cases.

That is the only time that Joseph Demarteau sent me a box of cigars, which I shared with my linotypist. Why cigars? I was seventeen years old and only smoked a pipe.

For forty-eight hours, or maybe a week, I was a sort of celebrity. But, of course, I was thinking much more of Rouletabille than of Maigret.

Novel finished this morning. Was going to be called *Le Cauche-mar*. Finally, it will have *Betty* as a title. Working full tilt for seven days. Nothing else seemed important to me. This morning, after writing the word "End," it all seemed wasted, almost absurd. I wondered why in a few months people would pay to read it. And I dread the moment when I will have to undertake the revision. The tragedy, to use a grandiose word, is perhaps that between novels I can't believe in the last one. . . . Funny profession!

On the subject of *L'Ours en Peluche*. What I'm about to say is at odds with the last entry. It is a novel to which I attach a certain importance (or attached?) perhaps because I had the impression of discovering a little area of humanity that only the psychiatrists had paid attention to. Then, when de Fallois, who seems to have understood all my books and who has read them all, read it he said to me:

"I followed the character [by followed he meant: I identified with the character] up to a little before the end. The three or four final pages escaped me."

Yesterday, young Mauriac, who also knows my work and who has written some things about me which I find to the point, wrote almost the same thing in *Figaro*. He saw the last page as a concession, or a set piece. I, who never write to critics to correct them or explain myself, almost sent him a few words.

For it is just the last three pages that are important and which could explain many crimes that are apparently inexplicable. For a long time my character was obsessed by the desire to throw in his hand, to get rid of his responsibilities, *while remaining the center of attention.* He needed to be a kind of hero, needed to be questioned about himself, to be discovered finally as not so simple as those around him thought.

For a long time, he has not seen any other means of obtaining this result than suicide, a spectacular suicide, which would create excitement. Then, at the moment when there seems to be no other way out, he discovers the possibility of a substitution. He can obtain the same result without dying and, thus, be present at the upheaval that will follow. The gesture will be almost the same. A difference of only a few centimeters in the angle of the revolver. It is another who will die. And, as assassin, he has the same advantages as he would have had as victim.

This substitution seems to me to happen often and could be, consciously or not, the basis of a great number of homicides and crimes of passion.

De Fallois and Mauriac do not understand. The other critics will not understand either, which means they do not understand the meaning of my novels. Am I wrong in not explaining, in not dotting the *i*'s, in refusing to use a moralistic or exegetic tone? I have the impression that if I did so I would betray my craft as novelist.

This shouldn't bother me. But there are moments when it discourages me.

Will they understand *Betty*? They will again talk about the sexuality in this novel when it is only secondary in my eyes. Mauriac mentions it in discussing *L'Ours en Peluche* where there can't be more than thirty lines that have to do with sexual life in all the novel!

I would like so much to be indifferent to opinion. Entirely indifferent. I manage to be in what concerns me personally. Not yet in what concerns my characters, as if, in my eyes, they are more important than myself.

Tomorrow Lyons. Criminology Congress. I'm curious to know the level of these men who indirectly dispose of people's heads. If I can judge by the works of some of them, it's rather frightening.

Three days at the Criminology Congress in Lyons. Jurists, doctors, psychiatrists, medical experts, social workers, chaplains, policemen, each one well versed in his profession. Assuredly professional conscientiousness (also many petty ambitions). But an astonishingly average level. Each speaks his own language and barely deigns to explain himself to the specialist next to him.

As for the criminal who, in the last analysis, is the foundation of this activity . . .

He *is examined*. With a microscope, or a scalpel, or with theories. He is made to undergo somewhat ridiculous tests, like those for the driver's license in some American states. And the man? All these people function as members of their background, their class. Once again, they examine. And the appearance of a photographer interests them more than the reports being made.

Too bad. I've already said that I have the same impression in politics. In almost every area, in fact.

I wasn't an anarchist, nor of the Left. On the contrary, though poor I recognized the necessity of social classes without bitterness.

It has been through getting to know—little by little, from close up, sometimes intimately—those who govern, who lead, who dispose, who decide, and who think professionally, that I've begun to be frightened.

If there were a scale to weigh men . . .

I've followed the path opposite to tradition. It is only as I've grown older that I've become "against." I would say almost against everything.

Man remains for me. I hope to be able to go on believing in him.

Lazy days, loving and paternal. Went to gather mushrooms, Johnny and I, and for two hours we were the same age.

Hurrying to revise *Betty* and to write another novel. I want this one to be different. It's a long time since I'd wanted to write a different novel, to give another point of view, a less tragic one

—that's not the exact word but I can't find another to fit. Then, at the last moment, sometimes after an almost ironic first chapter, as in *La Vieille,* in spite of myself I go back to my habitual tone. For a couple of hours or for several days (?) I can see things differently, but I find myself back again with my customary point of view.

Are my thoughts beginning to run in circles?

Many joys, in any case, these days of intermission, with my wife and my children. Are there any others that are real? I doubt it more and more and it is not—is no longer—unthinkable for me that one day I may no longer be a novelist. Later, of course. Much later, I hope. But I think of it now without terror.

In the meantime I am as anxious as ever to write my next novel—the one I would like to be, that I hope will be, different.

Zut!

/October 28, 1960

Corrections to a few sentences written yesterday. I'm trying to clarify my thought. It's not that I'm tortured by political matters. But, once more, as in 1936, at the time of the Spanish revolution, then the war, the Liberation, I see how politics inundates us again and I fear the moment—aren't we already there?—when France will be divided into two camps again and each will be forced, especially writers, to be "committed."

What I wrote yesterday about my scant sympathies for the Left at one time in my life, precisely when I had the most reason to oppose the Right, capitalism, etc., is not quite exact. It was more skepticism (easy!) on my part. Since there must be a government, and since, after a while, one government is as good as another . . .

And also: why ask the street sweeper or the village drunk for his advice on foreign policy?

I still believed that evolution of human quality more or less corresponded to a certain intellectual evolution.

E   123

It was only later that I realized how rarely this is the case, that the opposite is more likely to occur, that in raising himself in the social scale man grows harder and ends, perhaps unconsciously, by no longer perceiving anything but his own instinct. Not to speak of the need for power, which becomes overweening.

What criterion to use to weigh men, to judge them?

That's what I meant yesterday, but which I believe I explained badly and which I still explain badly.

Today I always trust the simplest, the least evolved man, most, the least provided with worldly goods who also, as the Scriptures say, seems to me the nearest to . . . To what? Difficult to answer that question without going into the domain of morality. And what morality? Based on what?

Even from the point of view of a certain individual serenity (not to say happiness), material evolution has failed. Man has lost his purity, which, if I were pushed to the wall, I might finally call an animal one. And I prefer the cruelty which accompanies that purity sometimes to the conscious cruelty, studied, political, of the more highly developed man.

Is it because I have scarcely any of this in myself? I haven't yet come to an understanding of the place assigned to what is called intelligence. In any case to its power.

Sometimes it seems to me a sort of curse, since most often it runs counter to all our instincts if not all harmony.

/November 9, 1960

Nothing special to say. Even nothing at all to say, anyway anything that is worth the effort of writing. However, a desire, since this morning, to bring this notebook up to date. Is it important?

Finished the revision of *Betty* and am well enough satisfied. Why not admit: very well satisfied? Sharp desire to write something else, to change. What I always promise myself for the next novel. I would like to be still capable of writing a novel with an intrigue, a plot, a host of characters. But, when I begin, my microscope only takes in a tiny segment of humanity.[1] I shall try again towards the end of the month after the visit of Henry Miller, who is arriving tomorrow or the day after by car.

Have S. here, and half his book. Much talk. Much too much. I swear each time not to talk. Then the need to convince . . .

The house is warm, well protected, folded in on itself. An anniversary that touched me more than the preceding ones: the 15th of our meeting, D.'s and mine. Fifteen years! The only years of my life I'd like to relive, Sainte-Marguerite, New Brunswick, Florida, Arizona, Carmel, and finally the house in Lakeville which I keep for no reason, out of sentiment. Fifteen really full years, in every sense. And three more children than at the start, not counting Marc's boyhood and adolescence.

I shall end up, I think, seeing no one but my family. Too bad if I've already said that and am repeating myself. Other people make me repeat myself even more by always asking me the same question to which I think I must answer like a phonograph.

Growing friendship with Johnny and, recently, with Marie-Jo, who is becoming a most attractive person.

A young Belgian, named N., just sent me his thesis on *Solitude in the Works of Simenon*. He isn't the first to have written on that subject. To my mind, they all deceive themselves. I am one of the least solitary of men, the least capable of living alone.

For example Miller, who is going to arrive with the two friends he picked up on the way (lady friends?), at seventy or seventy-two. I don't know what he'll say to me this time but we chatted at Cannes and he has written me since. He must have lived the whole of his life as a solitary. A vagabond, but a vagabond open to all comradeships, friendships, enthusiasms, loves . . . He has children from three or four wives, and today these women keep them from him. At least that's what I've understood. That, to me, is real solitude. But then, most often it is the solitude of those people who can only live surrounded by others.

[1] I hope it will be understood that this sentence is ironic and that I am mocking myself when I speak of a microscope.

I'll know on Friday or Saturday if I'm right. One of his last letters has a tragic tone.

I've known other men like him, happy Bohemians, and I've seen them at seventy; some have committed suicide.

Nevertheless, I'm a Bohemian too, in my own way. I don't think that it's ancient bourgeois instinct which forces me to live otherwise, to have deep attachments—not roots, however, nothing in depth. With me it's more a certain sense of animal life.

"You never talk about friendship!" S. said to me.

It's true. I looked at him a little stunned. If he had said companionship, comradeship, accompliceship . . . But friendship? This word means nothing to me.

He didn't understand me, from his point of view, while I was astonished by his concept of man, of a humanity barely twenty centuries old—when in my eyes it is at least a million years old and when prehistoric man interests me much more than contemporary man.

When I admitted to him that I envied the gorilla family in the equatorial forest, I must have sunk in his esteem, or else he thought it was an affectation on my part.

But the father gorilla fascinates me much more than Archimedes. I am sure a day will come when the lessons we learn will not begin arbitrarily either with Sumeria, or Egypt, or Greece, but with a much longer and more important past. More beautiful, too.

/Monday, November 14th

Miller just left, in beautiful sunshine. Fresh gay morning. Before his arrival, I had meant to speak here of two things, of no more importance than others, except, perhaps, for my children. My daily schedule and my reading, about which so many stupidities have been written. I'll come back to them later. I note it here, not to remind myself, since I don't reread these notes, but to date this preoccupation.

(Apropos rereading, day before yesterday it happened that I had to reread, for a new revised edition, two chapters of *Three Rooms in Manhattan* in proof. Not happy with the style, but how I was reminded of the beginning of my love for D.! What a road traveled since, better, without romanticism, with nothing forced or literary! And how, with Oona Chaplin . . . But that will come later.)

So, four days with Henry Miller. My fears proved groundless. However, I was afraid when I saw him getting out with two more or less parasitical "friends," whom he soon got rid of by sending them to spend the day in Lausanne, and whom, in spite of our polite invitations, we didn't see again until this morning for their departure.

Four very full days, fruitful, I think. D. and I aren't cut out to accommodate a third party, but in spite of that, of all those who have come here, he was the least cumbersome, the most tactful, and the one who fitted into the household best. The children adopted him at once.

He is a pure soul. Also a child, actually, in spite of his seventy years. Full of experiences, certainly, but always ready to leap to the attack against husbands and against . . . women. I shan't put down any indiscretions here. I have respect for my guests and for anyone who confides in me. But in the case of Miller, he himself has written the truth about everything that concerns him so one may talk about him.

A Bohemian, certainly, a sort of anarchist, but in the long run, less so than I, who seem to be a bourgeois because of my externally material life.

Pure? In a sense. He cannot refuse himself a toy, the first woman he sees. And he is incapable of refusing her what she asks, living with her, marrying her. From which results a situation so tangled that he can hardly find a way out. For he cannot break with any of them either. He does not cut ties. He remains bound to all these successive women, legitimate and illegitimate. He has children who go from one wife to another.

He loves these children. But for a simple whim, he will sacrifice them, send them back to their mother or back to a stepmother, take them back, send them off again.

In another man, this could be odious. In him, no. That is why I wrote the word "pure." He loves them. He continues to love, in his way, his wife or his successive mistresses. It is the organization of society that is at fault, not he.

Many points of contact outside of this question. I'll come back to it perhaps. Not a moment of boredom during these four days. No weariness. Joy, however, at being together again, D. and I, in a house without strangers this morning.

We are not good friends for others. I think that one cannot be part of a couple and have true friends. The proof is that the most solid friendships are those made during the war or in great calamity—when there are no women.

Saturday evening, a curious impression. Dinner here with Charlie and Oona Chaplin, the Millers—and us. At the beginning, Charlie tells stories, mimes, brilliant, gay, amusing. Then suddenly, to Miller and me, he admits:

"I always have to go into my act, at least in the beginning, first out of shyness, and then because I know it is expected of me."

Not by us. He realizes that. He knew that about me. But not about Miller. And, after dinner, there are the three men, not in easy chairs, of which there are plenty in the drawing room, but leaning on our elbows around the round table as if in a bistrot, while D. keeps Oona company in a corner.

A parenthesis. Oona is one of the rare women, maybe the only one, whom I would have married if I had met her before D.

Also, I had to betray D. last evening, and I ask her pardon. But first I must tell about it. Briefly, for what C. Ch. told us we will also find in his book of Memoirs, now finished and nine hundred pages long.

He tried to make us understand his reaction to the sudden,

cruel, pitiless turning against him in the U.S.A. (I wanted to give the same feeling, four or five years ago, in my book *Le Petit Homme d'Arkhangelsk* on a lower level, of course.)

Another parenthesis, because I am trying to follow the thread of thought rather than composing. Well before knowing Chaplin, in Los Angeles, around 1947 or 1948, I already had an idea on this subject which was not his, but which I continue to consider good.

When he made his first films and for a long time afterwards, Americans naturally (those who know them) believed that he was mocking the *little man* (as clumsy, ridiculous, useless, and petty). They laughed. They were enthusiastic.

Then they discovered, thanks to the critics and the reactions in other countries, that the little man was the hero, that it was the others who were ridiculous or odious. They discovered an anarchist! Whence their fury at having been duped. It was, for them, like a deception. For years, they had applauded the enemy of the system necessary to American civilization.

This isn't fully convincing. Chaplin doesn't believe too much in it. I've seen that this explanation does not satisfy him, that he prefers the one he gives in his book, which will not appear for a year: a certain speech during the war, in San Francisco.

I return to the three of us around the round table, to our three faces, the two women in their corner, talking about children. Oona indifferent to us, D., on the contrary, trying to hear and understand.

Chaplin tells us his most moving experience. An unimportant actor earning sixty-five dollars a week in Hollywood, he becomes, from one day to the next, a star with millions. He has to go to New York. He takes the train with his brother Sidney. And, at the first stop, he sees a crowd which overflows the station. He does not yet know it is for him. Music. Officials. He is seized with panic. At the next station it's worse, then at the third, and when he approaches New York the mayor asks him to get off incognito at 125th Street in order to avoid the crowd which is storming Grand Central and has got out of control.

The mayor and the chief of police come to meet him, drive him to the Plaza.

The same evening, when the crowd is looking for him, he takes a walk in the streets without being recognized.

"Everyone knew me," he says, "and I knew no one. I had no one to talk to!"

The crowd frightened him. He felt hunted. Solitude frightened him too. He was very young. I think that this marked him for life.

All this, he told us in a soft, intense voice. Oona wasn't listening:

"I've heard it a hundred times!"

D. tried to listen while talking about children and labor pains.

The Chaplins, who had planned to leave at ten o'clock, left at midnight. Miller, very much moved, went back to the drawing room with us, and we talked about it.

D. spoke the truth, calmly. I don't remember her words. It is no less significant that we have just been present at an act, that there was a great deal of "showmanship" in what we had just seen of a life.

I was obliged, although I share her opinion, to contradict her, brusquely, for the truth would have hurt Miller. To him, it was one of the greatest evenings of his life.

And he too brings a good deal of "showmanship" to his life.

To say it to him would not only be to hurt him but to take from him a part of his self-confidence. To take from him a little of his faith. So that there I was, in spite of myself, for more than two hours (for this all ended at three in the morning) obliged to argue, against my convictions, against my wife, whom I agreed with.

I betrayed her in order not to hurt a man whom I admire, of whom I have become fond, but who is nothing to me.

Stupid, isn't it? If only I had been able to give her a sign, let her know I was lying, that I was arguing against my own convictions.

For Chaplin continues his "act." A different "act," closer, very close to himself, but different from reality all the same.

All this is disconnected, on purpose.

Johnny understood. Wonderful Johnny!

I'll come back to it perhaps. I must go wake D., who finally agreed to lie down for an hour after sleeping three or four hours a night for several days.

Good morning again, D. Good morning, my old Kay, whom I never forget and who remains dear to me!

Without needing to reread it, I know that everything I wrote yesterday is almost true but not quite. I would have liked to make clear, through two lives, certain kinds of men who "take" without giving, quite naturally, because they have remained children. So cruel and egotistical, like children. That's what is called Bohemian.

And Ch. Ch. remains a Bohemian (in his soul) in spite of his seven children with Oona, not counting Sidney.

Amazing life. Up to the age of fifty-five, he felt no need to tie himself to anything or anyone. He meets a kid of seventeen, marries her, and here he is, at seventy-one, father of seven young children, the last of whom is six months old. He loves them. He loves Oona. He loves his present life. But . . .

Same for Miller. He is in love again. He is going to take her to Spain or somewhere else—he doesn't yet know—a young woman from Hamburg who has two children. His own? He sent them back, not to their mother, who no longer wants them, but to his third wife, who may not want them in six months either.

I don't judge him. Once again, they are sincere, both of them.

I feel I still haven't expressed my thought, my feeling. No doubt it isn't possible.

The 17th already! If I want to write a novel before Christmas, it's time. I hope to begin it the end of next week and I'll do my shopping first.

Yesterday I received a telegram from Georges Charensol, of *Nouvelles Littéraires,* asking me urgently for an article on the occasion of the *Prix National des Lettres* which my friend Blaise Cendrars ought to receive next Saturday or Monday unless there's some last-minute maneuver. I said Yes, of course. I've sent an open letter, since I haven't written any articles for a long time, and I am ninety-nine per cent sincere in it.

As with the *Grand Prix de la Ville de Paris,* this prize is not awarded until the winners are dying and it is almost always given to them on their deathbeds. Jean-Paul Fargue, Carco, were in that condition. Cendrars has been paralyzed for more than two years and if I haven't gone to see him it is because, according to what I'm told, he feels humiliated in front of his friends.

In my open letter, I speak of Henry Miller and of Chaplin. Cendrars is a Bohemian too, a sort of perennial anarchist, and I would like to modify what I wrote day before yesterday on this subject.

All in all, these notebooks are like my novels. I take up a subject or a character in a novel. It continues to pursue me because I have the impression of not having gone to the end of my thought, of having left it unfinished, or inaccurate. After a certain time, I take the subject or the character up again in another form.

There are some I've taken up five or six times and I'm not yet satisfied. Some critics reproach me for it, or speak pretentiously of my "themes" as if it were a matter of obsessions. But this is accepted in painters, who paint a *Pietà* or a vase of flowers twenty times over.

I'm coming back to Miller, to Cendrars, to Chaplin. We certainly belong to more or less the same family. And now, not speaking of them directly any more, I come to Bohemians in general, to rebels, to marginal lives.

I've known many of them, in Montmartre, in Montparnasse, in the South, then in Tahiti, in Greenwich Village. It seems to me that they become more and more numerous as man becomes more and more uniform, more and more domesticated, and there are veritable colonies of them in Rome, for example, and now in San Francisco.

But I am both very near and very far from them. I share their anticonformism, most of their ideas, their resentments.

Why do they trouble me? Because apparently I live like a bourgeois? I don't think so. It goes further. I've spoken of their purity—an infantile purity—and I have suspected for a long time that they are not always the weak or the maladjusted nor yet rebels by nature.

Many of them have realized that weakness, apparent or real, is the best armor in a hard world. Apparently unarmed, they get all the sympathy, all the help, all the indulgence. They are the ones whom the patrons not only adopt but seek out. It's for them that governments create useless positions or scholarships.

What is asked of them is to be awkward, ingenuous, uncompromising. They are that way with women, too, with their children, in the sense that they accept no responsibility, no rules.

At bottom, there is no doubt very often a real weakness, an authentic infantilism. Not always. And that quickly turns into a comfortable pose.

This pose, rightly, irritates D., and I understand her. Her almost pathological sense of justice makes her bristle before a certain tolerance which appears and which perhaps is undeserved.

What am I doing, I, in this brotherhood? It is simply that I have, basically, the same anticonformism, the same rebellions. I am a true anarchist, I too, but because I live in society, because in spite of myself I profit by it, I consider it my duty to follow its rules. Without believing in them. Without teaching them to my children. I follow them the more scrupulously because I do not believe in them, because that is my way of "paying my share."

All this is still not to the point, I feel. I love these Bohemians whom I would call planned. I am comfortable with them. There are almost fraternal bonds between us. At the same time they make me shudder as I must make them shudder. I remain conscious of the part they play, almost sincerely, and this is almost what constitutes the whole problem. Like children, they are marvelous actors. And does one ever know where "acting" begins and ends with a child?

Apropos acting in my last little chapter, D. made me notice that I used the word wrong, that in any case it is too strong. She is right. I should have written: "X did his act." And still this may be too strong. It is very difficult, above all with words, to place a boundary between a man's sincerity and insincerity, whether it is a matter of comedy, of tragedy, or of simple convention. I feel it. It triggers something inside me. But as for saying at what moment the insincere has begun, and to what degree someone has left sincerity behind . . .

That's all for today, for this morning anyway, and I would like to be as empty as possible to leave room for my next novel.

Should I add a little paragraph? Last evening, S. spoke on television of his new novel. He knows my work. He is writing a book on me. He told me, here, that his novel is directly inspired by one of mine. The subject is the same. Same situation. Central character almost identical. He added, still *here,* that he was so aware of this that out of honesty he had put a sentence from my book on the title page. But now, on television, he spoke of this case as a personal psychological discovery. Desgraupes—unless it was Dumayet, I mix them up—who knows my work too, did not bring it up either.

Bitterness? Honestly, no. A slight deception, which is connected with what I wrote above. I am not weak enough. I give the impression of being strong and it is possible that I am to a certain degree.

Basically, society avoids strong men. They are distrusted. They are envied. They are ignored. The weak man makes others feel good. The strong man makes them ashamed.

Sorry! I ought not to have spoken of that, but I know that this will interest Johnny, whom this question already bothers and who is learning to take his responsibilities bravely, the more bravely in that he believes in them no more than I do.

A little note just for myself. I am supposed to be a strong man, this is what they try to make me believe, what I appear to be, what I make myself believe I am, perhaps, while in fact I know that strong men don't exist. This week I was twice tempted to call for help. For nothing definite. For nothing serious. Only the person I could have called was the one who had failed me or whom I believed to have failed me. This ought to be deleted, I think. And besides it has no meaning except for me. "He who must be strong at any cost." He who is condemned always to be strong! Let's say no more about it. And excuse this weakness.

All erased, as if by a wind. Two-hour ride in the car, slowly, smoothly, over little roads and little byways in the country. D. asleep beside me three quarters of the time, and Pierre, on her knees, sleeping, looking contented as a bear cub in his mother's fur. We didn't exchange ten sentences. It was enough. I know it. I always know it. And all the same, each time, I despair.

Everything begins anew and I am going to cleanse my body of the whisky (I haven't once overindulged) of this last day.

Then a novel. And our good life.

How easy and how difficult everything is at the same time! And how much simpler it would be if we were never tempted to judge.

To live.

Welcome, D., as they say in your country.

I find you again, old notebook friend, sooner than I would have believed and than I would have wished. I was hoping not to see you again until after the holidays, in 1961.

Yesterday, at about 3:45, I settled down in this same study, the "Do Not Disturb" on both doors, the coffee beside me, four dozen new pencils freshly sharpened, a new pad too, of yellowish paper, and the brownish envelope with the names, ages, addresses of my characters—a pile of railway guides . . . Curtains drawn, typewriter and pipes cleaned . . . In short, my routine which finally has become superstition.

Eight to ten days of preparation, as usual, the most unpleasant, during which I'm in a bad temper. I try out subjects, characters, as one tries on garments in a store, or furnished apartments. . . .

I wrote the title: *Le Train*. Then ten lines, without conviction. Then I stopped and thought. No panic, no anxiety, as on other occasions when I felt that it didn't go right. In fact I could have written this novel consciously as homework, an exercise. Perhaps it wouldn't have been bad? Perhaps the spark would have come?

I stopped because I realized that I was not writing this novel out of need, but in spite of something, to prove to myself that I was still capable of writing four novels a year. But I have written only three, *L'Ours en Peluche*, *Betty*, and *Maigret et les Viellards*. Plus my Balzac broadcast, which took me more than a month.

I was writing out of fear. And the proof of it was that I had chosen an easy subject, with predetermined action, dialogue, and characters. But not one substantial character who imposed himself on me.

Wasn't that cheating? I preferred to stop. The end of the year is always a pressured period, preparation for the holidays, etc. And a short stay on the Côte d'Azur planned for the 15th.

I put my material away without depression, glad I hadn't pushed on at any cost. I hope to write a novel in January, perhaps a Maigret in order to get my hand in again.

Certainly not a manufactured novel. (I will have to explain someday why I don't consider the Maigrets, which are minor works, to be manufactured.)

A little shame, I admit, at D., the children, the staff, seeing me coming out of my office before time.

"No novel?"

But, the same evening, on television ("Reading for Everybody") there was a lady of fifty who just won the *Prix Femina*—an innkeeper by occupation. Why do you write? What inspires you? Do you put yourself in your novels? Etc., etc.

Then a mechanic of thirty, Bohemian, attractive.

Both of them just happen to write . . . yes . . . because . . . It's hard, but it's fun . . . they will go on. . . .

I was thunderstruck. Such frankness! It goes on every week on the same program, celebrities and noncelebrities who talk about themselves and their work in a way that amazes me.

Do I too . . . ? I can't believe that I am like them, that I write for the same reasons (except two or three of these colleagues whose words strike another note).

"When will you start a new novel?"

"Not for several weeks because that's the time I have to stay in Paris for the launching of my book."

And that one has talent and will be in the Academy.

I don't believe in a priesthood. But still—!

Still . . . when I was starting out, at twenty-five, at thirty, didn't I answer in somewhat the same way, often out of modesty, which falsified my interviews of that period?

Come on! Let's be frank. I had a certain cynicism and I was capable of saying of a novel that I thought had come out badly: "It's good enough for the public anyway."

It's now that I get stage fright, that I have scruples. Out of respect for what?

I believe in art, to be sure. It is the only human manifestation that seems to me to be worthy of some pride. But from there to believing that my own work, the words I set down, have importance . . .

Work well done? Certainly, I have a craftsman's conscience. This is not enough to make one impose on oneself the anguish that I go through.

To live with characters who . . .

I think I know the explanation. I am a happy man. Whatever one says and whatever I myself may have said in jest, I don't write to cure my complexes.

When I was very young, I dreamed of leading several lives at once. One of my first heroes in a popular novel, whom I called Jarry, had been a real peasant in the country, a real fisherman in Brittany, a man of the world in Paris, etc.

I too have done everything, as an avocation, been fisherman, farmer, horseman, sailor, etc. But it is in creating characters that I come closest to living a multiple life.

Each novel is an enrichment for me, an experience that I live. If a problem bothers me, it is through one of my characters that I find an answer.

I don't escape myself . . . I . . .

It's complicated. There is no real reason, however, I should live eight days with all sorts of characters—I don't say artificial ones —created for a specified action.

The Train started out with an idea. One of my characters was real and I was beginning to live inside his skin. The others, to move the action forward, had to be less real, or at least more schematic.

I preferred to give this one up, and today I'm glad of it, proud, though a bit lost to find myself free at the hours when I should have been working.

Once more I see that elderly innkeeper on television, so sure of herself, so self-satisfied . . . knit three, purl two . . . The difficult thing is to find the tone, she says . . . Once the tone comes . . . And the needles click . . .

There's a woman who's happy without knowing it. The young mechanic too.

"What I came up with is, roughly speaking, to write on two levels, the present and the past . . . the story takes place in the present within twenty-four hours but is constantly interrupted by flashes of the past, several pasts. . . ."

Yes, indeed!

I have a dream which I shall probably never realize. Still, I've been playing with it for more than thirty years, nearly forty years, it's come back to me over and over, particularly each time I've begun to see my next novel. It is to write a picaresque novel, a long story without head or tail, with stops, as in the course of a stroll, with characters who rise up and disappear without reason, secondary stories which, in turn, introduce others.

I don't think I'm capable of it. In spite of myself, by instinct much more than by dogma or conviction, I tighten. I cut short. I restrict myself, each time, to a precise, limited universe. Is this related to my phobia regarding crowds, which frighten me, to an instinctive reaction against disorder?

I've also dreamed of a house where nothing would have its proper place, a changing house, changing according to my mood or the moods of my family. I have a sixteenth-century Dutch painting, nothing special, which shows the common room of a country house. The men wear lace on their doublets, plumes on their hats, which indicates that they are, as one used to say, "well-born." However, near the baby's cradle and some children playing, next to the laid table, a pig goes its way, and hens and roosters. The bed is not far from the hearth where the meal is cooking. One feels that whoever wants to can come and go and won't disturb, that the house is open.

In my early days in Paris, I had a friend from Liège who got there a little before me, a painter, who had settled on the Rue de Mont-Cenis in a loft at the far end of a courtyard. There, too, there was only one room. My friend was married. He had a little girl. However, sometimes there would be ten or fifteen of us to feed (each one chipped in a few pennies to buy bread, cold cuts, and red wine for everyone), to smoke, to drink, to argue until three or four o'clock in the morning, sitting on the floor or on the only bed. . . .

You never knew beforehand whom you would find there, but you knew that you would find someone. It turned out badly. My friend died shortly after his daughter (dead at seven or eight years of age) of cirrhosis of the liver. And of all those I knew there in these three or four years I know few who stayed afloat. They came to sad ends.

Even then, observing them, I had the impression of being able to diagnose each one, to foresee his fate.

I am against every established order, against every imposed discipline.

But I cannot live without order and discipline and there is no object on my desk that is not in its place. I get up from my armchair to pick up a tiny piece of paper on the carpet.

Contradiction? I'm not sure. Protective instinct? It's possible, for I may have just missed becoming a Bohemian.

Can I risk another hypothesis without seeming arrogant?

I possess, I believe, a certain lucidity which makes me see causes and effects at the same time. I know what picturesque characters basically are and the fate that awaits them. In Montmartre and Montparnasse I met a good number of people about whom I could tell the funniest stories, all true, as Vlaminck used to.

Only, I also know the end of these stories, an end that is not funny at all. Vlaminck, sturdier than I, nearer to the truth, to a certain health, could adjust both to the funny and to the tragic.

For me, the fun was wiped out.

No doubt that is why I will never write a picaresque novel.

It would fail. One can write a book stuffed with dozens of characters. Not with dozens of destinies.

Or else I would have had to begin at twenty-five on a single work—a hundred or a hundred and fifty volumes long.

But isn't that just what I have done, more or less consciously?

140

I had just finished the preceding note when it seemed false to me, as almost always. In a picaresque novel, what counts most is the picturesque, the differences between men, the warts, the crossed eyes, the stammers, the limps, the phenomena of every kind. Each thing that grafts itself onto man as certain little white shells onto the mussel shell.

It is the accidental. The fortuitous.

But, in spite of myself, I always come back, not to the differences, but to the resemblances.

I couldn't have written a hundred-volume work with a hundred characters. But perhaps a work in a hundred volumes with one character.

Which is still not accurate, of course, but which appears to me already more satisfactory.

As for what that story is doing here, I don't know. I suddenly thought of it when I was 'dreaming after lunch, and leafing through the papers, about writing the novel of a whole street, or of a large apartment building. It would almost certainly be reduced to three or four characters!

We are going to take Pierre for a ride in the car, D. and I, as in Carmel each afternoon we used to take Johnny, then, in Lakeville, Marie-Jo. The same actions. The same peace. The same deep well-being.

/Sunday, December 4, 1960

Schedule! I haven't forgotten. I had noted that rather as if to remind myself of a holiday assignment (though I never had to do holiday assignments) and, since I thought of it, I might as well get it off my mind. There are many minor subjects that I mention here in a few lines so as not to have to think of them any more, as if it were exorcism.

It's somewhat in the same spirit that in 1941 or 1942 I wrote *Pedigree*, to finish with my childhood reminiscences once and for all, my aunts, my uncles, etc., whom I'm always tempted to put in my novels. I'm not sure of it but I think this was successful insofar as *Pedigree* was concerned and that there is very little in the novels that followed (at least consciously—I mean used consciously) from before 1918.

Good! Schedule. It's almost for myself that I do it. Journalists, colleagues, friends ask me what I do when I'm not writing. And as I only write sixty days out of the year . . . I don't know what to answer them. It seems to me that I do nothing and all the same I'm always busy and often on the run.

Once, younger, I rode horseback, or else, at Porquerolles, for example, I went fishing in a boat. I used to swim, I played volleyball. I traveled ceaselessly. I entertained a lot. I would go anywhere at the slightest provocation.

Now I feel I have become a stay-at-home, a stick-in-the-mud, still . . .

First the schedule of the year, which will be over in less than a month and which is pretty much an average year. What have I done, *grosso modo*?

First, in January, I think, a case of grippe that kept me in bed four or five days, then, for a week, I followed the debates of the Jaccoud affair,* which interested me less from a professional point of view than from a human one. I wanted to be sure that Jaccoud was indeed one of my characters.

Then, about a week of coming and going back and forth between Lausanne and Geneva, sometimes alone, sometimes with D. Afterwards, reading sixteen kilos of the dossier which I'd had here for a month, which took up another week or more. Indirectly, and I insist on this word, a novel came out of it which had nothing to do with the affair, a character who resembled Jaccoud in no way, *L'Ours en Peluche*. But let's follow the chronological order.

I had promised S. a television show on Balzac. Not on his work, which is not my business, but on the man. So I reread all

* The sensational trial for murder of a distinguished Geneva lawyer, Pierre Jaccoud.

his published correspondence, making notes on it, and also the works which told me about his . . . schedule.

A month? Six weeks? Almost. Then a sort of rough draft of one hundred thirty to one hundred forty pages which I used as background for my improvisation in front of the cameras. Six or seven days' more work. Finally, when the gentlemen came to film the broadcast, another five or six days of work, alone or with them.

In March, the novel *L'Ours en Peluche*. As usual—eight days to write it, several days of waiting, then a week to revise.

Now we come to April. In May I had to be at Cannes, where against my will I had agreed to be the President of the Jury of the Film Festival. Having accepted the presidency at Brussels, because I am Belgian, and because the government wanted it, I could not refuse Cannes.

Few days' trip to Paris for clothes and other things. Then the month of May, all or nearly all in Cannes, with several days at the Bernard Buffets' on the way back.

Second novel. After all this agitation, necessarily a Maigret. After abandoning another within the first day. I believe that I mentioned it elsewhere to emphasize that the Maigret, actually, repeated the same tonality. It was *Maigret et les Vieillards*.

We decided to spend ten days, end of July, with the children, except for Pierre, in Venice. This represented several days of coming and going between Echandens and Lausanne in order to buy them the necessary clothing.

Return at the beginning of August. Journalists. I wrote that. An Englishwoman for eight days.[1]

My dizzy spells began to worry me. D. and I decide to go consult a specialist in Paris, more exactly to see the neurologist who took care of me four years ago at the time of my cochlea trouble.

We were both tired. Anyway, we wanted to be alone for a few days.

We stayed there ten days, during the end of the Olympic Games, most often in our apartment.

[1] In my schedule I forgot an appendectomy, about the month of August, I think. And it was after that that I went to Versailles to convalesce.

143

And, as for the Jaccoud affair and *L'Ours en Peluche,* out of a chance meeting came a novel that had nothing in common with that meeting, while indirectly it rose out of it.

Return to Echandens. Third novel: *Betty.*

Family life, but with more visits.

End of October, five days in Lyons, where I wanted to attend the First Criminology Congress.

Return. Decided to write another novel this year. First prevented by the visit of Henry Miller, who spent several days here.

Then abandonment of novel and of the idea of writing one before the holidays.

Christmas shopping. This week, the 8th of December, departure with D. for Cannes, to meet Dr. Pathé at Grasse; he sees us there every year.

Then return . . . Christmas . . . New Year's . . .

So, only three novels. But how many really free, really empty days, in all that? Very few. If D. takes care of business matters, of virtually all the mail, I still write a number of letters by hand. I read. And a house where fifteen people live has its needs. To go to the city to buy this, choose that. Dentist . . . Clothing . . . Tailor . . . Dressmaker . . . Furniture in our offices which I had replaced . . .

This ends by filling up a year, and what I most miss, because of so many obligations which always seem pressing, are the hours alone with D. We have to steal them. If she is in my study with me, somebody bothers us every ten minutes, sometimes one of the children, sometimes a secretary or a maid.

We impose the discipline of eating with the family on ourselves, so we eat at children's hours, hours as strict as those of a boardinghouse: twelve thirty and, in the evening, quarter of seven.

Having sketched the year *grosso modo,* I will try to show a day, since they are necessarily a good deal alike. I don't speak of the times when I'm writing novels, when the schedule never varies.

Most often, when D. comes to wake me with my tea (since I'm

not allowed coffee) Johnny has already left for school at seven twenty.

It's Marie-Jo's turn to get dressed, to decide what she will wear, what she will eat, etc.

Boule (the cook) comes up for the menu. The telephone rings. One of the secretaries arrives. Errands must be assigned to Alphonse (the chauffeur).

Three days a week, massage. Three days without.

If it's a day with, D. spends from eight to nine having hers, I from nine to ten.

On a day without, I dress while the staff passes through the boudoir and the telephone rings.

I love this hour. Pierre comes and crawls around our legs. Only, among so many comings and goings, it's useless for me to try to have a moment alone with D.

I go down to my study at about nine fifteen. Read the mail. Glance at the papers. Light my fire. I go upstairs again five or six times during the morning.

Often, a short walk to the village to meet Pierre, who is taking the air with his nurse.

Then, almost always, something to do in Lausanne. Even if it isn't necessary. I like towns in the morning. Take photos to be developed, buy this or that, books or records . . . it doesn't matter. . . .

Return. The study. Read the dailies or the weeklies.

Luncheon with the family. Then D. comes to have her coffee in my study.

Day with errands or without errands? I mean for her. Purchase of things for the children, underwear, dentist, doctor, hairdresser . . . If yes, I accompany her and I wait from store to store, which doesn't bother me, on the contrary.

Return. Read the afternoon paper. D. downstairs with her secretaries. I again in my study, where the children come to see me one by one. Reading. Medical reviews or others. Or else a few lines of some historical work, or a memoir . . .

And already it's dinnertime. Pierre in bed. Dinner over, Marie-Jo goes up first and goes to bed, accompanied by her mother, who tucks her in while I watch the television news with Johnny.

At eight thirty I put Johnny in bed in my turn. D. briefs the staff for the next day, sometimes goes down to dictate in her office. Then I watch television for a little, if it's worth it. Most often I read, skipping from one book to another.

I wait. Around eleven or eleven thirty, D. comes up and we go to bed, after kissing the sleeping children.

This seems very little set down that way, perhaps empty, all the same there's not a moment lost, so to speak, especially for D., who juggles time from morning to night.

Not once, this year, have we gone to the movies. Nor to the theater. Nor to dinner in town.

Four or five times, around nine thirty, we have taken a break and gone for a walk, arm-in-arm, on the Rue de Bourg, window-shopping.

Then, when a journalist asks us:

"How do you spend your days?"

What to tell him?

Even this truth is only approximate. And, if one subtracts our trips, the novels, the periods during which we have a visitor in the house, how many days are left in the year?

Which do I like best? Two kinds. Those that I've just described, and those that we spend in Paris, in Milan, in Florence, or elsewhere (soon in Cannes!), D. and I, above all when we can avoid seeing other people. Then I have her to myself.

Today, Sunday afternoon, she is in her office. I in my study. Pierre is walking in the garden; the other two, with their friends, are playing music in the playroom. A typical family Sunday. And perhaps, soon, I will be able to persuade D. to go with me for a ride for half an hour. That will make it a lucky Sunday.

We didn't do it on purpose, neither she nor I, loading ourselves with all this work, taking all these cares on our shoulders. It isn't a question of ambition or a question of money. Letters pile up. They must be answered. And these novels written on this desk in eight days go from country to country, on the radio, on television, in films, make so much to-do. . . .

And readers demand to be told that . . . to be told if . . . to be sent this or that. . . .

Some ask for one or ten millions, or a house, or a car. This week someone demanded a cow from us!

But now, when I recall the time when I used to go horseback riding or when I fished, or when I went one hundred kilometers in the car to play golf and had guests almost every day, those years seem to me a frightening void.

And the present years are too short and so full.

Had just written this schedule when I realized that it is only valid for a rather short period. Three years ago, for example, I went twice in a week in the morning to do the marketing in Morges. I love markets. I rush to them each time I am in a new country or in a new region. After several months, when I know everyone, I'm tired of it. It was the same thing with Cannes, where, however, it lasted longer, because of the color, the unique atmosphere.

All in all, from time to time, we adopt a new routine which seems to us permanent.

With fixed points in the schedule, however, which have been the same everywhere we have lived, like our little rides in the car, D. and I, and like our brief trips together.

Same day, evening

Each person tries so hard to exist! It is perhaps the explanation of all human behavior. Each one wants to *be*, from the weakest, the most helpless child.

A little phrase from last evening, though it isn't very original, keeps running through my head. I think that if I rewrote "Le Roman de l'Homme" I would place this need to exist ahead of fear. Its importance is clear in criminology, for example, or in psychiatry and, I think, in psychoanalysis. It would come before sexuality, because it may be one of the reasons for sexuality.

Never mind. That's not my concern. In fact, I would like, only for this notebook, to know shorthand, in order not always to be slowed down by writing. I think some author kept his notes in shorthand, but I can't remember which one. I took one lesson in shorthand at about seventeen, when I was a reporter. It was in the evening, in a dreary place, a class for mediocre, slow, and also dreary adults, and I never went back.

I come back to my vacation homework. I had said: schedule. That's done.

Now, the other chapter: reading. If the idea came to me it must have been when I was changing the arrangement of books in the different libraries in the house, and I came upon a book by Quéneau in which, somewhere, among many others, I listed the books I would take to a desert island. I had no recollection of this. Each week one gets such questionnaires. I answer, because I don't want to be hurtful to a journalist. Briefly. Almost always in a word or two, for each question, on the questionnaire itself. And behold, it winds up in a work published by the *Nouvelle Revue Française!* (Parenthetically, I admire Quéneau a great deal.)

I've often been asked which books have had a formative influence on me and I may not always have given the same answer. Because you can't give an absolute truth in a few words. And one would get a false idea of my reading from studying my library. Each time we've moved, I've sold a quarter, sometimes half my books.[1]

---

[1] The truth is I've only sold books at the beginning of my Paris career, most of them first editions found in bookstalls during my adolescence. Afterwards, I gave them away or even threw them away (these weren't first editions any

For instance, I think I never mentioned that I read the Comtesse de Ségur, or Jules Verne, which I did, however, like all the children of my generation. At what age? Very early, surely. Between eight and thirteen, probably, for at twelve I was at Alexandre Dumas Père, and so on to . . . Paul de Kock. I also read several Fantomas, not many, with a certain twinge, as if this were backsliding, and at about thirteen or fourteen, after Fenimore Cooper and Walter Scott, the Russians, from Pushkin to Gorky through Tolstoy, Dostoevsky, and above all Gogol, my favorite.

I never liked Turgenev. Balzac before, during, and after, in smaller doses. That went by periods. Then there was, among others, the period of plays: all of Labiche, all of Augier, all Alexandre Dumas Fils, and even Meilhac and Halévy. Why?

Auguste Comte, around sixteen or seventeen (I'm not mentioning the authors I studied in school), and Dickens at the same time as Shakespeare.

Among my friends, I was the only one who didn't like Anatole France and didn't like any novels in yellow covers, which later turned into novels in white covers. I preferred Descartes, Pascal, and above all Montaigne, who, for ten years at least, was my bedside book.

Hated Barrès and Bourget, whom I put on the same level as Georges Ohnet or Jules Claretie.

Mad about Maeterlinck for two years.

Then even madder about Conrad and Stevenson (above all the Stevenson of Tuamotu, of whom I found footprints later, first in the Pacific, then in Monterey, in California, where one can still see the house near the harbor where he lived).

At about twenty-three or twenty-four in Paris, I bought at one swoop the entire Collection Budé Greek and Latin classics, in French, alas, since I only did a year of Latin before branching off into the sciences. Ate them up greedily.

A little later discovered Faulkner, Dreiser, Sherwood Anderson (whom I liked very much), then finally Dos Passos and . . . *The*

more!). They were replaced by others, then by others, and now there are only books I keep for my children.

149

Magic Mountain. My greatest admiration for an American writer went to Mark Twain and to the customs officer of the whale.

I read—and liked—Swann and *Within a Budding Grove* at twenty-two, at the same time that I was discovering the first translation of Freud.

For years, I devoured one to three books a day, from Goethe (*Dichtung und Wahrheit* is my favorite) to Napoleon's letters.

Then suddenly, around the age of twenty-seven, I decided to stop reading novels, except an occasional foreign one and the classics. It took an illness, in 1944, for me to reread from beginning to end, in sequence, first all of Proust, then all of Balzac, and later all of Stendhal (whom I admire but who makes me bristle, while Proust always charms me, and sometimes Claudel).

I must be forgetting some, but not a lot, in any case not the ones that count. If I try to sum up, I find the greatest enthusiasm for the Russians, then for the English, the Americans, the French coming last. Why? I don't know. Perhaps because they are moralists rather than novelists. Perhaps also because, in Balzac in particular, money is the basis of most of the conflicts. I prefer the soul, Protestant though it is, of Melville.

Read and reread the Bible and the Gospels many times, as well as the Civil and Penal Codes. Reread them still in small doses.

Tried to read Gide, with whom I was to become friendly. Couldn't. Never told him so.

I read, less for my novels than out of curiosity, almost all that has been written about criminology and continue to read works and reviews on this subject. Psychiatry fascinates me and, to keep things in balance, medicine.

Maigret wanted to be a doctor. And I? I didn't think of it when I was young. Later, yes. But without regret, and, as it happens, most of my friends have been and still are doctors. This interest grows continually and I now devour American, English, French, and Swiss medical reviews. I don't read all of them, of course. I don't have the scientific background. Many things are beyond me, or, in order to understand them, I'd have to do much research. But I'm lazy.

It's a curious enough mechanism that directs my present reading. I pass, for example and by chance, from a work on prehistoric animals to a work on paleontology which suggests several others, which in turn lead me to books on biology.

On a tangent apropos of blood types I'm off on a study of human races. The connection is unexpected and my bookstore is always surprised by my orders, which aren't suggested by the preceding ones.

Actually, I know nothing. I wander about in the knowledge of others, trying to establish, for my personal use, some sort of balance.

By the same token I am not good at any sport because I have practiced them all a little, in the same way that I know nothing in depth because I go into everything as an amateur.

Here and there, in all these works, in all these reviews, I am seeking, ultimately, clues that will permit me to understand man a little better.

And man today—this brings me to my little phrase of last evening—is very troubled. He who has so much need of *being* sees his sense of being diminishing as his knowledge of the worlds grows. The infinitely large of cosmic space on the one hand. The infinitely small on the other.

So here he is, caught between these two infinities, knowing everything except the essential, which means knowing nothing; contemplating innumerable worlds in which his place appears more and more puny.

Hasn't it become obvious, from the arts, from the press, from the mood of the people, that human beings are developing a complex?

Man is no longer "the chosen". . . . He isn't even "the least of these" any more.

He makes use of physical laws that he does not understand and he understands still less—less and less as medicine progresses—what goes on within himself.

One of my American friends, a doctor, editor of a medical review, professor of medical history, has written a fascinating book:

The Antibiotic Saga. It combines the history of the fight against the viruses, the story of their discovery, and, insofar as it is known, the history of the viruses themselves.

The book reads like an epic. One feels the author's awe before the infinitely small and, as it were, one even senses a certain envy.

I am scarcely exaggerating. We are on the way to a virus complex. Especially since the Russian scientists have made it known that these viruses can resist radiations twenty thousand times stronger than those human beings can withstand.

I am sure that there are millions of human beings today who are more or less consciously depressed by this idea—the idea of a world in which they will no longer exist, and where they will be survived by these entities which as far as we know may be nothing but a chemical compound, and which at this moment we track down more or less successfully.

The need to be! To be important! Not only as individuals, but as a species. To be here for some purpose. Not by chance or by accident. To be more than just a temporary form of life.

I wonder if scientists have done right in telling the general public about their discoveries. I even wonder if they themselves can accept their knowledge with serenity!

One can accept dying of the flu, of a painful cancer, of an automobile accident. Yet one revolts against the idea of a chemical explosion or a natural phenomenon that would sweep us from the earth or destroy the earth with us.

Halley's Comet (in 1910, I think?) brought on dozens of suicides.

When I see a psychiatrist, I must ask him—I am almost sure what he will answer—whether recent discoveries have not filled more psychiatric hospitals than any other causes.

I would have done better to write my novel!

Act of Faith
(if that's ridiculous, too bad)

I am happy to have been born at the beginning of the twentieth century. I am quite satisfied with my age. No doubt I would have said the same thing about any other since, unconsciously, I would have been imbued with the ideas and prejudices of that time.

Of course, I am present and I have been present at events from which I suffer or have suffered. I have known two wars, two occupations, which I consider worse than war. We have known mass assassinations, whether in Germany, Poland, or Hiroshima. Today we are still experiencing political events in which even the least informed people suspect small indecencies or great ones, whether in the East, in the U.S.A., in Africa, or in France. Have the human masses become better (this word must be defined and stripped of its moral sense) and are the leaders, politicians, financiers, or others, less self-interested than before?

I don't know at all. I don't try to know. It seems to me, however, that—being what I am—I would have suffered a great deal more in any other century than in this one. Even in the Great Ages of History, in Egypt, in Greece or in Rome, later in France, in Spain, in Florence or in Venice, in London or in Amsterdam.

Have we become sentimental? And is that good or bad? Is it a form of degeneration? Have we deviated from our origins and from human evolution and from laws unknown to us which have imbued this evolution?

I know nothing about that either.

I am happy to live in our time and I am quite proud of it in spite of its imperfections because:

Even if brutalities are still committed daily, for the most part brutality is condemned;

Even if man is not as free as he thinks, slavery has practically ceased to exist;

Even if questions of race and color are often nothing but a po-

153

litical platform, hundreds of thousands of men sincerely believe that each human being is human;

Tens of thousands of young people, all over the world, refuse to kill "legally," refuse to learn to kill and prefer prison to military service;

If many continue to kill animals for pleasure or vanity, a great number prefer to hunt with a camera, that is to study the animal world rather than to destroy it;

The American commander who directed the attack on Hiroshima committed suicide ten years later;

The pilot of the plane that dropped the bomb tried to kill himself twice, and today, after having stolen the most outlandish things, is committed to a psychiatric hospital (to be accurate, he has just escaped).

The "strong" have a bad conscience and to maintain their position are obliged to protect or pretend to protect the weak;

Even if social classes still exist, no one, in his heart of hearts, believes in them any more;

One dares to speak or write without too much fear—of ridicule or prison—things that once were only whispered, at the risk of martyrdom, within certain religious and philosophical sects;

Man in general has lost his pride and his self-sufficiency and is beginning to realize that he is not the lord of creation, made in the image of a god, but a fraction of a whole which can only be glimpsed by him;

The scientists, with every new discovery, admit that far from advancing them, it causes them to retreat; in other words, instead of leading to a conclusion, each new discovery poses new questions;

The . . . .

And many other reasons, if only small ones, throwing a more or less dim light.

There remain more "in spite ofs." Why cite them, when they still overwhelm us?

But those tiny lights growing ever more numerous, and scattered over a continuously expanding part of the earth, are enough to give me hope and even some pride.

I believe in man.

Even and above all if he seems to be going against certain biological laws (or what appear to us as such) of natural selection and therefore the elimination of the weak.

I believe in man even if my reason . . .

D. and I should leave for Cannes to see our doctor, who as a rule gives us an annual checkup. But because D., especially in the last few days, has had health troubles, we have been staying in a Lausanne clinic since yesterday. D. is in the room I occupied a few months ago when I was operated on. Yesterday, X rays. Tomorrow kidney and bladder tests, day after tomorrow the stomach, Wednesday, etc.

My mother used to say to me, as I've told in *Pedigree*:

"If you aren't good and if you wear me out, they'll have to take me to the hospital."

And she would talk to me about her "organs." I held it against her for a long time. I no longer do because I understand that these were the ideas, the terms, of her time and that lacking a superior intelligence, she could not react otherwise.

Something is not as it should be in D., something that isn't serious, as blood tests show, but that has to be tracked down.

Not only in my mother's time, but even in 1930, the great doctors admitted that aside from a few exceptional cases (mostly surgical) they could not cure but only help the patient to recover.

I am speaking of the great ones, because the others, like primitive sorcerers, solemnly played their role of omniscient healer. Some of these are still around.

F

Today, medicine often heals. The strange thing is that sometimes it does not know why. It only knows how.

Some admit it, others don't. I know I am repeating myself. I'm going in circles, with the intention of reaching the core.

Yesterday, this morning, this afternoon, de Gaulle is speaking in Algeria. The papers, and not only the French ones, praise his high-mindedness, his clarity, his courage, etc. But let us read his speeches coldly. They are only clichés and false Machiavellianism. A pastiche. There is fighting in the streets of Algiers. He has flattered this one and that one—for two years—and deceived them all.

Like the doctors in morning coats and top hats (they are gone now, for quite some time) in Harley Street.

Something to talk about with Johnny, just now. He's intrigued by it.

"Suppose," I'll say to him, "he served them up the truth."

To make it clear, I'll tell him the almost infallible method, if not of winning a woman, at least of making a friend of her: tell her that she is exceptional, that she must have an intense inner life, feel alien among others, etc. No more difficult with a man: he's strong . . . a real male . . . one knows one can depend on him. . . .

No one accepts being like others. No one accepts the truth.

Few newspapers, because of the literary prizes, no doubt, mention *L'Ours en Peluche*. Those who speak of it and praise it nevertheless rate it below what they call my great books: *Le Président*, *Le Fils*, for example.

But in *Le Président*, there was still a part that was "contrived." I didn't know how to be real from beginning to end. Nor in *Le Fils*, in which there is still some of the conventional, ready-made, artificial man.

All this is linked together. We use electricity, but as I was walking in town day before yesterday I saw that almost everyone is satisfied with a little yellow forty-watt light. I had to change all the bulbs in our room in the clinic to be able to see. Electricity may exist, but with our feelings we cling to gaslight. The same for the rest.

We discover . . . we discover . . . But, basically, we refuse to adapt ourselves to those discoveries. We live "as if" . : . And to change one small idea, one small habit of the masses, takes decades.

All this is confused and doesn't mean much. No more, to me, than the war in Algeria. What is important, at this moment, are D.'s tests, her health, finding the cog that is out of order and restoring balance as quickly as possible.

There are millions of us in the same condition and still the papers think they thrill us by announcing catastrophes in enormous headlines.

My wife and my children.

What good does it do me to get upset if man is not the way I'd like him to be? (By what right? In whose name?)

Four days ago for the first time I saw D. really suffering, giving in to suffering, without being able to comfort her. That upset me more than a war.

/December 17, 1960

Ouf! A week in the clinic with D., who took all the tests imaginable. I know that she entered against her will, and even, for the first time, with superstitious fear, for many reasons which I understand or guess. She said nothing, showed nothing of all this. She was a brave girl, as they say in the Midi.

And we left with a weight off our shoulders. Nothing organic. Metabolic troubles. Really exhaustion after a hectic, sometimes agonizing year during which she was spared nothing. Now it is a question of patience and will. In three months, I am sure, it will be all over. But we must be together more often, the two of us.

A new period is beginning, full of promise.

If only D. weren't so scrupulous and did not always want to do everything for everybody, as if it were their due! I would like to change this character trait of hers, as if her character weren't a whole.

Because they have created such a goodly number of these Jansenists I have come to hate religious educators, I who hate no one. And all those ostentatiously well-meaning people who do not suffer from their own scruples because these are only superficial, but who often spoil the joy of others who feel more deeply.

This leads us too far afield and I have always forbidden myself to speak of religion. It is true that this is not so much a matter of religion as of certain religious people.

Not exactly true, insofar as I'm concerned, nor with regard to D. It is truly Religion and Morality with capitals that spoiled my adolescence, which perhaps left scars on a part of my life, and which almost definitively handicapped D.

My God, how did anyone dare invent original sin?

I've tried to spare my children that. Have I succeeded? I hope so.

Marc is coming tonight, with his wife, for less than twenty-four hours. I'll go bring him from the station a little before midnight, like a guest.

When I became a father and a long time afterwards, I promised myself always to keep a room in my house for each child, to keep the child from feeling cut off (I think I mentioned the tepid fruit dish before, in which I dealt with this question in a pseudo-poetic form. Seen from the point of view of the son, since I was seventeen at the time). I was naïve. Children eventually need to feel themselves strangers in the paternal house.

I envy merchants, industrialists, certain craftsmen whose skills can be passed on from father to son. Two generations, sometimes three, work side by side.

It is a simplistic idea. I know cases of this kind. But I don't know one that is without friction.

So? Why must we spend so much of our lives getting rid of ready-made ideas? Why don't we teach everyone, from children to grown men, to face reality with equanimity? Why create false hopes, baseless enthusiasms, a whole mess of fictitious feelings?

This is linked to what I wrote about religion.

Why always turn your back on reality, by God!

/*Monday, December 19, 1960*

I feel embarrassed. When I started this notebook I wondered if I would let D. read it, as it went along. Not as with my novels, chapter by chapter as they are finished, in order to discuss them together. But whenever she wanted.

On the one hand, it would have bothered me to keep these pages secret, since we hide nothing from each other. On the other, as I knew that I would speak about her or about the children, I was afraid that some of my notes would seem to have been written with a purpose.

But that isn't what has happened. I don't want to put anything here that is not completely sincere, or to gloss anything over, for example thoughts that might diminish me in the eyes of others or make me ridiculous. All the more reason for writing nothing here to please.

I point out that D. will have the right, if this notebook is published someday, to suppress the passages in it that are about her. I don't want her to, or wish her to, but I insist on giving her this liberty.

This said, let's go back to the clinic then, where she underwent a certain number of painful tests. She is going to need to keep, for a certain length of time, to a regimen of half-idleness which, for her, is the worst thing of all.

Now this is the very moment when I feel a need to write things about her which might seem adapted for the occasion. That's not the case. If I note them today, it's because, in the clinic, I thought of her a great deal, about certain characteristics of hers, because I made a sort of assessment and because I must put it on paper before my ideas get out of focus.

Two or three days ago I spoke of her Jansenism. What I said is both true and false. I could say that even after fifteen years of intimate life with D. every so often I can be wrong about her, for a few hours or a few days, and always in the same way. Then I bristle and I suppose that I become pretty disagreeable.

What causes it? And why this consistency of error, its regularity, as it were? I think I understand and I would like to explain.

I'm apt to apply the word "perfectionist" to her. And it is true that she is one. Only, this word can be used for either praise or blame. In any event, it describes only part of her character. And the mystical leanings of a certain period, her adolescence in particular, and the rebellions that preceded and followed this mysticism, are not an adequate explanation either.

I've met many people. I've known them, very well, all kinds. But I've never seen anyone as tortured as D. by the need to do everything just right. Not only to do everything right, but to do her utmost. And even more than her utmost.

A need for intensity, in short. A need to excel, even in the smallest matters of daily life.

Also a need to exist, to be useful, if not indispensable. To be useful first to her own, of course. To me, to our children. An irrational need, instinctive, to smooth the path for everybody, to solve all his problems, remove all his difficulties.

This includes the staff, for whom she feels responsible, and, in fact, anything in our orbit.

"To take upon oneself the sins of Israel . . ."

The phrase flows naturally from my pen.

I don't think that this is either to punish herself or to win approval. In any case not to win approval in the eyes of others. Perhaps in her own? I'm not sure.

With her it is an instinct. To help. To ease. To remake the world, if she could, so that everyone would be happy.

Isn't it natural that occasionally, when I am nervous or ill, I should misinterpret this attitude, should see in it a sort of pride, of personal satisfaction?

That's what happens, and afterwards I realize that I was wrong.

I don't know if the children will remember, later, the almost animal passion (I'm thinking of a family of gazelles in the jungle) with which their mother brooded over them.

One day—we had known each other for a short time and were walking in downtown New York—we stopped in front of the window of a pet store. There were dogs, cats, parrots in it. There was in particular a monkey who held her little one against her breast and looked at us fixedly.

D. could not take her eyes from it, and I have rarely seen her so moved. We stayed in front of the window a long time and I believe that we went back.

When D. had children, especially when Pierre was sick and she protected him against the world, even against doctors, I found in her once more the same attitude, the same look.

All this is vague, forced. Perhaps I can best sum it up in one sentence:

Someone who desperately wants to do everything right, who desperately wants to do *everything*.

And who cannot understand, who will never understand, that there are limits to human powers.

All her life, behind her window, holding her own to her bosom, she will look out at the passers-by asking herself why . . .

Enough! I'll end on a lighter note: Why isn't she, why aren't we all, God Almighty?

And all her life she will be torn with anguish, other people's anguish and her own.

All her life she will eat her heart out, sure that she is inadequate to her task.

Against this, I'm helpless.

Even as a small child, as long ago as I can remember, I used to become so emotional that I would sob all by myself or clench my fists with rage, with helplessness—and this still happens to me at fifty-eight. The human being is capable of the greatest heroism, the greatest sacrifices. He is capable of devoting his entire life to the sole concern of making another being happy. Is this not what is called love? And yet, he is incapable of dominating an access of ill-humor caused by a trifle, a minor untruth, a troubled night, a headache, a fleeting irritation.

The same person who understood the other or others so well, who at bottom still understands, suddenly becomes unreachable, grippped by a fixed idea, and there he is, unhappy and humiliated, a victim of an objectless rage—or one whose object is ridiculous.

If this happened only to the weak, the ignorant, the obtuse, the violent-tempered. Not so! It happens to the best.

This, perhaps, is what in my eyes gives the truest measure of man. And the most humiliating.

In the same vein, man is capable of absolute sincerity and countless are those who have preferred death to retraction. Yet I would bet that even these were not above petty deceptions.

/December 22, 1960

In *Le Fils* I took an actuary as a character. These are unquestionably the people who cast the coldest eye on human life, passions, etc., since they study man only from the point of view of insurance companies. So many chances for such an individual to live so many years, to have a fire, an automobile accident, a personal tragedy . . . calculated in figures . . .

They don't, as for instance many doctors do, read a paper at the Academy of Medicine, write an article or a report for a journal, or present a daring hypothesis calculated to lend importance to the author.

The actuary is a boring gentleman. He may occasionally be mistaken in a particular case. Not too often. Never in his general forecasts, where it is not a matter of science but of money, the sacred money of the companies.

The world as seen by these people. No room for philosophy, for feelings, no place at all for the approximate, for the nuances of art. A sort of X ray of the world, of society.

All that has to be false. And yet close enough to the truth, since the estimates have to be more or less accurate.

Good risk. Poor risk. Bad risk.

In contrast to them, the psychologists, who, in place of figures, use abstract terms. It is true that psychologists, in their turn, make tests, establish quotas, norms, apply them even to children.

All this to lead up to a nomenclature. No inclination to describe a state of mind, a psychological state. Only a timetable: a schedule.

Woke at eight o'clock. Melting snow, still white on the fields. There are workmen all over the house. They have replaced the floors in the dining room and in the playroom. For a week furniture piled in the hall of the second floor and in the drawing room as if in preparation for an auction. Now, a cleaning team (of five or six) attacks the house floor by floor. This morning, it's the turn of my study and the kitchen.

Three or four cups of tea.

I shave and take my bath, listening to the radio while my wife has her massage.

Nine o'clock. Massage until 9:50. I dress, go down to read the mail in one of the first-floor offices.

In town with Marie-Jo. Take the five prints that B. Buffet sent me for Christmas to the framer. Then send chocolates to someone who was left off the list yesterday.

Florist. Sent flowers to different people in Lausanne for Christmas. The out-of-town ones were ordered yesterday by telephone.

Stationers. Buy paper for Christmas wrapping.

Then, still with Marie-Jo, buy a present for her little friend.

Back at eleven thirty. The Christmas tree has come. We'll trim it tomorrow when Johnny will be on vacation.

Glance at papers. At 12:45 we go to lunch at the inn (for lack of usable kitchen. The whole household goes in teams).

When we get back I light a fire in my former study on the ground floor. Papers. Leave at three o'clock with D. Errands. I to the tailor to try on some smoking jackets.

Then to some other place, to buy a sheepskin jacket. D. during this time is shopping for clothes for Pierre and underwear for Marie-Jo. We run into each other from store to store the length of the Rue de Bourg.

Choose a present for a woman who just had a baby.

Buy a mackinaw for D.

When we get back, the upholsterer is finishing hanging the curtains returned from the cleaner, the carpet man brings back the clean carpets too.

In the halls, on the stairs, we meet people we don't know.

The new jazz drums for Johnny have come and I spend an hour putting them together, for there are always mysterious things to fiddle with.

6:45 to the inn, where we all dine together, with the cook, the valet, and one of the maids.

Back again. News program on French TV. Put Johnny to bed after having looked at his school drawings, which surprise me.

Another half hour of television, alone in the drawing room. Then rejoin D. in her office. Back to drawing room upstairs, where we show the nurse our purchases for Pierre.

That's all. I forgot. This morning I ordered holly and mistletoe. And this afternoon I bought myself some gloves.

It is still snowing. It may be a white Christmas.

This time that's really all. We are going to go upstairs, kiss the children, take a phenobarbital, and sleep. I haven't done any thinking. I think of nothing. The proof! Tomorrow waking at eight o'clock. Tea. Bath. Drive D. to the hairdresser at ten o'clock. I will probably do errands and in the afternoon I will put the lights up on the tree. Then I'll watch the children decorate it.

I don't know just why, opening this notebook with the idea of writing: nothing, I thought of my actuary.

Incidentally. Met Geraldine Chaplin, who is sixteen. She was carrying Christmas packages. Everyone at her house has the flu.

/December 23rd

Hallelujah!

/December 24th

The Christmas spirit. At last!

/December 25th

Is it from Epictetus? I think so. Anyway, I'm too lazy to find the source, less than three yards from me. "Of the ten evils we fear, only one happens to us. So, we will suffer nine times for nothing." Very approximate quotation.

A perfect Christmas, in spite of my fears. One of the best, the most perfect, the most "complete."

Thank you, God!

And, last night, two good hours, real ones, with D. That makes up for everything.

Strange end of the year. We have everything. The children are in good shape. I too. D. has nothing wrong organically. Nevertheless . . . Three times, five times a day the color of life changes. In the evening, I go to sleep confident, D. in my arms, sure that the release will come. And in the morning it begins all over again.

She's trying, though. If not, all would be gray, without a ray of sun. The moment must not have come yet. It can happen soon, tomorrow, in ten days, and then our life will go back to its true rhythm. She is worn out and, suddenly, without energy, incapable of taking things lightly.

We are all subject to this and at this very point medical science, as a rule so cocksure, is the most helpless. An infinitesimal change in the quantity of such and such an acid and our whole equilibrium is threatened. It has happened before and I feel confident because I know she will respond suddenly. In the meantime . . .

The day I first met her, in New York, when, after our luncheon at the Brussels, we went for a walk in Central Park, she left me to do an errand, promising to meet me at the Drake. I waited for her for about an hour. I didn't know her.

At first I read peacefully. Then for the first time in my life I felt a painful contraction in my breast and said to myself:

"Maybe she won't come."

Since then, I have had that sensation again each time there has been the slightest cloud between us.

This time the cloud is not mental; it is neither misunderstanding nor irritation, none of the things that can separate, for an hour, people who love each other.

A chemical formula. A reaction which will come. She is in bed, this morning, which is best. Perhaps this afternoon? . . . Tomorrow? . . .

I am going to the tailor with Johnny. There is snow. It is freezing. The sun is shining.

I am waiting.

Soon, perhaps, to change my mood, I'll try to write, without much conviction, on another subject. But for the moment nothing outside of D. is important. I prefer that she should not read this before the reaction has occurred. Then she will be able to smile about it with me.

Four o'clock. Success? Partial success? I should know that it is not a question of hours but of weeks, and all the same I always count in hours.

Instead of going to bed as she meant to do at one point, D. came to walk in the snow with Johnny and Marie-Jo. All four in furred parkas in the white village, we must have made a winter scene for a calendar. Now, I am going out again with Pierre. I have had enough of my armchair by the fire. I need air, cold, movement, activity.

Five o'clock. I've been much more affected than I could have believed, yesterday and the day before, by pictures of the Belgian troubles on television. I don't feel myself any more Belgian than French, American, or Swiss, I must already have said so. Belgium is the country where, I think, I would least like to live, while, if I had a preference (I haven't for the moment), it is the only place that I would designate as the "resting place for my ashes." I say ashes, for I want to be cremated.

The pictures of slow, silent crowds in the streets lined with closed shutters recalled to me the strike in my childhood which I tried to describe in *Pedigree*. And suddenly I feel very near, very involved with these people (I speak of a social class that I scarcely know, that I never was a part of, and which, actually, I almost feared).

I also react to the events in Algeria, of course, and I am distressed by the behind-the-scenes intrigues there and in the Congo.

Last evening, however, in bed, I was tempted to make a gesture and only hesitated because it would have seemed theatrical.

In 1952 I had to be forced (correspondence proves it) to join the Belgian Academy. I only went near the place once. On the same trip, I was given the decoration of officer of the Order of the Crown, as a surprise, and I swear I wasn't expecting it.

The journalists thought I was moved while actually I was upset, upset above all at having to say thanks. At the Brussels Exhibition, for which I had reluctantly accepted the presidency of the Film Festival, I was given another decoration, Commander, I believe—I know nothing about it—of the Order of Leopold. And this time I blushed, furious, because I had been given this distinction . . . at the distribution of the Festival prizes, as if in payment for having accepted this boring job!

I don't belong to any society. I have never been secretary, treasurer, honorary president of anything whatsoever.

I confess that I would like to send my resignation to that academy of which I am only a nominal member, to send back the two decorations which I have worn just once and, at the same time, send back to France the Legion of Honor which I was given when I was in New York. (It was said that I had solicited it. It has been said of others. I know this is not so.)

This is how things happened. My friend Georges Charensol, of the *Nouvelles Littéraires*, wrote me that he and his friends had proposed me for the Legion of Honor; all he wanted me to do was to sign a form. On the face of it, it was an application. But I would have rejected Charensol and my friends at the *Nouvelles Littéraires* by not signing.

·In short, I would like to be rid of these medals which were given me by people whom I don't respect, who represent a world that has always been foreign to me.

I am tempted to send a telegram to *La Wallonie* which is at the head of the rebel movement of the Belgian people to tell them that I am with them.

But these are theatrical gestures that go against my grain. Where is freedom? And isn't silence sometimes the more difficult option?

I begin to understand a terrible saying of Léon Blum's in the French Chamber in 1936: "Bourgeois, I hate you!"

I know, I have met, I still meet here, in Paris, in Cannes, in Venice, in Nice, in the luxury hotels and in night clubs the people Léon Blum was speaking of and whom I knew only slightly at that period, because of whom there is fighting in the Congo, in Algeria, in Cuba, and, in some measure, all over the world, the people who are waiting for the end of the Belgian crisis in the hope that the government will be "tough". . . .

I even had one to dinner last week.

And I believe that I hate them too.

Or at least that I would hate them if I really thought them capable of the Machiavellianism of which they boast and if, in my heart of hearts, because of the close view I get of them, I did not know that they are pitiable.

But that they should draw me into their inner sanctums or cover me with their hardware . . .

I've given the medals I've received to my children to play with and make fun of. I swear, no matter what the circumstances, never to accept another ribbon, another medal, another title.

/December 31, 1960

Yesterday, December 30, 1960, when everywhere in the world cavalry is motorized, and even hearses; when horses are no longer kept for the big White House parades (too expensive), etc., etc., in 1960, yes, yesterday, I saw mounted police charge a crowd *with drawn swords.*

I saw them on television. It happened in Brussels. It was sudden, anachronistic, a Detaille painting in motion.

No doubt Algerian paratroopers' machine guns are more murderous, and even the so-called practice grenades.

I would be surprised if those horsemen and those waving

swords did not stay in the minds of tens of thousands of people who watched the spectacle on their screens like a sort of nightmare.

It is true that during the last war and after, torture was used in a perfectly official way, as in the Middle Ages.

However, the papers were amazed—and indignant—that some people, white or black, were dismissed during the recent and continuing troubles in the Congo.

I'm not speaking of us this morning, of D. and me. Chut! . . . Who knows? . . . I'm walking on tiptoe. . . .

/January 1st, 3:30 A.M.

Good, excellent New Year's Eve. All the staff out, including the nurse, Pierre and Marie-Jo in bed. Johnny with us at the television until eleven thirty. D. and I to bed at two thirty. Good awakening. Good morning. Johnny, Pierre, and I going to Morges, then Lausanne, while Marie-Jo paints a canvas for a present for her brother.

Everyone out again. Nana comes in and stays in the house with Pierre while D., the two children, and I go to lunch at the Lausanne-Palace. Almost perfect mood, perfect, finally, after a threat of storm.

It's a little like the time between two seasons. Such comparisons are overused, but one rediscovers them in experiencing them. Between our states of well-being—physical and mental—and the states of the sky, there are analogies, above all in the between-times, when the weather is neither good nor bad, when it is neither winter nor spring, neither summer nor autumn.

Everything can change in a moment in one direction or the other. One feels worried, sometimes oppressed. Perhaps, after all, the same laws govern these transformations. We make artificial ones for each kind, for man, for the different races, the different

170

categories, the animals, the vegetables, the planets, when there is probably a certain unity that we miss.

That's encouraging. If there is not yet secure, stable good weather on the barometer this time, still, for as long as it lasts, it promises that this will come soon.

I'm beginning to relax, to think of my next novel. A Maigret? A non-Maigret? I would prefer the latter but perhaps I'd be playing safe to put off a real novel until March.

The children have been delightful, all three, and Marc telephoned us before going to spend New Year's Eve with a friend in Versailles.

D. was adorable. Should I say that my only fear is that she became a little too much so, too quickly? With each of my little illnesses, flues, etc., the doctors got me up a day or two too soon and I've had to go back to bed.

I don't want that to happen to her. When one has reached, as in her case, the depths of fatigue and inner discouragement—the kind when one blames oneself without wanting to admit it— convalescence is slower than for a serious illness.

I hope that hers will be rather pleasant, almost voluptuous.

Now I am sure of a recovery. And it is because it is no longer a question of more than days, of hours, that I note the stages. This is not literary, psychological, or medical abstraction. It's a need, because our whole life is at stake. And I hope that she will only read these last pages when she is in top form—to smile at them.

Leave again for a drive with Pierre and Nana.

/January 2, 1961

Lausanne empty as in a nightmare or a Chirico canvas of the Montparnasse period. Neither weekday nor Sunday. An impression of tension, of waiting. But tomorrow, at five minutes of eight, the Place Saint-François will have its usual look, with its great banks devouring their hurrying employees.

Calm too, but without emptiness, at home, where D. has again made a step forward, and has almost regained her self-confidence. Just a little longer and she will be back to her real life.

A wish to invite K. (former chief of Geneva police, then called to the Congo by the UN to reorganize their police) to lunch and, afterwards, to chat peacefully by the fire. A little like passing an hour or two with Maigret.

K. and I speak the same language, or almost, and we understand each other in half sentences. It's rare that the desire comes to me to invite someone. Perhaps because he understands the workings of certain games, the need to assure myself that my own intuition hasn't deceived me?

I hope that he has read *L'Ours en Peluche*. Have forgotten to send him a copy. It is true that I never send them. Would also like the advice of Dr. D. of "Rives de Prangins," ° with whom I also feel on an equal footing, although most of his professional knowledge and experiences are beyond me.

In a few minutes the children and their two little friends are going to give a concert for the parents of those friends and for us. I look forward to it with more pleasure than to a real show. Johnny's face, leaning over his drums, fascinates me, seems suddenly adult, and Marie-Jo becomes a different person, which makes me think I don't really know her, that there is an inner life in her which eludes me.

Yesterday Pierre finally began to say "Daddy" after having resisted it for so long. And, at the same time, as if it came to him overnight, he calls everyone by name.

Soon, if I have the time, I want to talk about D.'s and the children's future when I am no longer here. The question is raised, in too brief a form, in my will. I have a few little thoughts on the subject. It is true that it will no longer be my problem.

° A sanatorium.

It's raining. The children are making music in the playroom. D. is in her boudoir. The secretaries are back in the office. Life has resumed its normal course after the holidays.

My last paragraph yesterday made me go back to the past. When Marc was born, in 1939, I was living in Nieul-sur-Mer, five or six kilometers from La Rochelle, one kilometer across the fields from La Richardière, where I had lived from 1932 to 1935, if I'm not mistaken.

As always, the truth is more complex. I had been living nearly six months of the year, sometimes more, in Porquerolles, in a small house oddly flanked by a minaret, and it was in that minaret overlooking the port that I had arranged my study. I had a fishing boat, with a pointed bow, which I had had built in Cagnes-sur-Mer, as many nets as a fisherman, and a sailor who spoke pirate's slang (of Neapolitan origin) named Tado.

In 1935, returning from a trip around the world (or 1936?), I rented and furnished, according to the taste of the decorators of the period, a conventional modern apartment in Neuilly at 3 Boulevard Richard-Wallace opposite the park of Bagatelle.

I had also rented the Château de la Cour-Dieu, in the forest of Orléans, near Ingrannes. Actually, it was the priory of a ruined Cistercian abbey. I had taken my horses, sulky, buggy, etc., there.

I had bought a clearing, a few kilometers away in the middle of the forest, with a dilapidated farm in it, with the idea of building the house of my dreams there, a huge one-story house with a large interior court, stables, kennels, etc. I had even rented a hunting preserve and I was organizing beats twice a week.

Having wounded a young deer at the first beat and being forced to finish it off, I gave up shooting. But I was obliged, by contract, to hold two beats every week.

What else was I doing at the same time? Today I am flabbergasted by that dispersion which left me nothing but confused memories. Ah yes, I was dressing in English style, was buying my hats in London, wearing a bowler in the afternoon, going to Le Fouquet's and, in winter, in Paris, I did not miss any chance to dress in tails and high hat. I was a member of the Yacht Motor Club of France, the Escholiers, the Sporting Club. . . .

I don't recognize myself very well in this picture. I was even wearing a pearl in my necktie!

One day, disgusted, unable to work in Paris, I left in a car for the North of Holland to find a simple house somewhere along the seashore where I could live like a peasant. I used to say, I remember: the house one would have liked to be one's grandmother's.

Traveled south, in short stages along the North Sea, then the Channel. After Normandy, Brittany, the Vendée, finally the outskirts of La Rochelle, which I had left five years earlier.

And there, tears came to my eyes, as if I had returned to my native land. I looked for a house. I found one. I bought it. I began work on it. Tearing down walls, opening bricked-up windows, once more I found that it was the remainder of an old abbey, and there were niches for saints in what would be my study.

I gave up Cour-Dieu, but I kept the clearing where the workmen had not yet begun. I kept the apartment in Neuilly and "Les Tamaris" in Porquerolles.

Marc was born in Nieul in 1939 a few months before the war, and I, who had looked so hard for a nest, I wondered where I would live when he was of school age. I thought of everything, of climate, of studies, of the university. Of myself, who would be getting old when he was twenty. (I'm there now!)

I decided that soon I would look for a house in Aix-en-Provence or near there. I would be two jumps from the sea, from Porquerolles, in a region I loved, in a town of the size I like, and where there are excellent educational facilities. At least—I still hesitated—unless I took up residence in the United States, for it appeared to me that the time had come for a young man to be brought up in both the European and the American way.

In September the war broke out. In August 1940 I left for the

Vendée in order to rest after the fatigue and emotion of working with refugees. I didn't yet know that I would never return to Nieul, that later I would give it to my first wife, that Marc was going to live at Fontenay-le-Comte first, three months in a house on the water front, two years in the Château de Terreneuve, then in the woods at Saint-Mesmin-le-Vieux, to end, with the Liberation, at Les Sables-d'Olonne.

After which several months in Paris, in my old lodgings at the Place des Vosges which my friend Ziza had looked after, and off to London, Canada, and the United States.

So that it was in Florida that Marc went to school for the first time, then in Arizona, then in California, and later in Connecticut, where I finally bought Shadow Rock Farm, which I still own, and where we were to live for five years.

Marc did not come back to Europe, to Cannes, until he was sixteen years old, with a brother and sister born in America.

Two years later, he continued his studies in Switzerland before settling in Paris and getting married there.

I foresaw everything except . . .

In the end, reality was not so far removed from my projects, at least one of them.

Will it be the same with all the plans that I want to make for D. and for the other children, of which there are now three, once I am no longer here, which will certainly happen someday.

It reassures me to try to imagine them in such and such a place, in a certain atmosphere. At the same time it is partly a matter of personal geography.

Plato considered that the ideal city would have, I think (the book is five yards from me, but, once more, I refuse to get up to make sure of the number), five thousand inhabitants.

Doesn't this correspond to a city of a hundred to a hundred and fifty thousand inhabitants today, so long as it's a university town? It is because Lausanne fits this concept that I settled here, and after four years I am still content with my choice.

Shouldn't it be almost the same, after me, for the children?

With the difference that, since they will not be able to live in such a large house, with as big a staff, distance from the town would complicate the least details of life.

If D. and they decide to remain in Switzerland, on the heights of Lausanne, near buses and trams, there are charming villas and even apartment houses which simplify life.

For I am the one who complicates it in this house, with my work and my demands.

Will they want to stay in Switzerland? Myself, if I am still here when the children are bigger, will I not wish to finish their education in France?

Apart from this, life must be made pleasant for D., and I fear the long distance from Paris, where we have most of our friends.

Versailles? I've always dreamed of it. But I've been there recently. It has become a tourist town and the neighborhood is inhabited by a restless crowd of snobs, as bad for the children as the Côte d'Azur.

Aix-en-Provence again? Maybe. Aren't there airfields, army camps, and a great deal of tourism there too now?

If they need or want the South, I'd prefer Nîmes, near Montpellier and its university. Only for D. that's far from Paris, and even if only on business she will have to go there often.

There remains, as for Maigret, the Loire valley, Orléans or Tours, Saumur, for example.

Rouen is depressing and rainy. Caen is too new a city, though it offers the advantage of being near the sea.

At the moment I incline to the Loire valley, a big airy house surrounded by a garden at the outskirts of the city.

Vain speculation, I know, I've had some experience.

Wherever they decide to go, wherever D. decides to take them, I know they will be happy and I hope they will never be sad thinking of me, that they will say that I had a full life, that they gave me all the happiness possible.

No museum of mementos. Nothing to make them sad. On the contrary. Let them remember me almost as a clown and sometimes, at meals, let them burst out laughing thinking of me, as they do now.

Loire valley? Lausanne? Nîmes?

I'm entertaining myself, children, thinking of you, preferably of you grown up, all adults, for I haven't the slightest wish to leave you and I hope to do it as late as possible.

But I sketched many plans for Marc when I was only forty. Isn't it fair that I should make some for you at almost fifty-eight?

No! D. is going to frown. Let's not talk about it any more. Long live Echandens and life in January 1961.

Who knows? Perhaps, after all, I shall see all my children married and then we'll have to find a house for two somewhere, and from time to time, my darling D., we will try, with our old legs, to climb the narrow staircase of your doll's house in Cagnes-sur-Mer. I doubt whether we shall get to that point—excuse me, that I'll come to that point, but I could always be carried upstairs.

Just now there may be fighting in Belgium. They may already be fighting there. They are fighting in Laos, in Algeria, in the Congo.

And I, nice and warm in my study, with the rain falling outside as in my childhood, I'm thinking of my old age.

/*Wednesday, January 4, 1961, morning*

It is sad to watch a being to whom one feels attached in every fiber struggling to regain her balance, her strength, her joy in living. One knows, as doctors know it, that in the last analysis this is finally only a question of chemistry, or glands, of a little too much of this or of that, or too little; that, little by little, the lack or the excess will be remedied.

It's a question of time, of groping, of keeping one's peace of mind, and, in a word, of confidence. But it is just this confidence that is almost impossible to achieve—otherwise, it would be so easy.

The patient—I do not say the sick man or woman since there

is no true sickness to speak of—attributes his or her state to different causes, most often moral ones. He argues with himself, lies to himself, a little as if he didn't want to get well. For to get well would be to agree, to admit to himself that all his phantoms are imaginary.

A subtle shifting of reality takes place (for physical reasons) and it is that reality which he begins to flee from. So he submerges himself, and when he comes to the surface, is tempted to plunge back down again.

How to help her? Every word, every attitude, runs the risk of being wrongly interpreted. The other day I wrote that I was walking on tiptoe.

Yesterday, the day before, I believed that we were coming back to the surface. This morning we have to begin all over. She is trying, with all her strength. But, *fatally*, she is trying in the wrong direction.

The experience of earlier depressions is useless. Each time she loses all confidence. Not her fault. Because we are at the mercy of a hundredth of a milligram of acid.

In a few days I will smile about it and she will smile about it.

Last evening, on television, another charge by mounted police in Belgium. And once again there is talk of separation between Flemings and Walloons as at the time I was reporter on the *Gazette de Liège*. This time the Socialists are at the head of the movement. Their leader is a certain Renard, editor of *La Wallonie*. This paper was almost a turning point for me, which very few people know.

I was working on a Catholic and conservative paper (it is no longer so) near the Place Saint-Lambert because it happened to be the first job on a paper I could find, on the day when I suddenly decided, at the age of sixteen and a half, to become a reporter. To tell the truth, I had no idea of its political color.

La Wallonie, at that period, was considered by conservative people, including my parents, as a sort of emanation of the Devil, and its editors had the reputation of men who carried knives between their teeth.

Among them, I was friendly (in spite of the difference in ages) with the editor-in-chief, Isi Delvigne, and a deputy of the party called Troclet, who still wore a very Bohemian flowing necktie.

I was only a kid. On the *Gazette* they were careful not to entrust me with any task that had to do with politics except, during elections, the accounts of electoral speeches by *our* candidates.

As is the rule, of all the journalists of Liège we were the worst paid (I noticed later that it is always the same: the further right a paper is, the less it pays its staff; if it is Catholic on top of that, you can starve).

One day Isi Delvigne took me aside and proposed that I come to work for *La Wallonie*, not just as an editor, but with the promise that when I was twenty-one I'd be listed among their candidates for elections, local and provincial at first, legislative later.

It was an assured fortune and future. At that period, in fact, the parties of the Left in Belgium had few educated elements, lacked cadres, as one says today, and I remember candidates and even men elected to office who barely knew how to read or write.

For a long time I had wanted to become a novelist. I had published a first book: *Au Pont des Arches*. I had written a second: *Jehan Pinaguet*, which my editor-in-chief had forbidden me to publish (I had found a publisher, or rather a lady-publisher, an older woman but very attractive, whom my youth must have stimulated) because there was a priest who smacked of heresy among its characters.

Politics? Literature?

Did I really hesitate? Anyway, I was tempted. The thought of manipulating the masses, of speaking from the podium, organizing impressive parades, fighting for a cause . . .

I said No. Without regret, I really believe. It is none the less true that one night, a little drunk, crossing the Passerelle in a fog, and also in a poetic mood, I declared to my friend Lafnet, who was taking me home:

"At forty I shall be a minister or a member of the Academy!"

At fifty-eight I am neither one nor the other. For I meant the French Academy, of course. I wasn't speaking seriously, just metaphorically, since, a Belgian, I knew that the Quai Conti was closed to me.

But a minister I would certainly have been at the specified age if I had joined *La Wallonie* and the party. It happened to several of my age group who were less well equipped than I.

As to becoming an Academician, there is no question of that, of course. I've expressed my opinions—sincerely—on this subject as on that of decorations.

I'm happy I never became a minister, never dabbled in politics wherever I was.

But still that was a turning point, a decision which it was necessary to make, at an age when I hadn't the slightest maturity. I certainly did not weigh the pros and cons. I followed my instinct. The other way was easier and put an end to my problems at the time.

I stayed on the pious *Gazette* until my military service, which I got over with ahead of the draft, and at nineteen and a half I went to Paris where, after some menial secretarial jobs, I was soon busy writing popular novels all day long under fifteen or sixteen pseudonyms before taking my own name again.

Yesterday there was fighting in Belgium, but no decisive battle. This disappoints me somewhat. On the whole, my instinct enables me to foresee events quite accurately, I have had proof of it recently in rereading my old reporting.

Where I am invariably wrong is in my sense of timing. Events always take longer to ripen than I think.

Perhaps it is the same for personal tragedies and even for illnesses. Whether it is a matter of nature, of men, of crowds, it could be said that there is a nearly immutable rhythm to which I am not attuned, which I have a tendency to anticipate.

This is also true for D., with whom I become impatient because she isn't getting well when she has scarcely begun to take care of herself and when she has to counterbalance more than a year of worry and extreme fatigue.

The children dismantled the Christmas tree this morning, with the same pleasure with which they had trimmed it, the same impatience.

Pierre, who has been eating with us for three days only, has proved the life and soul of the family table and meals have become delightful.

A relapse for D. yesterday, suddenly, at the same hour as in December. Same pains. Same utter fatigue. Fortunately less crushing, perhaps because we know. I watch over her from morning to night, look about fifty times a day into whatever room she's in, not because of restlessness but because I would like to help her.

Our five doctors have all been on vacation for the past eight or ten days and are not coming back until next week. Of course they need a rest, like everyone, and much more than most.

But that doesn't make it any less of a problem, linked to the social problem of the organization that someday must be set up, an entirely new organization, which is going to force change on us, the older ones, but which appears indispensable to me.

I would be greatly upset to find myself in a clinic before a more or less anonymous doctor "in possession of my file." But won't this be better than the present semi-anarchy? Three times in less than a year all our doctors were away when we needed them, and their substitute would have been helpless faced by a complicated problem on which he had no information.

D. is in good spirits today. Last evening, in the car, she told me a little of what oppresses her, almost all of it, in any case almost all she is aware of.

For my part, I'm still puzzled. I envy the clear minds of the seventeenth and eighteenth centuries, for whom man was so simple. They believed in intelligence. They believed in primary truth, in black and white, and were satisfied with caricatures (excuse me: with simplifications) almost as crude as the "Caractères" of La Bruyère.

Will we appear later as a gray turbid age, a time of gropings, of restlessness, of unresolved questions? Who knows? A period of sick men which, in the quest for understanding of life, will be brushed aside?

In terms of art, the passion for wretchedness has already been discussed. I am afraid, sometimes, of creating such willful wretchedness or "morbidity."

I try to remain detached, objective, not to succumb to sentimentality.

What comforts me is that professional researchers, scientists, arrive at almost the same . . . I was going to say conclusions, when there are none. . . . Say at the same difficulties, at the same doubts, at the same anxieties as I do; even that last word embarrasses me.

/Friday, January 6, 1961

Expecting Dr. R., who is in a hurry to see the book he has written about me published and who is also persuaded that he has discovered some subtle or secret things. He does not suspect— and I shall not say it to him so as not to hurt him—that I have the impression that all he writes about me diminishes me. I shall have to keep D., who is less patient than I, especially about what concerns me, from speaking her mind too openly. It's all the more difficult since I am very fond of him and admire his talent.

Am I not a bit like Anatole France taking umbrage at his portrait by van Dongen? But van Dongen was right.

What I would like to set down this morning is this. It is probable, if someday I reread these notebooks, that I will find the same subject taken up twice, twice in the same way. Loss of memory?

Certainly I have less and less—I never had any—memory for names or numbers. As it happens, this is not a matter of memory, I think. But, for example, doing errands in town I will say: "I must make a note of this." Then, as I don't attach any importance to it, it will go out of my mind to return a month or six weeks later. At that moment, I wonder: "Haven't I written that already? Or did I only mean to?" The opposite can happen too.

Same thing for my novels. Often a subject comes to my mind, haunts me for two or three days, and all of a sudden, when it takes shape and outlines itself, I am aware that I have written the novel five, ten, or twenty years earlier, anyway that I have used the theme.

This morning, I don't know why, perhaps because R.'s visit reminded me of studies written on me which speak of my sexuality in the falsest and most fantastic way, I wanted to bring up this question, quite simply and frankly, for if I have a sense of modesty in certain areas, I have none in this one.

But haven't I already done this? I don't remember and I am not going to leaf back through these pages to see. In any case, I haven't the time now. Dr. R. is about to arrive and I have spent a part of the morning, delightfully, walking to Morges with Johnny and Marie-Jo, buying dessert for lunch and flowers for the table.

It will come back to me. It isn't a matter of an account to settle with critics who are too naïvely Freudian, but a restatement of a question that seems to me natural.

In short, I consider myself a perfectly normal man in this area. Which may surprise certain people, in that I never mix sexuality, sentiment, and love.

With one woman only, D., sex and love were merged, are still merged. With the others, no. And this is neither cynicism nor vice. I consider sexuality, all sexual acts, as natural and beautiful.

I have no need of more or less forced and artificial sentiment to stimulate myself.

I like to see the beautiful body of a woman and it matters little to me whether she has this or that mentality, whether she comes from this or that background. A professional often gives me more pleasure than anyone. Just because she does not force me to pretend.

I will add that I feel for all women, when I take them, some sort of tenderness, what I would call human tenderness. This is not sentimental. I do not ask myself questions about them. I don't feel compassionate about their lives.

It is a tenderness for the human being, for the species, for the living flesh, for a body which, for a brief duration, in my arms, represents all life. That I can produce in that body certain vibrations delights me more than my own enjoyment, although that enjoyment is more often necessary to me than I might wish for my own peace of mind.

During my first days in Paris, for example, I remember that I would leave the arms of one woman at eleven o'clock in the morning to go back to another only a few minutes later, and be obliged to accost a professional or to go to a house of assignation to begin all over again twice the same afternoon.

Isn't this natural? It has been written that I was questing for the lost woman, the humiliated woman, the sinner, as for a kind of redemption.

Pure invention. If I slept more often with professionals or demi-professionals than with others it is, first, because I am revolted by the play-acting the others demand, by the wasted time, by what I call the height of pretense. Besides, the meddling jealousy of my first wife scarcely permitted me affairs, or, most often, even what are called adventures.

Also, when I think with nostalgia of any one woman I've had, it is rarely of a woman whom I had to pay court to.

D. is not jealous. She gives me complete freedom. Less than ever, however, have I any desire for another relationship.

I make love simply, healthily, as often as necessary, but I'm not in the grip of any compulsion. I am not driven by any neurosis; only by a need.

Perhaps someday I will again take up this subject. For the moment it doesn't seem necessary, but God knows what they will yet find in writing about me and my novels.

R. is still here, off with my wife, chattering. I have the impression that everything I've written this morning is both true and untrue. The sexual need . . . the need of the act . . . and that sort of tenderness which I've spoken of . . . I wonder if this is not part of a need that is more difficult to communicate, the need to penetrate humanity . . . This finally is reduced to an act that appears ridiculous but which is none the less symbolic. . . .

This would explain why the personality of the partner (except in the case of love) makes little difference, that on the contrary this personality anecdotizes (?) the thing, that the more ordinary the woman is, the more she is never-mind-what woman, the more one can consider her as "woman" and the more the act takes on significance.

All this is in the unconscious, for I do not indulge in such reasoning when I am confronted with a naked body.

Even nudity has a meaning. Isn't it a kind of return to innocence? To undress a woman is also to rob her of the superimposed, the artificial, of all the "contrived."

It is in itself a sort of penetration, of communion, if one can call it that. An attempt, in any case. Always fruitless. Always a failure. That is why one must continually begin all over again. Can't a miracle be produced?

The proof is that for me it has been produced.

Why, having found it, do I continue? Perhaps because at twenty I clenched my fists at the thought that there were women in the world whom I would never possess.

To touch, to absorb the world. To possess it.

But all this is so approximate that it becomes almost as false as what the critics write. Why the devil aren't they content with what I've said in my novels without trying to explain. Anyway, if I haven't done it myself, there is no possible explanation.

Certain men have a mania for "stooping" to women to raise them to their level.

How much simpler it would be if everyone, once and for all, would feel equal to every other.

I can say that this is the case with me. I examine no one. Each necessarily has her own qualities, some of which are clear to me, others of which escape me.

I have never stooped to anyone, not even, to return to the preceding pages, to the last of the prostitutes (why the last?), and that, no doubt, is why we have always had a good time together, they and I, in giving each other, for better, for worse, to the best of our abilities, pleasure.

Ten o'clock in the evening. How things that seem important to us at one moment can be forgotten the next! In the course of a crossing from Australia to Europe between 1930 and 1940 (I won't be more definite since the person I'm speaking of is no doubt married and has children, and surely also a reputation) I almost jumped overboard for a sixteen-year-old Australian girl.

On another evening, on the forward deck, I had a fist fight with a young man who had asked her to dance! She didn't speak a word of French. At that period, I hadn't a word of English. The ship was English. The mother and father were traveling with the girl, and occupied the cabin next to hers. But very early in the morning, very late at night, I found the way to join her, in pajamas, in her cabin. We did not make love. I was a grown man, a man of almost thirty-five. However, with the aid of a little dictionary, I stammered out my idiocies and I had decided to marry her once we arrived in Europe.

This seems to me unthinkable. Not just my state of mind, but the risks I took in an ultra-puritanical setting.

I only wrote to her once when she was in London. She answered me once, too, poste restante. And I returned to my own life. She to hers. How near to tragedy I came in that business! It took, just now, a map on television which reminded me of Australia, for that memory to come back to me.

But it was probably an important time in my life, for, from that moment, I knew that one day or another, in one way or another, I would divorce my first wife. She was at the end of her tether.

She knew this story. For the first time, I think, she felt dimly that I was a stranger to her, more exactly that she was a stranger to me.

Who knows? Without her constant jealousy perhaps I would have had more adventures in the usual sense of the term. Those that I did have were only of an evening's duration, a few hours, a few minutes, even with friends.

Perhaps this permitted me to discover the simple joy of loving with D.?

Another memory just came to me, very different, also the memory of a crossing, New York–Le Havre, or New York–Southampton, I don't know any more, with D., this time, a very gay, very happy crossing. The evening of the traditional party on board, I was joking with a pretty woman and asked her—without hope of her doing it—to come to my cabin.

I was with my wife, getting undressed, when she came in wearing an evening dress with several rows of flounces, of which she opened the zipper, letting it fall at her feet, leaving her naked and pink.

An hour of pleasure enjoyed without afterthought, without complications. And then when she had taken her pleasure several times, as I was going to take mine, a little phrase inspired by champagne and love:

"For her . . ."

To put it another way, she had understood that the essential was for my wife. D. will be able, of course, to suppress this passage. I don't think she will do it, though. And I am sure that, for her too, it is a pure and joyful memory.

I don't remember my partner any more at all, but I can visualize her movements. . . .

Nearly twenty years between the two crossings. But, if I would like to relive the second, I have no desire to relive the first, and its very recollection troubles me.

This time, here is really a subject that I didn't want to tackle and I hope that tomorrow I won't want to retouch it. In searching for a truer truth one risks being carried away. That is why, in the last analysis, these notebooks are in danger of being less close to the truth, in spite of my care for exactitude, than my novels in which I force myself to include nothing of myself.

We took a walk in the snow, this afternoon, around the village, D. and I. Then, the children not being home yet, I went to meet them and found them with the nurse, noses and cheeks red, walking fast in the snowstorm, with Pierre watching me proudly.

We like, he and I, to meet that way, as if by chance, in the village or in the vicinity.

Does he know I'm looking for him? Is he looking for me too? When he sees me, he puts on an indifferent air but cannot suppress a sly smile.

A delightful game, in which Johnny and Marie-Jo join during the holidays.

What a fine book one could make out of the day of a man, an ordinary day! How much life! But how much more difficult than a novel full of turmoil and passion!

/*Sunday, January 8, 1961*
9 o'clock in the morning

Yesterday, in bed, thought of many things that I want to write. But now I am going to the station to get the papers with D. and the children. I'll try later.

A marginal note, however. An explanation. I never try, in these notebooks, to get to the bottom of a subject, nor to tell a story completely. Out of laziness? Maybe a little. Above all because I force myself to follow the thread of the thought as faithfully as possible. I would like this to be a sort of shorthand, or transcription of thought, with everything that is capricious and incomplete about it. This is the only way to be sincere. I'm not concerned with style. On the contrary. If I can't think of the right word for a moment, I don't wait to find it, that would seem artificial to me.

Once, in *Je me souviens,* then in *Pedigree,* I proceeded differently and I've never dared reread these books (it is true that I never reread any of my books) for fear of finding them frightfully literary. *Pedigree* especially. It's a little as if I were watching myself write. Here, writing has no importance and I've even thought of a dictaphone. But then I would be afraid of starting to make speeches or to listen to myself!

It's odd that animals which we consider inferior, insects for example, possess more direct means of communication than we do. If thought, with all its haziness, its hesitations, its meanderings, could be projected! Speaking, and, even more, writing, make it necessary to be precise and, in doing so, to falsify.

3 o'clock in the afternoon

I came to this subject without meaning to and I would not feel honest with myself if I evaded it. However, I wouldn't want this to take on the aspect of an examination of conscience, still less a confession. On the other hand it is indispensable that I should be precise about the fact that when I speak of good or evil I never refer to my entirely personal morality, which also would be difficult, or too long and without interest, to define.

More than ever what I am going to write will be distorted by the fact that in a few paragraphs I can only outline the large elements of my thought, when to transcribe five minutes or an hour of this thought completely would take thick volumes.

Not only because five minutes of my thought today involves years of experiences, certain of which are forgotten, plus other thoughts, events, facts, faces, words spoken or understood. . . .

I was speaking yesterday of a novel to be written on a single day in the life of a man. It might also be possible to write one about five minutes in the life of his brain!

Enough! Often when I see a fault, a failing, a weakness, never mind the word, in one of my children, I keep myself from interfering by remembering that once I did the same thing. What reason could I give for asking them not to go through the same experience I have had, or to be more perfect than I?

I have always had a horror of the father image and mother image as they have a tendency to be created in families. I do not want my children to have a monolithic memory of me, or to attribute to me qualities that I do not have. On the contrary, I would like them to know the vulnerable man that I am, as vulnerable as they and perhaps more so.

That's the point from which I took off last night in bed, and my thought followed parallel lines: one about faults and one about risks. I have not made a balance. I fell asleep before coming to a conclusion, but I was no less frightened by what I discovered.

Suddenly, I blamed myself for having been so apprehensive about Marc when he was fourteen or fifteen years old—and even now that he is married and an adult. I will be just as apprehensive about Johnny when he reaches the age of imprudence, more still, no doubt, about Marie-Jo. Then, if I live that long, it will be Pierre's turn.

However, am I not the one for whom someone should have been afraid? I've told in *Pedigree,* more or less romanticizing them, but remaining faithful basically, about certain of my experiences from before the age of sixteen.

Haven't I, later on, and even not so long ago, nearly foundered a hundred times? And by that word I mean every conceivable catastrophe imaginable.

Could I have become a criminal? I don't know. I have studied criminology a great deal, not only at the time when I was writing only Maigrets, but especially during these last years. One of the branches least known to the general public is victimology, that is to say the responsibility of the victim in almost seventy per cent of crimes. Oh yes, I've deserved to be a victim a hundred times and I realize that I would have borne a large part of the responsibility.

But I have never been conscious of it. I am not particularly brave. I have a certain mistrust for physical bravery and, for example, I have a horror of getting involved in a scuffle, a scrap, even in a mob scene. I also have had a horror of brutality, of anything that injures the flesh, of what uselessly does harm.

How to explain my behavior, then? By a sort of innocence, of openness? I don't think so. More by a certain feeling that I am on an equal footing with men, whoever they are.

It is with the other column, of faults, that I want to start, since I began with my children.

Though, at the time of the *Gazette de Liège,* when I was sixteen and a half to nineteen years old, I had two women available to me each day, almost every day, at one moment or another, I would be like a dog in rut.

An example. A case that comes back to me. In Belgium at that time, as in Amsterdam to this day, there were strange houses: a dimly lit ground floor; half-open curtains behind which could be seen one or two women knitting or reading, raising their heads when they heard the step of a passerby.

These houses, the same as in Amsterdam, were not necessarily in deserted or disreputable streets. There was one on the Boulevard de la Constitution just opposite the largest secondary school, and I had to pass in front of it each time I came back from the center of town through the Passerelle.

I was passing this way one night at about ten o'clock. I did not see the familiar silhouette, but a splendid Negress, and suddenly I felt that it was absolutely necessary for me to enter and make love with her. I had never known a Negress.

I had only a small sum in my pocket. I hesitated. My father was already sick, dying. A little while before, he had given me his watch, a silver watch with the arms of Belgium on it, which he had won in a shooting match, for my father was an enthusiastic marksman (I still have three silver plates engraved with the same arms, won in the same way).

Shamefacedly, I paid with the watch, and it was one of the acts that I regret most, not for moral reasons, but because it would mean so much to me to have this souvenir of my father, who was to die a year later. At home, I was obliged to lie about it. Then to declare the loss of the watch to the police. And if it had been found it might have had far-reaching consequences.

It is only a small example. At the same time, I spent evening after evening all by myself in the most disreputable streets, where I risked being beaten up at every corner.

Later I did the same, almost all through my life, more out of curiosity than desire. When I was living on the Place des Vosges, as for instance around 1923–1924, the Rue de Lappe and other streets around the Bastille were not tourist attractions the way they are today.

In the dance halls they would pull a knife for a Yes or a No, and I have seen a woman's throat cut beside me in a bar.

At that time, my first wife was a painter and, to find models for her, I would go there to look for them, late at night. It was a curious world and one found girls there who had arrived in Paris from Brittany or Normandy only two months ago and were already on the streets.

I took them home. Men would follow me from a distance. Some of them threatened me.

During the same period I spent nights wandering, unarmed, on the old defense works which still existed, near La Villette, on the Rue de Flandre, and the neighborhood of the Canal Saint-Martin held no secrets for me.

I did the same thing in Montmartre and in the twentieth arrondissement and I admit that to my human curiosity was almost always added a certain sexual excitement. I have made love in the streets and the passageways where the unexpected arrival of a policeman could have changed my future.

Much later, in Cairo, I was wandering alone at night (with a revolver in my pocket) in the red-light district, which was as big as a Paris arrondissement, and I used to follow women through the alleys to houses that I could never have found by myself.

The same at Aswan, even in Panama, in Guayaquil, and almost all over the world.

I never had the sense of running risks. It is only now, retrospectively, that I feel fear.

As I feel it in the parallel area of which I have spoken. In Liège, at the *Gazette,* I already had the habit of borrowing two or three months' salary from the cashier and I wonder still how, finally, I managed to repay it.

In Paris I did the same thing, except that I had no salary. Having earned by a miracle, the day before the rent was due, the sum required to pay it, I would spend it in a night club. I earned money fast enough, with stories and popular novels, but even when the Maigrets brought me much more, when I had several houses at once, a car, a chauffeur, etc., I was only working to pay off debts.

"It's the only way to make myself work," I used to say.

Which was false, since I still have a middle-class soul and when I go several days without working I feel full of guilt, like a man who does not deserve the bread he eats.

I've owed money all over town. And I've seen too many cases where that has led to serious compromises.

Why did I have the luck to get out of it?

If I saw one of my children acting that way, I would shudder.

Sometimes when it seemed to be provoking fate, it appeared to me a natural act. I've mentioned my affair with a married woman. It has happened that I took her in her own house when her husband, busy in a neighboring room, was talking to us through the half-open door.

Isn't that a case where if there had been a tragedy I would really have been the one responsible?

The severity of American laws in sexual matters is well known. Well aware of it, one evening when I was feeling good I crossed the center of the city from east to west through the most brightly lit, the busiest streets and avenues, in a taxi with a woman, the two of us in a position . . . which, aside from any scandal, would have got us at least five years in prison and expulsion from the country afterwards.

Again, I did not mean it as a challenge. I am, by nature, a man who respects rules. If I do not believe in them, I pretend that they must be followed out of respect for others. And in forty years' driving I have never had a single ticket, not even for parking my car illegally.

I believe that I am a decent man, anyway in the sense that I give to that word. I have become more and more scrupulous in my own affairs and I am rarely satisfied with myself.

That is the reason why there are few years in my life which I can imagine reliving in a carefree way. I always feel uneasy in remembering myself as I was thirty, twenty years ago. Will I some-day be ashamed of myself today?

When I sent out my first press copies (*Le Pendu de Saint-Pholien* and *M. Gallet, décédé*) I was foolishly proud enough to sign those for the greatest writers and critics with only a ridiculous and cocky "Cordially," as if from one day to the next I had become their equal.

I've spoken of my suits cut in London, of the pearl in my neck-tie, of the apartment done by a "decorator de luxe" on the Boulevard Richard-Wallace.

How, in spite of all that, did I manage to find my way? And how many times, with the slightest slip, could it have been a ca-tastrophe?

All the same I have achieved a certain balance, at least I don't feel too ashamed of myself, I'm able, most often, to look myself in the face.

Then I think of others, some of them for a time my friends, my colleagues, or my relatives, who ended badly.

The responsibility of parents we talk so much about today! Would my parents have been responsible if something bad had happened to me? God knows they took their roles seriously, fol-lowing to the letter the precepts of morality and religion.

Me, I don't presume any right to interfere, except to speak gently to them, and, as I do to Johnny, to tell them things of the sort I tell here.

I hope there won't be other details coming back to me, as with the preceding entry. There are hundreds, buried in my memory; I don't want to tell them, or to remember them. Not out of shame or embarrassment, but because they are without interest and this would take on the tenor of a pose.

Isn't it simpler to say, without searching further:

"I'm only a man."

Either my children will understand or they will not. I hope they understand, although that assumes certain risks. I mean that they must run some risks.

Amen!

I took a walk to the village with Johnny. We came back with Pierre and the nurse, whom we met. I played the drums in the children's playroom and they did not make fun of my clumsiness but seemed rather troubled by it, they who have rhythm under their skins!

Then an errand in town, to leave something at the laboratory. When I got back, I found D. at her typewriter. A joyful noise, which delighted me.

I want to raise my hand as if in school, to say that I've forgotten an important detail and to ask permission to explain. It's a matter of the question of drink, the question of alcoholism. There's a great deal about it in my novels. There are legends on this subject. I would like to take my bearings on this. That will be for tomorrow.

Now I am going to listen to the results of the referendum knowing that I will suffer, for I am persuaded that all the phonyness we have watched in the last few weeks will bear fruit, especially since fifty-five per cent of the voters are women and they vote emotionally or sentimentally. It's none of my business. I am not French, I don't even live in France. But when I speak of it, I still say, without being aware of it:

"At home!"

Even if it were happening in China I couldn't stop myself from getting excited and agonizing over it. Trickery on both sides, certainly, and bad faith, and intrigues. There is nevertheless a certain tone, a certain conceit, a certain contempt for men, of what those people call the mob, which makes me shudder and want to fight. Soon, in front of the television, my toes will contract. And it is I who, when D. gets indignant, tell her that she will get over it in time, that she is not yet quite grown up!

Is one ever quite grown up? For myself, the longer I live, the more I doubt it. And I don't hide it from my children and I avoid saying to them:

"When you're grown up . . ."

"Behave like a grownup . . ."

If they took it into their heads to do it?

/Monday, January 9, 1961

Last night, after a perfect day, followed by a marvelous hour, a brutal, unexpected relapse for D. I wanted to comfort her, first tenderly, then by reasoning with her.

What did I say to provoke a painful crisis? I don't know at all. I search in vain. There she is, depressed, beaten, and anything I say hurts or wounds her. Words are like drops of acid on a burn. I must be quiet. And go on waiting.

Everything I've learned about men, ironically, is useless to me when it is a matter of the one I love the most. I must be calm, not panic. I admit, however, that I am tempted to call for help, that I need someone to reassure me, to take the situation in hand. Alas! There is no one and she no longer has confidence in doctors.

Afternoon

The obsession of aging. I've known it for several years. It is a subject that has rarely been treated in depth, without romanticism, without sentimentality, even by doctors who have only just now managed to invent gerontology.

Goethe's *Faust* seems to me as false as the rest. The only sentence which struck me with its truth was Trotsky's and I no longer know where to find it again. At present I think I've rounded the cape, at least if this isn't only a remission.

It's even more pathetic when one suffers from this obsession falsely, in anticipation. That's the case with D. at the moment, and with her, I believe, it is not so much herself that she is thinking of as of a certain part she plays that she wishes to go on playing forever, and which indeed she plays admirably, lover, mother, wife, mistress of the house, businesswoman.

She is afraid that someday she will become to her children, especially the youngest, only a kind of grandmother. She is afraid of not fully playing her triple part with me.

Falsely, I repeat, because of I don't know what, because of an as yet unknown organic or metabolic trouble, probably, which will have disappeared in a few weeks.

In other words, in a few weeks she will be completely herself again, with all her activity—and her physical well-being restored.

Meantime, she refuses to believe it. She is buried in her conviction of a definite decline which medical opinion contradicts.

She no more believes what I say than she does the doctors. I'm sorry not to have recorded the telephone conversation she just had with one of our medical men, a professor of the Lausanne Faculty. I am sure that if we played back the tape in a few weeks we would both find it high comedy.

It's tragic not to be able to help, not to be able to transmit my trust, my certainty.

How approximate all this is! Speaking of my novels, I have said that I would like to write with a burin on copper, like an engraver. In this case, it would take a scalpel to get to the truth.

/*January 10, 1961*

Day before yesterday, or yesterday, it doesn't matter, I thought of alcohol. I wasn't able to write what I had in mind at the time and I'm doing it today—exactly as I thought of it day before yesterday.

There will be legends about this too. Certain people have seen

197

me working on red wine, others on cider, on muscatel, on whisky, on grog, I don't know what else, and for each it is an eternal verity. Those who have seen me drunk will always see me as drunk, and the contrary is also true.

That, precisely, is a question that has preoccupied me because, of all the dangers I have run, some of which I have cited, this is undoubtedly the most serious. It preoccupied me so much that I have studied the question as only some specialists in Europe and in the United States have done, in medical works as well as in reviews, and in the domain of criminology too. I could fill a notebook with statistics.

Why? Perhaps because I just missed becoming an alcoholic—and the worst kind, the worst for me, I mean.

When I was a child there was neither wine nor liquor in the house, and when someone came to visit I had to run down to the corner store to buy a deciliter (retail) of Cusenier. (?) My father never drank, occasionally a bock, less than a pint of light beer, on Sunday mornings, when he went to play cards in the Café de la Renaissance. For a long time I went with him.

The words "He drinks" were uttered in our house with consternation. For the strongest of reasons, my mother had a horror of alcohol. Her father was ruined by drunkenness, her eldest brother, Léopold, became a sort of bum (an occasional house painter, after university studies) of whom the family was ashamed. One sister, an alcoholic, died very young in an insane asylum and another, my Aunt Maria, made such "Novenas" that she had to be shut up in her room, from which she managed to escape sometimes.

Nothing of this on my father's side. But hadn't he something to be afraid of? Drink spoiled my father's life too and one could say that indirectly he died of it, but that is another story.

My first introduction to alcohol took place during the war. We were hungry. Food was very inadequate. All this I've already mentioned. In "the sideboard" there was a small decanter containing eau-de-vie meant to impregnate the circles of waxed paper with which jars of jam were covered.

One day, at about the age of fourteen, alone in the house, I drank a swallow, out of curiosity. Then, as it gave me a feeling of well-being, I tried it again the next week, being careful to replace what I had drunk with water, so that soon there was nothing but water in the decanter. For a long time it was believed in the house that the alcohol content had evaporated.

I don't think this incident has anything to do with drunkenness, with the taste for alcohol, but that it was both the attraction of forbidden fruit and the need for a certain comfort in my empty stomach.

As a reporter, I eschewed drinking for a long time, until a friend who worked in the front office of the paper took me for a glass of ale to the Café de la Bourse at five o'clock. It was strong beer, pale ale, served, as is the custom in Belgium, in silver goblets, and I think that it was the goblet, with its rich metal and its reflections, along with the cozy atmosphere of the café, that seduced me more than the beer. In any case we got into the habit of going there at the end of each afternoon and having a glass or two of pale ale.

Next, at seventeen, I met the little group of painters and "poets" of Liège and we formed a sort of club, "The Keg," which I've had occasion to describe (particularly in *Le Pendu de Saint-Pholien*) and where, at least once a week, we got drunk deliberately.

Nevertheless, I felt no need to drink, and never did I go into a café alone, preferring to spend my money on cherries, in season, or on pastry; preferring, when I had to go into a public establishment, a *café-filtre* dear to the people of Liège (with the filter in silver, again!).

It was in Paris that I began to see on my table at the "Dîners de Paris" (3.50 francs for the meal, including wine, Passage Jouffroy) a small bottle of red wine whose contents couldn't have exceeded a quarter of a liter.

For several years that was all I required except when, with friends, we decided to have an orgy.

It was at Montparnasse that I began to drink more, because it

199

was the fashion; all the painters of the period (except Vlaminck) were heavy drinkers, while the American novelists whom we were beginning to admire, Hemingway, Steinbeck, etc., were even more so.

Actually at that time I drank mostly to do as the others did, and when in 1925 or 1926 I took the second-floor apartment on the Place des Vosges (up to then I only had lodgings on the ground floor) I installed a superb American bar there, very "modern art," where I officiated almost daily as barkeeper. That was the period of complicated cocktails and I knew all the recipes. The biggest part of my income, obviously, went into liquor.

An anecdote, in passing. One morning, at about eleven o'clock, a painter friend brought one of his clients to see me, a big wine merchant from Béziers. Of course, I went behind the bar. I served. At the moment of leaving, I saw the merchant coughing, turning towards my friend, going through his pockets, murmuring in an aside to him. Scarcely out the door, I found out afterwards, he said to my friend:

"I think I did something stupid. I didn't dare pay. . . ."

The poor man had thought I kept a commercial bar in my house!

On board the *Ginette*, during my tour of France along the canals and rivers, in the Midi, I used to fill a ten-liter demijohn at pumps that looked like gas pumps. I drank when I was thirsty, never to get drunk.

On board the *Ostrogoth*, in Holland, it was rarely wine, too expensive in that country (I had a barrel sent to me from France at Stavoren), but from time to time a glass of gin.

It was at about this time, and after my return, at Morsang, still on board the *Ostrogoth*, that while writing the first Maigrets I got the habit of working on wine. From six in the morning. And as I was writing morning and afternoon, that is to say three chapters a day . . .

At Morsang, there was a barrel in the fork of a tree next to the boat. The habit was formed. I went on like this until 1945. Wine, white at Concarneau (cider in the afternoon), red in Paris or elsewhere, grog when I had a cold, brandy and water at other times.

Once again, I was rarely drunk, but I needed, as early as the morning, especially to write, a pick-me-up. I was persuaded in good faith that it was impossible to write otherwise. And, away from work, I drank anything, apéritif, cognac, calvados, marc, champagne. . . .

I was not at all aware of being an alcoholic, but only a temperamental fellow, and the fact is that my days were long and full, that I was intensely active. I traveled a lot and while traveling I drank more.

My lowest consumption of wine, a little before and during the war, was about three bottles of Saint-Emilion, which I considered very modest, since the farmers of the region (Saint-Mesmin) drank their eight to ten liters of white wine.

In 1945 I left for the United States and I admit that I then began to drink American style, no longer wine with my meals, but before them, Manhattan after Manhattan, then dry Martini after dry Martini (with an onion, which is called a Gibson).

I began to have painful awakenings, hangovers, attacks of gas pains during which I thought I was dying of angina pectoris each time.

With D., we had two or three months of wild life, which I don't regret and of which I often think nostalgically, but she had the courage, from the beginning, to propose to me (which meant to force me) to work . . . on tea. The first novel written on tea is *Three Rooms in Manhattan* written in a log cabin on Lake Masson in the Laurentians in midwinter.

We got around on skis. We crossed the frozen lake in a car. Logs blazed in an immense fireplace. I was sure I would never come to the end of that book.

Trembling, D. waited behind the door of my study (neither she nor anyone else has ever seen me write a novel) listening to the rhythm of the typewriter, and ceaselessly bringing me hot tea. I left the door half open, stuck my hand out, and grabbed the cup without a word.

She had reason to tremble, for if the experiment had failed I would, in all probability, never have tried it again, and I would be dead at this moment.

We continued to drink pretty seriously from time to time. Then we cut the liquor, allowing ourselves only beer (very strong in Canada, also strong in the U.S.A.).

We had an occasional sherry or a port, and finally, one fine day in Arizona, we decided to put ourselves on the wagon (complete abstinence).

Not out of virtue. Only because we knew that we were, both of us, incapable of stopping in time.

I am not trying to write an edifying story and I don't pretend that I'm saved for good. Every two months, every three months, we get off the wagon for an evening or for two or three days, whether because of some occasion, a celebration, or simply, I would say, out of hygiene, so that this does not come to seem a deprivation, thus an obsession.

Wine or liquor, because of the fact that we are detoxified, and because we have lost the habit, has much more effect on us than it used to, and I have got drunk on two or three glasses.

The rest of the time there is no wine on the table, no beer, nothing—water—Coca-Cola for me the rest of the day. And we have managed, for example, when I was presiding over the Film Festival of Brussels, then the one in Cannes, to get through a luncheon banquet, three or four official cocktail parties a day, without touching a drop of alcoholic beverage.

We started our abstinence in 1949, which makes about eleven years. This does not keep me from considering myself an alcoholic.

I may add that in my current life the odor of alcohol has become disagreeable to me and that I, who was a wine expert (I bottled my wine myself and I bought from the winegrowers in all the winegrowing regions of France), I have come to find the first glass unpleasant, to barely appreciate the second, and to drink the rest only out of habit.

Few of my French friends understand it. And I resent those

who have made drink the indispensable complement to every friendly, worldly, or even official meeting.

In an hour D. and I are going to the radiologist for the last test. Radiology of the gall bladder. Then the doctor will pore over a file as thick as a criminal dossier. May they find something!

I should add a note to what I wrote yesterday on alcoholism. It is quite striking, I think, that I did not become truly alcoholic with an alcoholic consciousness except in America; put another way, after having drunk for more than twenty years and often having drunk much more than I did there.

I'm speaking of a particular, almost permanent state, in which one is dominated by alcohol, whether during the hours one is drinking or during the hours when one is impatiently waiting to drink, almost as painfully as a drug addict waits for his injection or his fix.

If one has never known this experience, it is difficult to understand American life. Not that everyone drinks, in the sense in which my mother used this word, but because it is part of private and public life, of folklore, you might say, as is proved by the large, more or less untranslatable vocabulary, most often in slang, that relates to drink.

We knew that state, D. and I, only intermittently, and I admit that alcoholism for two, accompanied by love, by passion, by exacerbated sexuality, is not at all disagreeable, quite the contrary.

All of life is colored by it. New York, for example, seems made to be seen in this state, and then it is an extraordinary New York and, strange as it may seem, comradely.

The crowds cease to be anonymous, the bars cease to be ordinary ill-lit places, the taxi drivers complaining or menacing people. It is the same for all the big American cities, Los Angeles,

San Francisco, Boston. . . . From one end of the country to the other there exists a freemasonry of alcoholics (like the one that exists for Alcoholics Anonymous). . . .

Then a couple lives folded in on itself. The hotel room becomes a home. The bed takes an unexpected, unforeseen importance, whether for sleeping, for making love, or for suffering. The hours of the day are different from what they are for most people, measured by successive drinks, a little as in a convent they are marked by religious rites.

I'm not exaggerating. It is another world in which certain preoccupations disappear, where the order of importance of things changes. For two, I repeat, it's marvelous. And, because it is marvelous, it is vital to leave it as soon as possible, for after a certain time, as with drugs, this exaltation and privacy become a hell. Intoxication begins.

We fled in time, D. and I. We went on the wagon (the wagon, that is to say the water cart from which at one time drinking water was sold in the streets).

Nevertheless, I have a nostalgia for certain nights, certain mornings on Sainte-Marguerite-du-Lac-Masson, for certain days at the Drake in New York. . . . We tried at Cannes, soon after my return to Europe, to rediscover these sensations when the occasion presented itself. It wasn't the same thing.

Because we were in Europe? Because we had been detoxified too long and for that reason the mornings after were too painful.

Or, again, because we had acquired a sense of guilt? For that too is a part of the problem. For twenty odd years in France, until 1945, I drank without remorse, without seeing anything wrong with it, I was going to say: quite the contrary.

In the United States I learned shame. For they are ashamed. Everyone is ashamed. I was ashamed like the rest. Which contributes to that sensation of solitude, of isolation, to a certain withdrawing into oneself and at the same time to that solidarity with all other men. A solidarity which is almost universal there.

Utterly overwhelmed. I discover once more, with D., that everything you know, everything you have learned, counts for nothing, that the truth is always different. But I wasn't far off. And God knows if my love ought to have helped me in what I dare not call my diagnosis. Impossible to talk about it here, because the form is too specific. I would need a novel, a transposition, which would be nearer to reality than what I could say here.

This morning I almost wrote: Is she perhaps right in spite of and in the face of everybody else? I didn't because I feared her reaction to this question when she read it.

/Friday, January 13, 1961

Yesterday I had my best (I hope our best) evening in the last two years. Dinner tête à tête, slowly, quietly, at the Grappe d'Or and, as happens to me rarely, I was in no hurry to leave the table. Because of this, the Grappe d'Or, where we scarcely ever go except when we have to take out friends who are passing through, has almost taken on, in my eyes, the aspect of our dear Brussels in New York, where we saw each other for the first time and where we go back so often on a pilgrimage.

I am happy, I am thinking about my novel, and we will be able to escape for a few days, D. and I. It seems to me that this will be our first real holiday in a long, long time. We've earned one.

/January 14, 1961

Last evening received and read the book that Bernard de Fallois devotes to me. It seems to me the best of those written about me (including the less important studies). He speaks less of me than of my work, which is a relief. However, I always feel the same

205

embarrassment reading studies of this kind. Of course I believe in the importance of what I do, or I wouldn't have been writing for forty years. But from my believing in it to hearing someone else speaking of this importance, seriously discussing this or that passage in a book . . .

Strange as it may seem, it's unpleasant.

From another point of view, it's equally unpleasant to me when my work is treated cavalierly.

An hour later, D. is reading the Fallois manuscript and is overwhelmed by it. I wouldn't want the above note to be misunderstood. I, too, was happy to see the importance of my books to a fellow I'm very fond of.

Certainly, D. is capable of protecting my books, on my behalf, not only from the material but from the literary and moral point of view. In my successive wills I've designated the Société des Auteurs my executors, as a last resort, and for want of a better. (I have a horror of the Gens de Lettres.) I must correct my will and write in de Fallois's name instead.

The "embarrassment" I mentioned earlier is not aimed at him. It's what seems to me the natural reaction of any creative person to an analysis of his work. One is divided between pleasure and pain. Difficult to explain.

It appears the three books will come out at the same time. This one, then Dr. R.'s, and finally the one by S., which I haven't read.

I hope it will be de Fallois's book that will receive the attention of critics and readers.

What I'm most grateful for is that he doesn't speak of me as of a "phenomenon," hasn't tried to analyze the "creative mechanism," hasn't looked for "sources," but has tried to understand a certain number of novels—and has understood them. When I say a certain number, I mean all my novels, for he read them all scrupulously, some of them two or three times.

Later, perhaps, I will be able to read this kind of work without being thrown into a panic.

I mustn't form an idea of myself yet, much less of what I write.

In the middle of a novel: *Maigret et le Voleur Paresseux*. Today, page 100. I want to get rid of an idea that came to me suddenly last night. I think that my work will have much less importance later than certain people would like to think. I am speaking very sincerely.

If that came suddenly to mind, it is because I had the impression, I don't know why, that I was mistaken in thinking that I was at the beginning of a period, that I had in some way found a certain way of feeling, of penetrating man, of giving importance to his surroundings and even to the objects, etc., as well as to a certain rhythm in my novels. So I would have been at the beginning of a period:

1 9 3 0 – 1 9 6 0 . . . .

and that would have given a certain weight to my writing. But if the opposite is true?

1 9 3 0 . . . . 1 9 6 0

Well, too bad, I'll never know. All the same, it bothers me a little and I mustn't work with any less faith in what I do. Above all, now.

There now! Another novel finished. Feeling of relief first, as each time, because I got to the end, that I'm no longer at the mercy of any touch of flu, any headache, any moment of discouragement.

And also, because once more I've done my job. Then, almost at once, a wavering, a dull worry: readjustment to everyday life. Not disagreeable at all, though, rather the opposite.

Tomorrow morning I shall be surprised not to be wakened at six o'clock, not to have to build my fire, make my coffee, not to follow the routine of work days. And I will plunge joyfully into the life of the house.

169th, 170th novel? I no longer know. So many figures are published. It is enough for me to ask D., who keeps the count up-to-date. The number doesn't matter.

Whatever it is, it suddenly seems to me ridiculous. Less than two hundred times, this impression that I've just described . . . It isn't much when you think that I've been working at my trade for about forty years. How many times does one make love in a lifetime? How many times does one get off a boat, a train, a plane, does one make contact with a different world?

I envy painters. They do many more canvases than we do novels. Yet pictures are works that are just as complete, as finished. Why?

I don't yet know what I shall think of my last Maigret when I revise it. It's a fairly disorganized sketch, by design, two stories that intertwine, I don't quite know why. Some passages will make the reader laugh. I purposely put in a lot of light touches. And I wonder if I could have treated the same subject in one of my harder novels, if then it wouldn't have been unbearable, at any rate to many people.

That's one thing that de Fallois, who is coming tomorrow, understands very well—the first person who has, except D., of course—that in Maigret I often take up subjects that are more serious than those in my other books. But in a playful manner or, at least, with the poise of my police chief as a counterbalance.

The next week a holiday at last. D. and I will fly to Cannes, where we will spend several days together. Ouf!

And already I am thinking of writing, as soon as possible, my second novel of the year, with another holiday in mind, in Paris, probably. I'd like that very much. Many books in order to have these brief moments alone together, no matter where.

If I took these holidays without having written first, I would have the feeling of not having earned them.

As I foresaw, I woke up at six o'clock and couldn't go back to sleep. By tradition, I went to the barber.

Last evening, happened to hear on television (heard, because the pictures broke down) Giono talking about our profession. I haven't read him. As with other contemporaries, I once skimmed through one or two of his books, but, from what I know of him and his work, he is a writer whom I respect. (Not responsive to his lyricism, personally, which is perhaps a lack in me; I wonder if I wasn't a little jealous, before and during the war when he was one of the novelists most popular with the young. He isn't any more, but I'm not either. End of parenthesis.)

Giono said that he did not understand novelists to whom writing is a sort of agony. In his eyes, this is a hangover of romanticism. The creator, he says, is like any craftsman, like a shoemaker, and one cannot imagine a shoemaker suffering over making a shoe. (The shoemaker is his analogy.) He added that if writing were painful for him, he would have chosen another trade.

I envy him. The shoemaker, having finished his apprenticeship, is sure of being able to finish the shoe he has begun. There is a simple, known technique which he has learned. There also are norms. And everybody knows whether a shoe is successful or not.

But with a novel? With any work of art?

So Giono is sure of himself. He is sure, in beginning a book, that he will be able to get to the end and that he will succeed in saying what he means, of getting the right vibration, the right degree of emotion, of communicating it on the right page, of finding the words, the rhythm. . . .

For me this is so miraculous that I never dare believe in it.

If it were a matter of a novelist working commercially according to proven formulas, this wouldn't bother me. I didn't worry either when I was writing popular novels and adventure novels, and I used to go to work whistling.

So I find that not everybody suffers from stage fright. By contrast, Maurice Chevalier, on television the night before, admitted openly that for the past sixty-six years he has always felt his throat dry up and his knees weak when he went on stage.

One is not necessarily right and the other wrong. Just the same, it bothers me.

/*Wednesday, January 27, 1961*

Yesterday went to have a film screened, the film of the Balzac television broadcast that I did about a year ago and which de Fallois (who left last evening) had missed at the time. Odd impression. Last year, seeing it on my own screen, I was preoccupied with knowing if it had been cut much, if it held up, if I hadn't stammered, etc. Yesterday, I realized that while I can't stand my photographs, even those taken by the best photographers, because I don't recognize myself in them, I recognize myself very well on the screen.

This had never struck me, although I'm used to seeing myself in the movies or on television. I think I understand. The still photo inevitably gives a false image. The moving image is much nearer to the truth.

The painting, the portrait, without showing the man in movement, does not freeze him at a precise—hence artificial—instant, but gives an illusion of time passing.

Now, however, we have the moving pictures and voices of men.

Would we have the same idea of a Hitler, a Mussolini, a Churchill, a Stalin, etc., without those pictures and voices? Isn't our whole perspective on great men—or small—transformed by them?

This presents another problem that I have not yet seen raised, but which one day will call for supplementary texts in the Civil Code. Certain North Africans, for example, refuse to allow themselves to be photographed because they believe that in this way a part of their soul is taken from them.

Without going that far, there is, it seems to me, a question of property. I'm not speaking of money. As to political men, the pictures of their public life and their speeches pass into history. But how about all the others whom radio and television interview each day?

I'm lucky to own a print of this Balzac because I refused to be paid for my work and they kindly offered me a copy. That is very unusual.

So, here are a man's picture and voice which no longer belong to him. He has collaborated in a broadcast at a given moment. In two years, in ten, in fifty, in entirely different circumstances, in other perspectives, they can be used again without the least authorization from him or his heirs.

Radio and television networks thus possess a prodigious capital over which there are no controls.

I'll take a case. Day before yesterday, out of the year's literary broadcasts, a *single* sentence was taken from each writer, a single sequence, and these extracts were shown back to back, out of context, in a sort of symposium in which one or another of them ran the risk of being misrepresented.

The papers complain that some people attack photographers and break their cameras. But for an actress, for example, for an actor, for people from other professions, a *stolen* picture, taken extemporaneously, can really be prejudicial, even tragic.

Our picture is taken, our voice recorded, with or without our consent, and we subsequently lose all control over them.

There is something there contradictory to the very basis of the Civil Code, and this must finally be recognized. How can it be remedied? I don't know at all. If I had written the Balzac instead of speaking it, the text would belong to me and no one could use it without my permission. I could also destroy it if later it displeased me.

Because it went on television, and because it was recorded on film, I lose all my rights, moral and material.

In the crowds at a festival or an opening, someone sticks a microphone under my nose and asks me a question (sometimes after a banquet). I answer anything, quickly, without reflection, because it is almost impossible not to answer. This sentence that I speak is only valid in the circumstances, at a certain date, under certain conditions.

But now it can be shown again in other countries at other times, may perhaps be inserted in my obituary.

Are the North Africans so wrong? Don't they steal a little of our souls?

Certain television journalists pretend to catch their "subject" at the moment of truth with difficult questions.

I would not be surprised if one day this will come to seem incredible—and outrageous.

This is not the reason why I refused the close-ups they asked me for but, after having seen Balzac again, I'm glad I refused.

Johnny delights me more and more. As for Marie-Jo, she "tries" so hard, like her mother, that she touches me and I would like to rid her of her scruples. As for Pierre, he now occupies such a large place in the house that one wonders how we could ever have lived without him.

D. herself is getting well all by herself, as I secretly hoped she would before our visit to Dr. Pathé. Good girl!

/*Saturday, January 28, 1961*

It's difficult not to become a "man of letters" (the word has always sounded a little like "general houseworker" to me: "all-round man of letters") and I understand my colleagues who adopt it. We are continually asked for everything: interviews, lectures, articles on everything under the sun, to preside over juries, etc., and people, sometimes the government, are annoyed if we say no.

This time I have been asked to do something that tempts me: a play for Eurovision planned to be produced the same evening, at the same time, in different languages, in Paris, London, Berlin, Stockholm, Copenhagen, etc. Television has fascinated me for nearly twelve years.

On the other hand, it's not my trade. I'm afraid of failure. I'm afraid of the days or weeks of anxiety it would cause me. I'm wavering. Will I allow myself to be persuaded? Or, more honestly, will I give in to the temptation of trying a medium that is new to me? I was promising myself a novel at the end of February or the beginning of March. I am going to think about it for a week while I revise the last Maigret and then be on my way to Cannes. If a subject comes to me . . .

The same thing happened when the *Illustrated London News* asked me for a long novella for its Christmas issue. I answered: "If I find a subject in two days, yes. If not, no."

I wrote *Sept Petites Croix dans un Carnet*.

We'll see if something will materialize this time or if, more wisely, I'll stick to the novel.

D. is better and better. I was counting on three more or less difficult months of convalescence. She's coming back to herself with surprising speed. In the last analysis, with her, one shouldn't try to interfere. Let her go along according to her own logic, which is after all only instinct.

/February 4, 1961

Revision finished on the 2nd. Refused the television play. Last evening, Raoul Levy telephoned from Los Angeles. Purchase of movie rights of *Three Rooms in Manhattan*. That is a film I would like to see made, and at the same time it makes me more apprehensive than the others. It would give me an odd feeling to see Jeanne Moreau in the part of Kay.

Leaving for Cannes soon. As I don't want to take this notebook along (for fear of losing it, I admit) I'll take a new one, Notebook III, so that this one stops here, even though there are several blank pages left.

End of Second Notebook

Third Notebook
1961 – 1963

"My beautiful new notebook," as I used to say when I was still in school. (I just came·back from a walk with Pierre in the sharp cold and my hands are still stiff. The logs are just beginning to burn. Eleven thirty in the morning. Marie-Jo has come back from her music lesson and Johnny will be back at noon. D. is in her boudoir.)

That's all, really, I just wrote all I have to say this morning between the parentheses. I wanted to begin Notebook III as soon as we were back from Cannes (yesterday afternoon, but the Nielsens were here waiting for us) and most of all to begin it in a peaceful and joyful atmosphere.

Wrote nothing in Cannes. Did nothing. Good news about D.'s health and mine (which wasn't bothering me). Like certain animals in spring, we both felt a sudden rush of health, of cleanliness of body, and next week we will probably go to the clinic for two or three days for a small correction D. needs after her last childbirth. A stitch broke.

Finally saw P. after all the other doctors. Someday I must write all I can on this subject, which I'm beginning to understand.

So, back at the house, our own bed, my study, clear cool weather, and we're going to a wedding this afternoon.

Is it because of the mimosa, the orange trees, the flowering almonds in the Midi? For me, whatever the weather is tomorrow, spring has already begun.

217

Officially I am fifty-eight years old. In reality I won't be until to-morrow.

So, yesterday we went to the wedding. Mostly doctors, most of them university professors, the bride being the daughter of a professor. Among them a man of sixty-five, known around the world as much for his writings as for his international practice.

Two or three years ago, I think it was, he abandoned his chair, his clinic, and his practice, because he became addicted to drugs (morphine, according to what I was told). I expected to find him physically and mentally diminished. I spent more than two hours in conversation with him. Of all those present, he was the most lucid, the most human.

Did he notice that I wasn't drinking anything but water? I'm sure of it. Whenever he was offered a whisky, he would hesitate and refuse most of the time. During those two hours he must not have had more than three drinks. And I felt a sort of question in his eyes.

For the past year he has been living by himself most of the time (he has a wife and a child), in a country house, to write a work which will deal largely, he told me, with instinct and intuition. He asked my permission—as if he had to!—to show me his manuscript.

This is a subject that has fascinated me for a long time and which I've found worth researching in works of all kinds, including those on primates, for example, and on the training of wild animals.

Someday I hope to have that man here in my study and to talk with him at leisure. I did not say to him yesterday: If I had accepted a glass of that champagne or of that whisky continually passed under my nose (though I had a long wait for a glass of water, which was very difficult to get) I would have taken a second, then a third, I would have begun to talk volubly, and instead of leaving at nine o'clock I would have been one of the last to leave—at four o'clock in the morning, no doubt. And Sunday in bed, sweating out my alcohol, with palpitations.

That's the way it was during some twenty-four days of the Cannes Festival.

"You aren't drinking anything?" people marveled.

Oh no! Nor do I eat any of what is served at all those luncheons, dinners, and receptions. For years, however, I thought that gastronomy was an essential part of my life.

When he comes, shall I tell him that someday I may be tempted to write, uninitiate that I am, a book on medicine and doctors? I have been observing them since my mother's house was filled with them when I was barely six years old, first medical students, then doctors from the neighborhood, from the countryside around, and finally the big guns of all kinds.

Is it accidental that more than eighty per cent of the friends I've had, the people I've made companions of, belonged to the medical world? When it has been called to my attention, and when I've been asked the reason for my choice, I freely answer that doctors and novelists have almost the same interest in man, study him from the same angle.

But yesterday, watching those around me, I realized that this is untrue.

The closest to myself was the man who was no longer practicing and who is going to write a book not on medicine or his specialty, in which he has made a number of discoveries, but on instinct.

Is it necessary or indispensable that a man touch bottom at least once in his life to become wholly a man?

Touch it himself. Not just be present. . . .

Seriously, if someday I no longer write novels, for lack of creative energy, it is possible that I might try to write a book on doctors. Hasn't one of them just written a book about me? And a psychiatrist like Delay an extensive work on André Gide in which there is no question of psychiatry?

We promised Johnny to be back at nine thirty and we got back at nine thirty sharp. He was as happy as I to know that his mother danced three wild Charlestons in succession, which exhausted her seventeen-year-old partner!

Today the whole family went for the papers. The house is quiet. Soon we will take a ride around the village, D. and I.

We won't go to the clinic next week as I'd hoped, nor the following, because the doctor won't be free, so that my next novel is postponed to about mid-March. A novel on what? I haven't the least idea. I'm going to begin to empty myself, little by little, to feel myself out.

As almost always when I'm beginning, I promise myself an optimistic novel. I know what I mean. Not conventional optimism. A novel tasting of life. Then, when it is finished . . .

I'm thinking about a couple I've known for forty years. They have both struggled. She must have had virtues, since he used to love her and they were happy. At fifty, she became another woman. A caricature of herself, morally as well as physically. And at any slightest difficulty, she falls ill. But he goes along without a word, smiling. . . . Do some people laugh at him, taking him for a fool or a simpleton? He surely knows it. He pays no attention. . . . He is paying.

He had "the other one" for thirty years. He is used to her faults. Which is the real woman, the one today or the former one? Does he ask himself that question?

I don't think he submits silently just because it is the only way to have peace. I think it goes further than that, that he is aware that this deterioration, which must have come about imperceptibly, is part of a complex process, a sort of law. . . .

There used to be vaudeville skits about this sort of thing, which made people laugh. Now we try to understand and don't laugh any more.

It is the same with all known and unknown laws in nature. Man always submitted to them whether he liked it or not, reconciled himself to them.

Today we no longer reconcile ourselves.

And I come back to medicine, which I hadn't meant to say any more on today: to heal or not to heal?

For the question is asked. I'm not talking about finding the remedy for this or that affliction. I'm talking about caring for and healing the individual, this individual, in these circumstances, with the consequences that this entails. . . .

I just read a phrase of Littré's. Is it true or false?

"Imagine how sad one must have been to have composed a dictionary."

Is there a link between my different notes today? It doesn't matter. Yesterday, at the wedding, few young people. One, however, who asked me, he too, for permission to come to see me. He is the son of one of the most famous contemporary orchestra conductors.

He is twenty-five years old, paints, seems to be giddy, charming, and aggressive all at once. I wouldn't be surprised if he became a personage himself, but I foresee an eventful life, if not a tragic one, for him. At the moment he is engaged, in love, full of life. He behaves as if he needed someone to look after him, or cajole him.

At his age I was already saying (and I've often repeated it since) that a novelist must live to be an old man, as old as possible, in order to see mankind from every point of view, that of the adolescent, the old man. It is even truer than I thought. One must have led a certain number of lives, been present, from beginning to end if possible, at those experiences which make up human life.

Professor X said to me yesterday, on a parallel subject: "As a young man one can express ideas. It takes a lifetime to discover them."

To rediscover them, rather, even the simplest ones. To experiment with them, to *feel* them.

It was only last week that I suddenly understood that one of my good friends, also a doctor—another one!—could quite easily become the character in *L'Ours en Peluche* in spite of his apparent stability. And he too, like my other friend, is silent, silent, with a wife who overflows with vitality. Smiling.

Always with a look of . . . I finally recognize these eyes, which others accept so easily as serene, but which, it comes to my mind, are the eyes Monsieur Monde had—when he came back. Didn't I have that look myself for years? It is neither tragic nor moving. It's worse!

I'm very glad I went to New York! If I hadn't gone, how long could I have continued to have anything to write about? *Monsieur Monde . . . Le Cercle des Mahé . . . Les Noces de Poitiers . . . Bilan Maletras . . .* And then? The balance of what?

/February 13, 1961

So, fifty-eight years old. Sun. Lovely birthday, flowery, affectionate, leisurely, with an afternoon walk in Lausanne with D.

The thought I write here is yesterday evening's. Taking off on some idea one wants to get rid of, there it is again at the end of the line in a different form.

We often joke about old men—or middle-aged men—saying that whenever they get together they can't stop talking about the good old days, about what they've lived through and experienced. Now that I have been a middle-aged man for some time and many of my friends are really old men, I know the truth.

There's no doubt we sometimes recall old times with a kind of exuberance, but that's only superficial talk after a good dinner in good company.

What an old man wants to know when he meets another is whether the other has come to the same conclusions he has, the same results, though of course the question is not put so crudely. It isn't asked at all. It's the young men who ask questions or answer them.

They arrive by soundings, prudent, veiled. They are looking for the flaw. For they know that everyone has a flaw.

A few words, certain silences, looks, are enough to inform the questioner and he rarely goes further, because what remains to be said cannot easily be expressed in words. Or because words seem trivial or absurd.

So many years . . . So many experiences, hopes, joys, pains, springs, journeys, discoveries, doubts, successes . . .

And what were they looking for?

Shall I be foolish enough to tell, when I'm still only a half-oldster; won't they, the real ones, accuse me of betraying the brotherhood?

Like Diogenes, they were looking for a man. Because one would be enough! They have sought outside and inside themselves.

If one of them, at the end of his search, finally found one—even more if it were himself—I haven't met him yet.

That would change everything. On that, one could build . . . I don't know . . . not a morality, which I don't care for . . . build a world, perhaps, which would really be made to our measure?

Short of that, they speak in brief sentences that are noncommittal, that are like bait on a line, they watch, they smile, they open or close their mouths, and from time to time one is tempted to wink at the other.

Don't primitive peoples express all these things—and much better!—in their sculptures and masks?

Since last night a small machine weighing as little as a 4-CV (and which may make no more noise) has been on its way to Venus.

/February 14, 1961

(Children, I wouldn't want you to imagine, because of yesterday's notes, for instance, that one day in February 1961 your father thought of himself as an old man, or even felt old. He doesn't at all, and I undoubtedly owe that to you, for by living with you I am plunged into youth once more. If I'm talking about old men, then, or middle-aged men, it's because I am at least halfway between them and you—more than halfway, alas!—and I'm beginning to understand them while still able to look at them from the outside. Finally, I should say that I am surely at the ideal age to see both sides. How wonderful it would be to stop time!)

Still on the subject of old men, there are some left—not for long, though—who in my eyes belong to a particular species which I always observe with curiosity mixed with some envy. They are country people from the little villages, whom one sees congregating at the fairs or in the inns.

They are eighty or more. They all were babies at the same time, went to school, to all the burials, all the marriages, all the baptisms of the countryside together.

They remember their games together, their fights of other days. Their life has passed in an enclosed world, which must have been reassuring. And yet, looking at them closely, in spite of their simplicity, their lack of philosophical curiosity, it seems to me that I've found that same question in their eyes that I was talking about yesterday.

Also, I wrote a sentence that doesn't really make sense and I want to correct it. But I can't see how to do it. I spoke of building a world made to our own measure. This doesn't stand close examination. Build a world? Who? Us? How? Why? And what is *our* measure? Whose measure? The measure of what? How did I fall into such bad writing? And yet, behind these clumsy words, I feel that there is something.

Lumumba has been assassinated. I wonder if his death isn't going to speed up the end of a certain soeiety which I despise. Somewhere in this notebook I was wondering if cynical people really exist, people strong enough to be cynical. Is this one of the proofs?

I'm not sure yet. Men are obliged to make themselves believe that they are right, and they manage to do so without much trouble. From that point on, everything becomes easy, including a certain Machiavellianism which is more apparent than real.

The African business is no closer to me than other world affairs and still Lumumba's death makes me as sad as if he were someone I knew well.

My son Pierre has got into the habit of dropping in on me in my study. Yesterday he devoted himself to the inspection of my drawers, respectfully, without touching anything. At a certain point, when I was busy writing, he came to take my hand, led me to a piece of furniture, and showed me a key that he could not turn in the lock.

I discussed with D. the changes necessitated by the ages of the children. Johnny is inheriting Pierre's room in the spring, and vice versa. We're putting in a bathroom for Johnny, who then won't have to share his brother's and sister's, etc.

It's like a wave, advancing slowly, imperceptibly. All of a sudden you see the landscape has changed. Difficulty of organizing vacations that three children of different ages can enjoy equally. And all these little problems change from year to year.

Delicious, almost complete relaxation. Last night D. and I worked together on the translation of an article by Miller about me. More precisely, D. made a first draft and together we then tried to reproduce the spirit of the original. No arguments. Everything very smooth.

I believe this is our first collaboration of this kind, since as a rule each of us does his own clearly separate work. I was delighted by it. The crocuses are in flower. Soon the tulips will be. And I'm forgetting to think about my next book. Next Tuesday I'm going to have a wisdom tooth pulled, because my cheeks are too thick for the dentist to work on it.

Lessons with my daughter now, then to town with D. Life is beautiful.

Full of a gentle euphoria. Then a letter from Marc, and here I am, suddenly anxious, upset. Why are we so apprehensive for our children when they are becoming men while we had no fear for ourselves as we rounded the same cape?

Isn't it because of a retrospective fear which overcomes us at the thought of all we risked without realizing it? I was a hundred times more foolhardy than he at his age, and I'm no less frightened by the least of his follies.

I've seen young people become men in spite of and against all odds, some of them, often, the very ones a psychological observer would have classified as almost hopeless cases. It is also true that I've seen others who failed, and for almost as long as I can remember, I have felt an anguish over spoiled lives, which made me invent and describe, when I was fourteen, maybe in 1917, the profession of "restorer of destinies," a sort of Maigret as doctor, psychiatrist, etc., a kind of consulting God-the-Father, in fact, and I had no idea that this profession was actually in the offing, replacing that of confessor: the psychoanalyst.

I just made a mistake. The expression in my childish mind was not restorer but mender. "Mender of destinies!" If only there were such a thing!

And my good friend Miller, who believes me strong, invulnerable, and who, in his article, attributes to me serenity in the face of every test! In what concerns myself, perhaps. And yet! When it is a matter of my wife, my children . . .

Wasn't I unconsciously thinking of that impossibly serene man, of that God-the-Father of my old dreams, when I spoke the other day of the man without flaw?

End of my serenity for a few days. Went out with Marie-Jo and we got ready for her eighth birthday. Just now we were walking along gaily with our arms around each other's waists like lovers, on the Rue de Bourg, and I think she was happy to see people turning to look.

Three times since lunch have gone up to Johnny's room, where he had taken refuge to read, to tell him funny stories I found for him in papers and magazines. This morning I went to meet Pierre in the village, but because of the fog didn't find him.

Later on, how will those two find their way to be men? I hope to be still around, although I know now that a moment comes when we are no help to our children—except to rescue them when they've got themselves into trouble.

In an article on Gide I read that he always seemed a bit strained, tentative, that people who spoke forcefully like Malraux or Saint-Exupéry, etc., impressed him, and he seemed to envy them. I knew him enough to know it's true. But I also believe that I know the reason for this reaction. He did not affirm. He doubted everything. He hesitated to offer an opinion.

And he regarded as wonders those men who knew everything, decided everything without hesitation, as if they were in possession of the truth.

I suddenly have the impression of knowing him better, of appreciating him more than when we saw each other and wrote to each other.

/Monday, February 20, 1961

I may have found a subject for a novel, which is none other than the one I failed at last year (before the Maigret), *The Train*, but written in the first person, which would change the lighting, the rhythm, and, except for the opening, the story. I must grope about for a few days to know if I'm getting into it or not.

Last evening, after a peaceful family Sunday, during which only D. worked straight through, a passing remark of hers amused me. She had gone on dictating after dinner. Towards ten thirty she came upstairs and joined me in the drawing room, exhausted. As usual, she read the papers for a quarter of an hour for a change of pace. But when she finished reading them, she asked me quite naturally:

"Can't I read your notebook?"

"But you read it three days ago."

"I thought you'd written in it since then. . . ."

It's becoming a habit, then. And the fact is that I sometimes want to write for the sake of writing, or rather of relating, going over the small events of the past.

These have been so distorted in the press, or by my friends in the telling, that they don't correspond to any reality.

But last night I realized that the things I've done that have taken on a quasi-legendary quality were done quite naturally, quite logically. The very fact that they are too natural and too logical makes them extraordinary. To relate them in detail seems to me long and tedious, yet if I abridge and simplify, I'll fall into another sort of artifice.

The business of the canals, for example (and perhaps someday the one about the wolves), takes on an exaggerated importance under a journalist's pen, and also a meaning I don't recognize. They talk about canal boats. I have never had a canal boat. Before the *Ostrogoth*—a fishing cutter ten meters long that I had built at Fécamp, and on board which I lived all the time I was in Holland and in Germany—I did indeed travel through the rivers and canals of France, but not in a canal boat: on board a five-meter mahogany craft that must have been the lifeboat of a big yacht.

Why the rivers and canals? I had been living in France for three years. Outside Paris, I had made only a few trips to the provinces. I had observed that most of the cities and towns faced not towards the road or railway, but towards the river, the stream, or the canal, which is natural.

The memory of the canal from Liège to Maestricht, opposite my Aunt Maria's house at Coronmeuse, must have had some influence too. I always had wanted to travel around France by navigable waterways.

I wasn't rich. I must have been writing from forty to eighty pages of a popular novel each day. No question of buying a yacht. No question, either, of sleeping in inns or hotels.

It was almost a problem in arithmetic. I looked for a good fishing boat, which I found on sale at Sartrouville. In order to be able to sleep on it, I had the center thwart removed, which left a place to put two kapok mattresses at night. I had uprights installed, and removable supports for a solid waterproof awning with canvas curtains on the sides, forming a regular cabin.

The boat was called the *Ginette* and I didn't unchristen it. But it was necessary to take the maid, Boule, who was then twenty years old and is with me today, and my dog Olaf, a slate-colored Great Dane who measured seventy-five centimeters at the withers.

I also had to take along my typewriter, supplies of paper, a tent (for Boule, and for me to work in in the mornings), a folding table, also folding chairs, pots, dishes. All this wouldn't fit on board, so I bought a light flat-bottomed barge three meters fifty long, for which I got an awning made. So during the trip the supplies followed in our wake.

That was in 1925. Camping wasn't yet fashionable, still less this style of navigation. Aluminum motors didn't exist in Europe so I bought an outboard *Archimède*, bronze and cast-iron, that weighed more than forty kilos and could work up a speed of about ten kilometers an hour.

We left, my first wife, Boule, the dog, the typewriter and I, in March, by the Marne, then the canal from the Marne to the Saône, before sailing down the latter, the Rhône to Avignon, and from there to Grau-du-Roi.

As a rule we would stop in the country in order to pitch the tent in a meadow, near a wood if possible. In the morning I would work there. Sometimes we would stay two or three days in the same place.

Sometimes we had to stop in a town, as for instance at Châlons and at Lyons. To supply our needs my typewriter had to turn out its daily pages. So at five o'clock in the morning, I had to put up my folding table on the dock and type there until eleven in the morning.

As I tell it, this sounds like forced eccentricity when it was only the logical outcome of a decision I had made. . . . Same at Grau-du-Roi. Impossible to stay in port because of the mosquitoes and noise.

It was in June, out of season (at that time!). I took the *Ginette* out to sea, opposite the beach, and I anchored securely. I continued to sleep aboard. The tent, pitched on the beach, served as a dining room, workroom (very early in the morning, because of the heat), and as a bedroom for Boule.

I like to have my coffee as soon as I get up. Result: I would blow a horn to signal Boule. She, tray in hand, would go into the water and wade out to the *Ginette,* where the waves would be up to her breasts.

If we went to the Casino at night, how to get back on board? By stripping naked and swimming.

There are a thousand details of this kind, improbable or comical but, again, not forced.

This lasted six or seven months. Sometimes editors' money orders didn't reach our next stop and we would have to wait, living on our supplies.

Along the Canal du Midi, I would occasionally arrive, at nine at night, at a village several kilometers inland, wearing a bathing suit, because it was midsummer. I had come to buy bread, canned goods, and the villagers wondered where on earth I came from.

Again, this was in 1925.

So no canal boat, no barge, nothing out of the ordinary except the desire to see France in a certain way. I was not disappointed.

Later people talked about my wolves as if I had a passion for wild animals. It's a great deal simpler than that. We were in the garden of the French Embassy in Ankara when a sort of tramp stuck his head over the wall, showed us a sack, and said something in his own language. Chambrun, the ambassador, translated for me:

"He's just captured three young wolves."

"And he wants to sell them?"

"Yes."

I was very fond of dogs. I immediately thought of crossing German shepherds with wolves. I bought the three little beasts, which went to Istanbul in our sleeping car. At La Richardière, where I was then living, cages had to be built where the wolves could live once they were grown. In the same way I had also brought a Karabakh bitch there (I was told the word means black head)—a very savage breed that herded huge flocks of sheep in that part of the country.

The wolves grew. The female had to be put to sleep when she got a skin ailment that made her vicious. One of the males was hurt and also had to be killed.

The last of them lived for several years at La Richardière and used to follow me on a leash on my country walks—in the evening he played in my study. There never was any crossbreeding. When I left for my trip around the world, the servants refused to take care of him in our absence and I sent him to the Vincennes Zoo. I went to see him a few times there and we recognized each other.

Nothing eccentric here, either. We were having coffee in a garden . . . a tramp passed carrying a bag . . . Wolves . . . Why not? And out of that it all grew.

Today I have something better than a boat or wolves. I have children. Quite naturally, logically too, my life revolves around them and my wife.

But on the day when I suddenly asked myself what I was doing in America, this did not prevent me from deciding to move my whole little world.

And here we are. In Switzerland! Why am I, a Belgian, a French writer, with my Canadian wife, and my children who were born in the United States, why are we in the Canton of Vaud?

It is just as simple, just as logical, provided you don't form it into something fanciful, aren't looking for something picturesque, for a good story, or, in other words, as long as journalists and biographers leave it alone.

Unfortunately, they don't leave it alone, and the simplest things become so false you could scream.

Tomorrow I'm having a wisdom tooth pulled and I'm nervous about it because up to now I haven't had a single tooth pulled in at least twenty-five years. I'll take D. with me to the dentist.

/*Tuesday, February 21, 1961*

Wisdom tooth pulled this morning, no pain, which proves once more that . . . etc., etc. Friday he's taking out the one above it. Delicious harmony between D. and me. We always live in harmony, to be sure, and even intensely so, but this time there is the kind of agreement between us that couples have who walk thigh to thigh as if with a single movement. It's very pleasant.

A while ago I was setting down my schedule. Here's another example for this week. Yesterday went with Johnny to buy paper hats, harmonicas, etc., for Marie-Jo's friends.

Tomorrow, Marie-Jo's birthday. There will be some people here whom D. and I will have to take care of, and I will have to take a run into town to sign a paper at the notary's.

Friday, taped interview for the Swiss radio in the morning and second wisdom tooth in the afternoon.

Saturday, dinner at Dr. D.'s, the psychiatrist who heads Rives des Prangins, with another French psychiatrist.

And Monday I go with D. to the clinic, where she is having a minor operation. I'll stay with her for the three or four days she needs to be there. Tuesday, dentist. Friday too. And, if everything is all right, the following Monday, novel. Of which, during all this time, I will think without thinking, trying to put myself into a state of grace.

We've become so contented at home, so absorbed in our routine, that a dinner like Saturday's takes on the proportions of an event.

There are people, especially in my field, who have dinner in town every evening. I did once. It now seems horrifying to me.

Yesterday, on television, once again they were discussing today's youth, who are represented to us as being different from the youth of any other time. I don't understand. It is the leitmotiv of the newspapers, the radio. . . . One would think that my whole generation, and even those who are in their forties, were afraid of these emerging young as if they were afraid of being brought to trial.

Bad conscience? Maybe. Not I. I feel, perhaps wrongly, on an equal footing with youth.

They talk about scientific progress, technological progress, of the conquest of space. . . .

The rhythm of these various progressions, like the growth of populations, inevitably takes on an ever greater acceleration. But the discovery of Asia, then of America, were just as overwhelming in their time as that of the planets—which has not yet taken place.

Fire, then gunpowder, brought about as much change for young people as the atomic bomb.

They also talk about the transformation of traditional morality, as if a traditional morality had ever existed—especially for the young!

More words. What do they mean? That they no longer marry for a dowry, become civil servants, wear a certain kind of suit? Even that is false.

They are trying to find their way as we have all tried to find ours, and, as the young have always done, they mistrust the solutions that their elders tell them are final.

What change is there in the basic instincts, common to all men as to all animals: to bare one's claws, to conquer one or more females, to reproduce, to raise offspring—and to eat, of course?

Gide used to talk to me about how the novelist must remain unattached. Must not love (in depth), must not have children, so as to dedicate himself to his art alone. Must not worry about money, he would have added if he'd dared, he who never had to worry about it.

Which is exactly the same as escaping (trying to) from the basic instincts. What is left? Some words, some sentences, some mental acrobatics, which to my mind is nothing.

Was he aware of this in his last weeks when he was surrounded by his daughter, of whom he had seen so little, and his grandchildren? I received no letters during that period and I don't know anything about it. A film shows him with children on his lap. But what was he thinking?

Yesterday again they declared that youth no longer reads. Always the word "youth." As if they were talking about a homogeneous group. As if anyone knows what youth reads! As if it were not as various as the rest of the population. What about old age? Why not assume that it thinks this or that, reacts in this or that way, reads this book and doesn't like such films. . . .

Is Mauriac representative of old age, or is it the serene Rostand observing his frogs? Or, again, is it that still curious and lively André Siegfried, younger at eighty than so many others at fifty? Or my worthy grandfather, in the old days, sitting on the stoop of his hat shop on the Rue Puits-en-Sock?

After dreaming, one often has the impression of having had that dream before, even several times. I have the same feeling about writing these words, and I wonder if, rereading, I wouldn't find the same thoughts expressed two or three times in the same terms. It's very possible, for my mind goes in circles and I suppose I'm no exception. How long it takes to encompass the most modest subject! And how it always seems we are rediscovering it!

/*Wednesday, February 22nd*

Re sex. Inexhaustible subject. I've already written about it here. I'd be curious to know what I would have written about it twenty years, thirty years, forty years ago, what I shall write (or would write) in ten, twenty, thirty years.

Desire to explain this need for "light sex," as one says "light conversation."

For me, physical love with a beloved person has always something serious, even dramatic about it. It is akin to religion, to worship. It is a thing complete in itself, total.

I don't dare say that it is like my "difficult" books as compared to my Maigrets, but I'm tempted to make the comparison.

Once, when I was young, these kinds of adventures, more or less without future, probably served some need to reassure myself. Such a woman, from such a background, apparently inaccessible, would allow herself to be had. . . . The distance was bridged. . . .

It's a long time since that has happened to me. Why do I go on? Why does it remain a near necessity for my stability? I've written elsewhere on the subject. I was asked to treat one of the seven deadly sins for the radio, and I chose lust.

"A Panegyric to Lust," which never went out over the air, needless to say. If I remember correctly, I said that lust, pure sexuality, was man's means of restoring himself at the springs of vitality. Of finding the purity of childhood again.

I am still of that opinion. In our complicated society, in which we are only pawns, the solace of being naked, of committing certain acts, without need of complication or explanation, without sentimentality.

This relates to what I was writing about the boat trips, about the wolves, etc., in the context of the logic of my behavior. In order not to feel a prisoner of society I need to pat a passing thigh, to make love without declaring it, without passion, to have sex on the spur of the moment, in my study or any place else, as it was once done, as it is still done, in the equatorial forest or in Tahiti. I know whereof I speak. I've been there.

It puts all pretenses in their place, all conventions. Five minutes between two doors is enough to turn values upside down.

A great surprise to me when I first came to Paris and in the years after that: no women, whether "good" or worldly, no movie star, has as beautiful a body as certain professionals do. Not one of them could earn her living by making love.

For me, it is a kind of righting of balance. False values go down, true ones go up.

And above all, as with the Maigrets, it allows me to keep the same separate place for love that I give my real novels. No comparison.

D. will understand. It doesn't matter if others don't. For a long time now she has understood, but I have the impression that for the first time I have discovered a really satisfying answer to a question many people have asked me—but that she and I have never needed to ask.

Because, instinctively, we have understood.

/*Friday, February 24th*

Hangover. Because I took a drink the other day when I came out of the dentist's office. Again the next day. And yesterday, with my English Maigret, much too much. Today I'm licking my wounds like an animal. Always this feeling of shame. Feeling of melancholy. This is the only time when I've known what that word means. In spite of it, gave two radio interviews this morning.

Also, as always, extreme sensuality. Once, in Paris, after a fairly wild night (in 1952) while D. was packing the trunks for our return to the United States, I called three or four women to our apartment, one after another. That was sexuality in its natural state.

D. is in town. I know where. I know for how long. It's barely twenty minutes since I woke up and already I feel quite lost. I find the paper that she was reading during my siesta in my study, along with her cigarette butts. I look at the clock.

Yesterday morning, by accident, and without my expecting it in the least, I lived through ten minutes that I think will remain in my memory as do certain childhood scenes. I had a hangover. I was waiting for my two radio reporters at eleven o'clock. I went into the garden and the sun was as warm as in April or May. The blackbirds were hopping about. All the crocuses were in bloom, especially the yellow ones.

Then, surprised, enchanted, I saw some tiny bees, so small in fact that at first I took them for some other insect (there are hives five hundred yards from our garden as the crow flies).

They were awkward, hesitant. Some barely knew how to use their wings. All the same they penetrated the flowers, bumping against the petals, hardly able to get out again. I imagine they were the first bees of the year—on their first excursion, just as last year at the same time, also in the garden, Pierre took his first steps.

I finally located several larger, more practiced bees, and I wondered if they were not there to teach the others, to show them what had to be done.

I stayed a long time watching them and I treasure my poignant memory of that clumsy ballet. Soon I shall go to see if they are back at work, if they have gained confidence and skill. But the same sun never shines twice.

D. not here. Gone to the hairdresser and I had to wake up, get up, alone.

Is it possible that this can create such a void and make me so restless?

Another beautiful Sunday. Children in the garden. D. is dressing and we are going for the papers in Lausanne.

Dinner yesterday (which I found fascinating) with a half-dozen psychiatrists, among whom were the head of one of the most famous clinics, another who is the director of a prison-asylum where four hundred criminals are held, and a third who is the author of authoritative works—two others more interested in psychotherapy.

Almost all of them were trying to reassure themselves, to be sure they were on the right track, that they were doing a useful job. Same look as the professor I spoke of earlier.

And for me too an occasion to reassure myself. More and more, even from the beginning, my characters, to my mind, go to a point where the psychiatrists can take them over. I mean that my patients, carried a few steps further, would become theirs. And there is an overlapping in their lives, a common zone, where those patients are both mine and theirs. I take so-called normal men and carry them as far as possible without reaching the pathological.

In Case of Emergency was published when Jaccoud committed (?) his crime and I was struck by the similarity of that affair not only with that novel but with another one written earlier. I followed the trial. I studied his dossier in depth. Of course I was not doing this for literary or journalistic purposes.

Later, when I felt I understood, I wrote *L'Ours en Peluche*, in which I tried to set down that part of the affair I felt no one had understood.

That was an extreme case, and in my heart I was not sure of my interpretation. The discussion yesterday fully reassured me, and I was delighted, for, if I'm not mistaken about this one, there's a chance that many other characters of mine are also true.

Only one of the guests yesterday was making an effort to shine. All the others were trying . . . trying to what? Like me, to reassure themselves. Man needs the conviction that he is doing something "worth while," something "useful," something that couldn't be done by somebody else.

This explains many disappointed hopes, many lives dedicated to a very small segment of human activity—and many breakdowns when this conviction is suddenly shaken. Man needs faith, not in a god—unless to be told that he is right—but faith in himself.

Many of these people envy me and often admit it: they imagine that a large audience is reassuring, whereas all they have is the respect of certain of their "peers" all over the world.

Or their titles and decorations, which, I think, have never reassured anyone.

/Monday, February 27th

Yesterday (after so many others) read a work on criminology (American) tracing the definition of crime—and the criminal—through the ages.

I wonder if the essential characteristic of crime isn't its illogic, which would explain why in the Middle Ages it was attributed to demons taking possession of a human being, and why today the psychiatrist is more and more often called in. But doesn't psychiatry, the kind which is less concerned with lesions and traumas than with behavior, also go beyond logic?

Following a recent airplane crash, specialists in charge of the investigation (which will take several months) have been stressing that an airplane is a man-made machine, that airlines are managed by men, pilots are human beings, etc., concluding that for this reason a certain percentage of errors and failures is inevitable.

Doesn't the same thing apply to crime? And isn't a certain percentage of human beings almost inevitably destined to . . . etc.

Lesson in humility for judges and moralists.

/Saturday, March 4th

A notion that seems new to me but which seems more and more to have taken root in the minds of the masses: the right to health.

Not just to medical care, which will soon be entirely free, to hospitalization, etc., but to being cured. For the doctor is expected to cure by hook or by crook and governments have a ministry of health, they recruit doctors, nurses, specialists of all kinds. It has become the most expensive piece of administrative machinery.

I suppose that the sorcerer, precursor of the doctor, as still today in primitive tribes, was once a man who assumed power for his own ends, like chieftains, then kings, emperors, dictators. The idea came not from the community but from an individual.

When was this process reversed? Today it is the community that demands doctors, teaches them, pays them.

Curiously, the number of doctors per patient is nearly the same, it would appear, as that of sorcerers in the primitive forest.

In the most highly developed countries, one doctor to eight hundred inhabitants. Wasn't there one sorcerer to a tribe and weren't those tribes made up of about that many individuals?

I am writing at Johnny's bedside. He's had the flu since Monday with a pretty high fever, while my wife is in the clinic where I go to see her, shuttling back and forth.

Human values change with circumstances. During the war of 1914, life, the survival of a unit, often depended on a jack-of-all-trades, a sort of tramp or ignorant woodsman who suddenly became more important than the officer or the specialized soldier to the comfort and morale of his comrades.

Suddenly the nurse has the same importance to the individual. To the point where men of a certain age who are rich enough to afford anything choose to marry theirs to assure themselves care.

I always hesitate to tell stories, above all about third parties. However, these two seem to me so significant that I shall try to tell them so that it won't be possible to guess the identities. They came to me firsthand and I know that all the details are correct.

More than twenty-five years ago, a gynecologist then in fashion received a telephone call.

"This is Mr. So-and-So. I should like to have an appointment with the professor."

"The professor does not see men."

A quarter of an hour later, another telephone call.

"This is His Highness, Prince . . ."

An internationally known name. A colossal fortune. The professor received him. The prince, already an old man—dead today —explained that he had two children by former wives, that he had just met a beautiful lower-class girl whom he would like to marry, but by whom he first wanted to have a child.

He was not sure that one of his sons was his own (he was wrong about that, since the son resembles him unmistakably), and this time he wanted to take all precautions.

What he wanted from the gynecologist was this. The young woman was to enter the clinic during her fertile period. The prince would join her there and give semen for artificial insemination. The woman was to stay incommunicado for a month. No man was to go near her. So that . . .

And without waiting for an answer, the prince went to get the young woman in question from the waiting room.

"Examine her first, to make sure she can give me a child."

The doctor examined her from head to toe in an adjacent office and discovered she had an atrophied uterus which ruled out all hope of maternity. The young woman pleaded, wept. Her future was at stake. . . .

"Please don't tell him, I beg you. . . ."

Why give this information to an old man who, anyway, already had two male heirs?

The gynecologist said nothing. The couple left, came back three weeks later, was shut into one of the rooms, the prince with a bottle which he was to fill.

An hour passed. Suddenly the alarm bell rang through the clinic. Nurses rushed in, found the man naked on the bed, the room in disorder. The woman also naked, neither of them understanding what all the excitement was about. The prince had simply pushed the wrong button. He wanted to see the doctor. The latter came, saw that the bottle was still empty.

"I wanted to ask you if it matters if the sperm is mixed with saliva."

The doctor shrugged. "Not at all."

And the procedure continued. The bottle was returned. A little later, the insemination which could have no effect took place. Some time later, the prince telephoned from a foreign capital to complain of the lack of results.

"Had you considered," the doctor asked, "that you might be the one who was deficient?"

I forgot to say that in the course of the first conversation, the prince had suddenly lowered his trousers and showed his member to the doctor, who had said:

"I examine women, not men."

So he complained on the telephone:

"But I showed you . . ."

"I can't come to any conclusions by examining you. It will require an analysis. . . ."

This was done. The results were not promising.

"Your spermatozoa are barely active. Many of them have no tails, etc."

All this is entirely authentic. The prince married the young woman, who is a princess today and received in every court that still exists. She did not have a child. She is one of the best-known women in the world and newspapers are continually publishing her picture.

The other story is also connected with gynecology. It happened in another clinic, several years later. A couple introduced themselves. Also princely, belonging to one of the reigning families of Europe. This time too it was a matter of artificial insemination. But the husband, who was impotent, could not be the donor. The couple asked if the procedure was possible, and spoke of going to Rome to ask for the Pope's authorization.

"You won't get it."

"You don't expect me to take a lover. . . ."

The couple insisted. The doctor, to get rid of them, got out of it with a vague promise. Some time later, telephone call from the wife:

"I'm coming tomorrow morning. Get everything ready."

How to find a donor? The gardener? There wasn't time to make the necessary tests, Wassermann, etc. Someday the child might be called on to reign.

The next morning the doctor got out of it by injecting some physiological serum, counting cn hearing nothing more of the matter.

But six weeks later he received a telephone call from the couple to thank him and congratulate him. The wife was well and truly pregnant. . . .

In other words, before coming to the clinic she had taken her precautions, had had relations with a lover, and the artificial insemination was only an alibi!

This is a very, very great lady, an old woman today, about whom there never has been the slightest gossip and who leads an exemplary life.

Aren't these stories rather extreme?

I hope that without being inaccurate I have shuffled the cards enough so that names cannot be attached to the people and that, anyway, the interested parties are or will all be dead when these pages are published, if they someday are.

The world closes its eyes and behaves "as if." These things didn't happen today, to be sure, but doesn't the same thing happen today in another sense? Must it go on forever?

This week, three hundred children died daily of starvation, in one small Congolese town. Airplanes are flying in dried fish for them.

5 o'clock in the afternoon

Clinic. Came back to see the children. Accident on the road. Cyclist knocked down by a car. Saw another this morning at the same spot.

Difficulty in harmonizing the "pity for the masses" so peculiar to our times and our sense of responsibility, if not of guilt about them (a New York financier talks to his psychoanalyst about the starving people in India or China and makes a real neurosis of it), with the discoveries of biology.

Not a difficulty of personal morality but of a way of life, of behavior which will harmonize with "biological law."

On the one hand our evolution moves in the direction of the individual, and our duties towards him.

On the other, science moves in the opposite direction and might arrive at a point of absolving Hitler.

Sentimentality? Instinct?

And our reason, which might impel us to wipe out millions of beings to preserve the species?

I write novels which I feel. I tell about men whom I try to understand, and at the same time I wonder if this isn't a kind of new romanticism, this time a romanticism of the masses, which would be worse than romanticizing the individual, and which could lead . . .

Tea, now, with D., in our sunny room.

Shit on abstract ideas!

/*Sunday, March 5, 1961*

Another real Sunday, though at the clinic, with even a Saint-Honoré with whipped cream for dessert, reminding me of my childhood.

At home this morning, Pierre pulled me into a corner of the room where I was changing and was annoyed because I couldn't understand what he wanted. Finally he took me by the hand and gave me the telephone receiver, saying: "Mamma!"

He wanted me to call his mother so that he could talk to her and more especially hear her, and he got his wish.

He does not go into his brother Johnny's room (Johnny has the flu) but stands in the doorway. This morning, however, he purposely dropped some small object a foot or two inside the door, then hesitated, jumped in to snatch it, the way you see kids jump into the river just at the edge.

Marie-Jo, who envies her brother for being in bed, constantly touches him, hugs him surreptitiously, in the hope of catching the flu.

I have watched the awakening of intelligence in each of my four children. It is so quick, so impressive, that one wonders how such a progression can end . . . in what we are.

Why, when, how this halt, if not actual regression? We should all become geniuses!

/Wednesday, March 8th

At home since Monday. More and more often a terrible temptation comes over me not to write any more. I'm speaking of my novels, not these notebooks. And yet! Why not stop entirely?

I comfort myself by saying to myself that in the two or three years that this has been happening to me I've written novels like *Le Président, Le Veuf, La Vieille, Betty.* . . . What discourages me is that each time I decide to get to work, obstacles arise. But before? Wasn't it the same? Isn't this the way it is for everyone? Isn't it an excuse, an alibi?

We shall see.

To write with joy, what rubbish!

/Friday, March 10th

All right, then, I won't begin my novel on Monday as I planned (why?) and it will probably not be—or may not be—the novel I was trying to write around March 20th. The idea had already been rattling around my head for some time. At the clinic, in particular, and since I've been back I've been thinking of it in spite of myself and that's always bad.

I've noticed that nothing is gained, quite the contrary, by "worrying" an idea. We'll see. It doesn't really matter. My biggest mistake is announcing in advance when I'll get to work, as if I were ashamed of doing nothing.

It also serves as a kind of alibi. It's a way of getting out of invitations, of putting off demands for interviews and appointments until later. And when the moment comes, I'm ashamed to back out.

This must have begun during the period when I was working on assignment because I had to. For a long time I signed an annual contract with Gallimard every year for six novels, because in terms of income that corresponded to my style of life. The novels had to be done well within the year. I had to turn them in on fixed dates. So I knew, in a less pressing way, the difficulties that weighed so heavily on Balzac.

You could say that now that these difficulties no longer exist, when writing no longer has anything to do with my material needs, I have instinctively kept the habit. I made it my trademark then to get the manuscripts in before the deadline, never a late one.

Today, it's funny, I force myself to write them on the date I have fixed for myself or that I have happened to mention to someone else just to get rid of him.

It's quite unexpected. I have to take myself in hand when a delay upsets me. And if I become less prolific anyway? Anyway, it doesn't signify that I'm losing interest in people, quite the contrary.

Is it because I no longer have as much confidence in my little discoveries, or because I judge people more severely, that I reject some as uninteresting which I formerly would have delighted in?

In short, here I am on vacation again for ten days and I can only hope that during that time, at some moment or other, the spark will come.

So I'm still a wage earner. I revolted early against my parents' servitude and that of the people in my neighborhood. I ran away from them to be free of it. But I have ended up in a voluntary servitude. It doesn't change anything to call it discipline and, all things considered, it isn't accurate. It is almost a conditioned reflex.

Next week I shall give myself a little pleasure that I've been promising myself for some time: go to the automobile dealer in Geneva to buy a new car for D., who gave hers to Marc.

A drive and a walk in Morges with Johnny. First walk in the garden with D. .

I read an interview in *Newsweek* with one of my Irish colleagues, Frank O'Connor, best known for his short stories, whom I met "once upon a time" while at Harvard for several days for a seminar on novel-writing.

"The writer," he said, "has to have a good streak of solid selfishness to get his own work done. He should throw his wife out and make his children go out and work to support themselves at a really early age so he will be able to concentrate on his own writing."

If I write down that sentence it is because it sums up the attitude of many writers, of artists in general, who pretend to have a right to a life different from that of common mortals, and who demand material aid, whether of their families, or rich patrons, or governments, etc.

This coincides with Gide's opinion, of which I believe I spoke, that the life of a couple and the obligations created by a family, thus paternity, are incompatible with the profession of writer.

This contention has always irritated me, first because I think that the artist is basically a man like any other, without special rights (he is often a dangerous element to established society, but to my mind this is not a bad thing, rather the contrary, though it explains the harsh measures of this society against him, as for instance under almost all dictatorships), and then because the novelist, at least—I freely exempt the pure poet—needs as total a knowledge of man as possible.

Is that why I'm incapable of reading certain books, highly

praised by critics? From the beginning I feel in them what I shall call an incomplete man, a man who does not accept his responsibilities and who, I'm sure, has chosen art—whether it is literature, painting, the theater, or the cinema—only to escape daily realities.

At a meeting of the "Belletriens" of Lausanne to which I was invited, one of the provincial luminaries to whom I remarked that I was doing certain things—receiving journalists, photographers, for example, though it meant being asked the same questions over and over again—to whom I said, then, that I did this so as not to hurt anyone's feelings, answered me with assurance:

"That's where you make a mistake!"

But for an hour I had been listening to his quite tedious lecturing and I had tried to answer his questions. I was in a hurry to meet D. at the clinic, where I knew she would be worrying. What would this gentleman have said if I had not gone to that meeting, or if I had left him in the midst of his chatter?

In every book, in every work of art, I look for the man, and I don't think I'm alone in this. The fuller a man's life is, the more complete it is, the more it covers the gamut of human experience.

Perhaps that's why I hate the words "man of letters," "literature," "artist." . . .

"I am a man and everything that that . . ."

An American university gave Frank O'Connor asylum, as the kings of other times named a poet or playwright gentleman of the bedchamber, or what have you, and as France now appoints them curator of a museum or a library, or traveling lecturer.

Among modern writers, none of those, to my knowledge, has given us an important work, while a Bernanos, for example, had his six or seven children trailing behind him.

Enough! What is the use of discussing these things as if pleading a case? Won't we always end by believing in what suits us best personally? It's for this reason that I can never convince myself that any man is wholly insincere, even a politician.

A curious phenomenon. For about a fortnight during which D. was either at the clinic or convalescing here—and so, when I was more or less missing her—I pondered the subject of a novel that only half attracted me, which I resigned myself to writing at the risk of stalling after the first chapter, which would no doubt have happened.

Yesterday, first day of reunion. We don't need many external elements. This morning, visit to the gynecologist. A drink in a bar, not for the sake of the drink, but just to be together, to be close in the atmosphere of a charming little bar.

In the afternoon, walk on Place Saint-François and Rue de Bourg. Then, later, dinner alone together in a good restaurant, television at home with Johnny. That's all.

But it was a perfect day, what I called a day of perfect happiness when I was fifteen (then it was a matter of reading alone in my corner, eating and drinking coffee and smoking my pipe. It was during the war. To eat, drink, and smoke were very important things).

Result: the novel in question dropped into darkness and another was born in my head and skin, full of warmth, of animal tenderness. . . . Provided I am able to write it. It is a subject (like the other one) that I abandoned last year at almost the same time for technical reasons, and I seem to have suddenly struck on the solution, a perfectly simple one.

Man was not meant to live alone!

Just now, papers at the station, as every Sunday, with D. and the children. In the afternoon, the two final world championship hockey matches on television.

We're talking about cars. We are promising ourselves to be extravagant at the Auto Show—we've earned it, haven't we?

Still sunshine, the garden full of flowers, and I took a lot of photos of the children there yesterday. They will never know what a state of euphoria I was in when I took them.

My first contacts with psychoanalysis date from 1923 (?) when Gallimard published *Three Essays on the Theory of Sexuality*, and between 1927 and 1928 I must have bought *Journal Psychanalytique d'une Petite Fille* and then *Leonardo da Vinci and a Memory of his Childhood*.

I was then twenty when I discovered Freud. Since that time I have read Adler, Jung, others, but I think I never allowed myself to be influenced by their theories when I was writing my novels as, for example, the American writers are today.

A psychoanalyst said to me recently that in his way he was a novelist, adding that the discipline of his profession is sometimes less scientific than that of the novelist.

It doesn't matter. If I speak of it, it's because it came up yesterday in a television broadcast in which they resorted, as usual, to the mother and father complexes.

I wonder if it isn't a matter of a certain distortion or, more precisely, if we haven't been fooled by a label.

The child who cannot break away from his mother—the one who revolts against his father, or, on the contrary, needs his exclusive protection, aren't they simply more afraid of life? I mean natural life.

I would like to propose a change of labels. The more I observe men and the more of their confidences I hear, the more the title of a bad novel my mother used to read comes back to me: *The Fear of Living*.

A different fear, like the Freudian complex. For some, fear of the artificial life of society, the need to stay in the primitive cocoon, to return to passivity and the dream.

For others, on the contrary, fear of leaving the beaten path, of finding oneself suddenly off the track, of losing the support and approval of society: and so, fear of instinct, of the primitive life we find within ourselves.

With a simple change of words, Freudianism and the theories

that result from it lose, in my opinion, their somewhat simplistically systematic character.

I shall be told that the father and mother are only symbols.

All right! But even in these symbols the truth seems to me simpler, more human. At fifty-eight, I am frightened by the number of people who are afraid of facing life squarely. This relates to similar thoughts I noted a few days ago.

It's a little as if we were taught everything from childhood—except how to live! Where would we find teachers?

Science has taken centuries to evolve rational nourishment (?) for us, for the nursing child and for the adult. Nutrition has become an entirely new branch of medicine—like the art of aging. But what have those other doctors who are psychologists, moralists, and philosophers evolved to satisfy our other needs? I've known a few of them, three or four, and they were afraid of the man in the street.

As my psychoanalyst concluded the other day:

"We teach our patients nothing. It is they who teach us."

The ones on television yesterday, however, seemed rather smug. Of course they were aware of families, friends, and acquaintances watching them on the little screen.

/*March 15, 1961*
9:15 in the morning

It's odd how certain tastes persist for long years, even most of one's life, and how one finds them again passed on to one's children in one form or another.

Johnny loves to trace maps for his geography class, to write the names on them in careful lettering. He has just finished a notebook on Brazil for school which he worked on with positive ecstasy. I have always loved cartography too.

And this morning, while shaving, I planned to give myself the pleasure of telling about my successive houses and of describing them, with a photograph of each pasted in the middle of the page.

It's childish, especially since I've never kept an album. I'll have no time before my novel—if I write it—but I shall do it someday. For the first stages, it may appear to duplicate *Pedigree*. In spite of what people think and what, out of laziness, I have let them think, *Pedigree* is not really accurate. I remember how in writing it I thought of a book of Goethe's which impressed me very much: *Dichtung und Wahrheit* . . . *Fiction and Truth* . . . Transposition of truth.

Here, by contrast, I intend to set down some precise information. For my amusement. Anyway, it entertains me today, which doesn't mean that it will still entertain me two weeks or a month from now.

I realize, as I may already have noted, that if I have lived in many houses, I have never, outside of here, spent time in my study except for the hours strictly necessary to write my novels, and before D., to get through the mail as quickly as possible.

I don't think it's just a question of age, of a lessening of my curiosity. Never mind. This morning I'm going to do the last cleanup on the manuscript of *Maigret et le Voleur Paresseux*, which for me is in the nature of homework to be done in place of an anticipated pleasure.

Tomorrow, Auto Show. Easter soon, already, which doesn't give me much time before starting my novel. Either I begin on Monday, or once more I must postpone it.

/March 25, 1961

Novel finished. Ouf! Promised myself to finish it before the holidays. It's done. I suffered. I failed with the same subject last year. It seemed easy and at the same time awkward. Perhaps, in the end, it will be understood. Euphoria? No! Exhaustion, like my character's. I am happy to have succeeded. In my own terms.

It annoys me to see the best-intentioned people—above all the best-intentioned—look for parts of myself in my novels.

They don't realize the harm they do me because they make me conscious of a certain chemistry that I shouldn't become aware of, and they sometimes keep me from writing as I please. How, out of what, a novel is made, is nobody's business, and especially its author shouldn't know.

/Sunday, March 26th
11 o'clock in the morning

Back to the mail. Played with the children. I find the above notes 1 and 2, which are typical, alas, and furnish an example of the effect of alcohol on me. 1 was written after one whisky, an hour after finishing my novel, and 2 after several other drinks.

It's plain why I no longer have any right to drink. I came near to self-pity—and now, the next day, I cringe, most of all because it is those who are dear to me who invariably get the blame. Without meaning to I have set down two fairly eloquent specimens, on which I needn't elaborate.

This morning I am full of tenderness, but because I had to be with the children—Johnny with his skates bought yesterday, Marie-Jo with her scooter, Pierre, who has a substitute nurse—I shall not be able to go on the wagon until tomorrow.

Give myself a good cleaning!

/Friday, March 31st
(Good Friday)

As foreseen, with my novel finished, I had two days of euphoria. Then the corresponding letdown. I've already spoken of it. It never fails. I ought to be used to it and not be bothered by it. For three or four days, great fatigue and a kind of depression. When I had promised myself such joy! Of course it's physical and now I'm back to my normal state.

The Rolls delivered day before yesterday. I think I've wanted it for a long time and was looking for good or bad reasons not to buy it. Because of the snobbism attached to it. So much so that I drove it cautiously at first, almost fearfully, as if it were some unknown monster. An hour later, we understood each other perfectly.

Yesterday D.'s car came—almost a work of art.

Children on vacation, my mother here in the house. Each day I wait for D. to be free to go driving with me.

Next week, as usual, I'll begin the revision of *Le Train*. Invariably also the same slight anxiety before a revision. The novel always seems bad to me. I change it. I cross out. Then, little by little, I get into the spirit of it again. I hope it will be that way this time too.

Theoretically, I don't believe in the importance of anything except love. In fact, however, I panic—over a novel, of all things, which is only words on paper, dusty copies of which someone, someday, may find in an attic, shrugging his shoulders.

/*Easter*
10:30 in the morning

Easter morning family style. Johnny, the only one up, made a scene, and that reminded me of my dramatic first communion. It's hard to be eleven years old, to feel like both a child and a man at the same time. It passed very quickly, and now he is his delightful self, just a little sensitive in eyelids and heart, as one is after crying.

For the first time Pierre hunted colored eggs in his mother's boudoir, because it rained in the night and the grass is still wet.

Marie-Jo, who loves to give presents, bought everybody chocolate bunnies, ourselves included.

In a few minutes, in pale sunshine we leave in the car, all of us together, for the station—to get the papers, as we do every Sunday. Marc wished us a happy Easter by telegram.

Yesterday I happened on a sentence of Gide's that I recognized: "Family, I hate you!" The counterpart of Léon Blum's words: "Bourgeois, I hate you!"

Poor Gide, who, for fear of losing some small part of himself, had his daughter brought up to believe he was a stranger—who later suffered from his malice—and who ended his days with her, his son-in-law, and his grandchildren, having himself filmed as a doting grandpapa two or three months before his death!

Kierkegaard, Nietzsche, assumed similar attitudes, out of pride, I think, maybe from laziness, and hadn't the luck to recoup their losses.

How good it is, and how it takes me back to real life, to have a Johnny who makes a scene for us on Easter morning, a wife who understands, a little chick to offer chocolate bunnies knowing we won't eat them, and a Pierre to hunt eggs for the first time!

States have their compulsory military service. No one has ever thought to institute an obligatory family service—if only for a short term—so that all men would have to learn certain elementary truths, acquire a base, as in learning Latin.

11 o'clock in the evening

Because it's Easter and the staff has the day off, I just took the dog out this evening, and was surprised to realize that it was the first time in a long while. The first time in a long while, too, that I've been out of the house walking in the evening—we usually stay in behind closed shutters after nightfall.

I saw the nearby café-bar with its reddish lights, like the little cafés of my childhood in Liège. I saw the ill-lit rectangle of a window and felt as always the mystery of hidden lives. I noticed a couple in the shadows.

There is much talk about the upheavals of the atomic age. We seek new truths, new bases for life. But windows like these are still the same in the time of electricity as they were in the time of oil, of kerosene, or of gas. Couples too. Noise and lights of a train in the distance. A plane flew over, going towards Cointrin, and it was only a buzzing, a very small light in the sky.

I can't believe the world has changed so much, and in Paris, in London, or even New York I've found the same lights and the same evening shadows in the streets, the same smell of night, the same echoes of human footsteps. At six in the morning, there must still be little boys walking fast, a shiver of fear on their skin, going to serve early mass.

Yet how many investigations, probes, studies, researches, on the new generation and the world of tomorrow!

This afternoon the whole family went to the country together as I used to go to Chèvremont with my parents on Easter Day, when I was a child. We would go there by tram. Today, we were in a car. But we saw the same faces. There were the same sudden showers. The air had the same taste of grass and dust, and when we came back Pierre's cheeks were redder than usual because of the first spring sunshine, and he was the way children always have been, shedding a few tears of weariness.

/*April 8th*

We've had a relative of my wife's in the house for a week, charming, tactful, nineteen years old, who took up as little space as a guest can. She leaves tomorrow.

Ouf! Just by her presence she has managed to spoil my Easter vacation—and the children's because of that—which I was so happy about.

I can't stand a strange presence in the house any more. It

shocks me to find her seated in my study, to see her at the table, then, in the evening, in front of the television. Suddenly I become impatient, nervous, especially with the children.

I feel any presence as a violation of our intimacy. And I don't think it's a question of age. I suppose it has to do with the fact that I've always considered (actually, it began only with D.) that the couple, then the family, are the real human cell, the true unity.

It doesn't matter how many strangers spend an hour or two, the time of a meal or a chat, with us. But I consider it an attack on our intimate life to meet one unexpectedly in a hall, to find one seated in "my" armchair, or in D.'s, or one of the children's. If, on top of that, they join in the conversation . . .

However, I am full of good intentions and I do my utmost to make our relative happy here.

Monday, I hope, I shall plunge into revision of *Le Train* and, I also hope, recover.

/*Sunday, April 9th*

Alone at last! And a lovely family Sunday. Oddly, I have recently rediscovered odors, the vibrations of ordinary things as I felt them in my childhood and adolescence. I'd lived for a long time without feeling these small daily ecstasies.

I used to seize passing impressions which remained in my mind, isolated ones, which I probably didn't enjoy much at the time I perceived them. Now, for the past few years, I have been newly aware, as I was at fifteen, of a ray of sunshine, a scent, the color of a flower.

At fifteen, it was intentional—I called it my theory of little joys. Now it is less conscious. Perhaps it has to do with a state of balance that allows me to enjoy time passing. Or else with the fact that I attach less importance to questions which from twenty-five to forty seemed vital to me.

Not detachment. My curiosity is no less. Hard to explain. Each thing takes its place, its true value and, for example, it delights me to see D. coming down the stone staircase in a certain house-coat, to smell the odor of earth and grass that Johnny gives off when he comes in from the garden (as when I used to come in from playing at the water's edge) . . . a look from Pierre . . . Marie-Jo's straw hat with the orange ribbon.

In fact I'm happy to have an excuse for putting off our trip to Paris. Too many people are expecting us there. Would prefer to go elsewhere, it doesn't matter where, even just ten kilometers away with D. And to continue to inhale the spring.

For tomorrow morning, I promise myself the joy, in the peace of my study, of beginning the revision of *Le Train*, in which I've tried to put certain impressions I've set down above. For my hero, it took a war. And it didn't last. But who knows, when he's my age. . .?

One of these days I must talk about abstract art, because it bothers me.

/*Monday, 10* A.M.

Began the revision this morning—one chapter—and, as usual, incapable of saying if I like it or if I hate it. I will know after three or four chapters, otherwise at the end.

If abstract art is preoccupying me, it's not in an impersonal way but very much because I feel involved. All my life I've been closer to painting than to literature. From the age of sixteen, my friends in Liège were painters, students or former students at the Beaux-Arts. Some are now teachers, but none has really arrived as a painter.

In Paris, at nineteen and a half, I met one of them again. I've spoken of his studio at the foot of Sacré Coeur where some of us used to go virtually every evening. (I remember a young man from a bourgeois family coming to ask my friend to teach him—not how to paint, but how to handle colors. He had his own plan. To do modern painting and make a lot of money. But I recently learned that he is the quite famous painter whose name never even struck me as familiar.)

So from the time I arrived in Paris I often hung around Montparnasse, Foujita, Vlaminck, Derain, Kisling, etc., who, for the most part, became my friends. I used to go to the shows every week.

My childhood was especially influenced by Impressionism and Pointillism (the gayest, happiest painting, where every spot of light is like a song) and I'll gladly admit that my novels reflected them.

I liked the Fauves, too—then the period of guitars, matchboxes, gray packets of tobacco. Matisse was one of my gods.

I saw life through those men, or rather I loved its surfaces as they did.

Later, at La Rochelle, then in the United States, I lost touch, and today I find myself faced with abstract art, which baffles me. It happens—rarely—that certain paintings please me, but I admit that I don't understand them, that I mistrust them, that I sniff them as if I were detecting a fraud.

On the level of logic, these painters seem to be right. At a time when we are discovering (?) the mechanics of the universe, the atom, the genes, antimatter, etc., perhaps it is natural for painting to interest itself in a dissociated world.

Very well! But . . . Am I going to object that art should be difficult, that fraud has become too easy? Isn't it just as easy to make a chromo as today, let us say, to do *tachisme*?

Last night on the television screen, I saw faces of serious, sincere painters, and their words troubled me.

So? The *roman nouveau*, the novel that isn't a novel of which there is so much talk (I haven't read any), isn't it the literary equivalent of such painting?

I would have liked to understand, to feel enthusiasm, not to be reactionary. I can't manage it. I doubt. I look for reasons.

The parallels with painting in my work, in my life, have suddenly stopped. Is it the fault of painting or of me?

It ought not to bother me and I should go on my way without asking questions. That's what I try to do. But in spite of myself, more and more often, when I'm beginning a novel, I hesitate. I don't like to be repetitious. I would like even less to imitate current fashion—a question of principles.

Vlaminck used to dismiss all abstract painting with a shrug and a laugh, but I'm not sure that deep inside himself he didn't have doubts too.

Bernard Buffet is no less categorical, though he is only thirty-two.

At fifty-eight I am less sure of myself, less sure of being right. To the point where I go over my predecessors to reassure myself, to see if one of them was able to understand up to the very end.

It isn't a matter of following the movement or the surface. I said understand. But not gently, imperceptibly becoming a stranger in a world whose sap is continually renewed.

Is this too ambitious? Perhaps. Anyway, there is nothing else to do but jog along quietly without wondering too much where I'm going.

At ten years old, when I served at mass, each day I looked with new eyes at the richly embroidered altar cloth, at the complicated patterns where I saw new images each time, mainly very strange personages.

After so long a time, certain of these images still appear on my retina. I've had the same experience with a cracked, flyspecked ceiling, and staring at certain stones with odd veinings, or even just in a pond where the reflections of clouds were distorted by the evening breeze.

Last evening, on television, a connoisseur declared that this was how he looked at his favorite modern painting each morning, which was facing his bed.

In that case . . .

But where is creativity, if it is only a matter of giving the viewer—or the reader—a point of departure for dreaming?

Finished revision of *Le Train* last evening, after four days, by
dint of eight to ten hours a day. Impression? Less bad than I
feared. Less good than I hoped? Maybe. I haven't any idea. Now
the book must begin to live its own life.

Today it was photostated. Then it leaves for the publisher, then
the printer. A cover will be suggested. It will come off the
presses. It isn't so much reviews I'm waiting for. It's a ripening
process that takes nearly two years. Little by little I shall see the
novel go into different languages, take different forms, and then it
will be filed away in my mind between this book and that. I have
nothing more to do with it.

It's taken me years to have an opinion on *Three Rooms in
Manhattan,* which will soon be coming back to me in the form of
a film.

It's raining. Have done the errands. Have listened to a friend
I'm very fond of talking endlessly about famous, rich, titled,
glamorous people. Her husband is famous too. Why do these people interest her? I wonder. At a certain point it irritated me just
because I'm very fond of her, and my wife tells me that I was a
bit short. I'm sorry.

But after finishing a hard job, hearing this talk about false values has something depressing about it. I needed peace and intimacy so much!

Next week, probably, I shall revise *Je me souviens* for a new
edition. In the first one, I cut some passages from the manuscript
that I considered too personal. I'll see if there's a way to put them
back in.

This is a kind of work I'm not familiar with, the work of a man
of letters, which I'm not.

This afternoon, on the other hand, I revised and corrected a little "novel" that Marie-Jo wrote as vacation homework. It was delightful.

How much better it would be to spend even only forty-eight
hours with D., nobody else, no telephone, no mail, walking unfa-

miliar streets, eating anywhere, going to bed and getting up any time! Real luxury! The only one virtually forbidden us—or granted so sparingly! We end up loving in shorthand.

/*Saturday, April 15, 1961*

Last night I almost forgot the lion's socks—D. reminded me of them when we went to kiss the children before going to bed ourselves. That's the first time this has happened to me.

It made me think of the importance of traditions, of habits, of rituals. We live in a period when nomadism reigns anew. In Russia, entire populations are dumped in Siberia. In the United States, factories, offices, and all who work in them are shipped from New England to the South. In France, heads of businesses that leave the Paris area for the provinces are given a bonus. Few people still know where they will be in ten, even five years. Families separate.

(It is curious to note that it is just at this moment when furniture and objects of daily use are interchangeable, mass produced, that the purchase of an apartment is indirectly imposed, of a cell in a huge co-operative where the man who occupies it has nothing to say, where he will have nothing to say, where he will not really be the owner. To my mind, it's a cynical swindle.)

I have always thought that the human being needs the landmarks which traditions are. As a child, I was impatient to leave my family. I pretended to be a rebel. Our way of life was a burden to me.

But I am still grateful to my mother for having, for example, taken me to market with her from the time I was three years old. I've kept a taste for markets, for baskets filled with fruit and vegetables, for odors. Later I took each of my own children to market in turn. One or another of them will probably continue the custom.

These habits are a need so natural that children, even very

young ones, demand them, each according to his temperament. Perhaps to reassure themselves? Probably, for the first ones have to do with bedtime, always an anguish for them.

One evening when Marc was two years old I told him a story of a little Chinese named Li. For years after, each evening I had to invent new adventures for Li. When I met D., he asked her for a story too, so that for a long time one or the other of us gave him a daily installment every evening.

For Johnny, the ceremony was just as complicated, but different. He was the most watchful, the most jealous of these little traditions, and he is very unhappy if one is forgotten. I understand him all the better since I am rather like him.

Putting him to bed one evening, I put the socks he had just taken off on the ears of his plush lion. This amused him. That was at least three years ago. He is eleven. Every evening I have to cover the lion's ears the same way.

And I must leave his door open just enough so that the nurse can come in without touching it if he needs her, for he likes to think I am the last to touch that door before he goes to sleep.

There are passing traditions that last for several months or a year, and others to which he remains attached.

Marie-Jo seems less concerned with these trifles.

Is that really true? She has always had a more secret life. The entire house is her domain. She may be found all by herself in the most unexpected places.

In the morning she goes to the kitchen to prepare her scrambled eggs, Daddy's eggs, made according to my recipe; she says the ones the cook makes are not as soft.

She can also be found in the secretaries' office, working near them. Finally she follows Pierre's tracks, knows where he is at each moment of the day. So she has a whole personal life and, I am persuaded, her own secret rituals.

At twenty-three months, Pierre has some too. After meals, for example, he dawdles, eating his dessert in the dining room while D. and I go into the drawing room and my adjacent study. By the time Pierre gets there, I often have a newspaper or a book in my hand, and my reading glasses on. Pierre takes these off and puts my other spectacles on my nose. If he sees me without a pipe, he goes to get one from the rack, insists that I fill and light it.

Finally he takes his mother by the hand, leads her to *her* armchair in the drawing room. Then me to *my* armchair. Then the nurse to a chair which he has decided is hers.

If Marie-Jo and Johnny are there, they must sit down too, in definite places.

And then the *bss . . . bss . . .* begins, a game he invented a few weeks ago. He plays at flying, his arms out like wings, running around the center table very fast imitating the noise of a bee.

Useless to try to drop this ceremony. There would be tears and we would have trouble getting him to sleep.

"Bsss . . . Bssss, Mamma."

After which he goes to bed himself.

I could cite other fads, for each of the four. Four experiences, then, with children of different temperaments. We haven't discouraged them. We haven't invented these rituals for them. They established them themselves, when they were still young, when they could barely walk.

Human groups, small or large, act in the same way. You might call it a need.

A holiday with bells ringing today, and festive meals, processions, etc., which have more or less lost their meaning. Automobiles speed along the roads. Nomadism is reborn. I am sure that traditions are being established just the same, different ones, but just as deep-rooted in those who follow them, or will follow them.

Fear of the void!

I forgot that every evening in bed, Marie-Jo, for whom we bought a little plush monkey, for months, nearly two years, if I'm not mistaken, has demanded stories about her monkey, named Bob. But she has a very well-developed critical mind.

If the stories are not funny, she is so disappointed that sometimes I spend more than an hour during the day on them. Finally I had to throw in the towel! She always sleeps with Bob near her in a doll's bed, though she has never played with dolls, and she dresses him and makes clothes for him.

Johnny, at eleven, sleeps with a clown that was given him eight or nine years ago in his arms, and his plush bear. He is so attached to his clown that every time it is worn out or dirty D. has to remake it with a new sponge rubber inside, so that it no longer has its original body.

For a few weeks Pierre has slept with a wooden cart and horse in his bed. He doesn't ask for stories yet.

/Monday, 17th

Our friend left this morning at eleven thirty. It's one thing to meet friends in Paris or elsewhere, to dine with them and pass the evening, and another to see them here twenty-four hours a day. Then we realize how much separates us from them, our almost complete lack of shared tastes. It is a saddening experience.

This afternoon between the time when I drove Marie-Jo and D. to the dentist and the time I had to get Johnny after school, I went into a brand-new little coffee bar where I spent nearly an hour all by myself playing the pinball machine.

At the moment (nine thirty in the evening) television commentators are still talking about the man shot into space last week—who has come back. If these pages are read later, won't it seem odd that the day after this event I didn't devote a single line to it?

It affected me, certainly, even moved me; above all, the pictures of the crowd in Moscow; but it remained no less external. Why do I note it here today? I've forgotten, and I'm not going to look back.

I wonder if pity (human, as we always call it), which has replaced religious pity, born of Catholicism, isn't more likely to generate stress, isn't more traumatizing, both for the one who feels it and the one who is its object.

Religious pity accepted evil, pain, misery as necessities and a Christian's duty was only to give "comfort."

Today, man believes it is his duty to "suppress" it. And I am always the first to share this feeling. More from a medical than from a philosophical point of view.

Journalists, for example, are told to go after "blood and gore." Whether in the daily papers, the weeklies, on radio, on television, in newsreels, everything is set up in such a way that the reader or viewer will be in the middle of the action, inside the skin of the victims.

Nowadays, in Europe and most of the developed countries, no one can escape news broadcasts, even in the depths of the countryside, and they affect women and children as well as men.

Here, *grosso modo*, except for unintentional omissions, is a summary of the past few days:

A man in space. General rejoicing, while we begin to talk about military possibilities and the vital necessity of colonizing other planets eventually, to accommodate the surplus population on our own which we won't be able to feed.

Bombs dropped on Cuba, and yesterday a landing on that island. National funeral services for the first victims. Antiaircraft on the rooftops. Tension between East and West and possibility of world conflict.

Eichmann trial. Photographs and films of German atrocities rerun. Three times a day we are shown piles of naked bodies, children marching to the gas chamber, skeletal prisoners.

The Sunday and weekly accidents in detail, of course. The young bridal couple, leaving the wedding in a car, who drove off a railroad bridge. Seven young people in a car that crashed into a tree . . .

The Congo troubles go on, cases of cannibalism are cited.

Troubles begin in Angola. Series of murders with machetes and firearms. Torture.

The weekly victims. The woman who drowned herself in a river trying to save her child. A madwoman who tried to hang her child in the Père-Lachaise cemetery rather than have it left in the care of her mother-in-law . . .

Plastic bombs in Paris, in the provinces, in Algeria . . .

Machine-gun attacks in the eighteenth arrondissement and elsewhere . . .

De Gaulle, in a speech, says in substance:

"Count of war dead in Algeria used to be as high as seventy a day. Now it is down to eight or ten. . . ."

An expert sounds the alarm (there's at least one a week) warning of the end of the world if atomic tests aren't stopped.

Another, backed by statistics, demonstrates that in 2020 men will be crowded nose to nose all over the earth.

Not to speak of earlier news items kept alive in the papers.

The doctor who announces a new cure for cancer, causing cancer patients or those who feel threatened by the disease to dread that they may die too soon.

Etc., etc. All this through the medium of voices, of pictures of haggard or convulsed faces, all the suffering of the world right in your living room several times a day, pleas for funds for refugees, for polio sufferers, for heart victims.

A doctor told me about the case of one of his patients, a rough fellow, whom he saw arrive one day from a sawmill two or more miles away with one arm completely torn off. It is a truism that the more man evolves the more he suffers, not just physically, but from fear. A dentist is the worst patient another dentist can have, a doctor for another doctor.

Peasants of earlier times knew that of ten or twelve children they would lose half at an early age, and accepted this without too much grief. Death, disease, hunger, cold, poverty, were accepted as part of everyday life.

All social levels have evolved. All have become sensitized.

Each man suffers not just from his own suffering but from the whole world's. Each man fears for himself and for all humanity.

One might even say that fears for the future of the species subconsciously trouble man even more than those that concern himself.

(Joys too. At the parade in Moscow, there was more joy over this triumph over space (?) than over some event that might have touched each individual personally.)

All of this piled up, accumulated, overlapping, entering each life.

There are not enough mental hospitals, and disease has become more moral than physical.

Is this attitude of man towards his fellows, towards his fate and theirs, rooted in evolution, or isn't it rather a passing style, like romanticism?

Will we return to a cynical acceptance of the law of the jungle and what seems to be biological law?

This bothers me. My instinct is on the side of compassion. My reason sometimes pulls me in the opposite direction and I'm not sure that this is not the condition of many men, and an important cause of unbalance. As I believe I have already said, the world has a bad conscience and insists on it, increasing instead of placating it.

The Fascists may not have been buried forever, and who knows if Rome will not return to life?

Same day, 6 o'clock in the evening

I just reread the first fifty pages of *Je me souviens* for the final (?) edition (the title is not mine but my publisher's, because I was traveling across the United States and he couldn't reach me in time). I just reread, I say, this text, which served as a point of departure for *Pedigree*, and I'm troubled.

I wonder if my style wasn't more intense, more lively, than

today. I worked faster, drinking a great deal of wine. I find little to correct—unless I rewrite everything. It's loosely written, often inaccurate, but I dare not touch it for fear of demolishing the whole thing.

It also seems to me that I have already written many things that I am rediscovering, hence that I repeat myself. Is this inevitable? Is it the rule? Or do I, after all, see the world differently now, more maturely, or, on the contrary . . .

It's because of my fear of this impression, which is depressing, that I always refuse to reread myself, even to correct proofs. In the case of *Je me souviens* it was necessary for family reasons, because of the people I quote: which has not prevented certain among them from bringing suit against me.

Marc, for whom I wrote it, since I had only that one child at the time and had no hopes for more, has never read it. He is twenty-two today. Could he have read it and not talked to me about it for some reason I don't understand? One day he told me he had skimmed over a few pages.

Will the others read these notebooks later? Johnny, almost certainly.

Curious feeling, this noon, hearing him coming in from school (his first day of Latin) shouting: *Rosa—the rose*. How little these things change—or rather how little men change—in the midst of so many changes in things!

D. in town. I decided not to go with her, not to wait for her during her fittings. I didn't so as to stay here and work, and now I feel a sort of emptiness, a lostness, a "hunger."

My dizzy spells have got better in the past few days. I'd rather not talk about that, nor about my slight depression; rather not play at medical diagnosis.

I think that this morning again I wrote nonsense as I do every time I take off on abstract ideas. Why should I, when it isn't my trade?

As I foresaw, end of discouragement—touch wood—and end of bad weather. Yesterday seemed like autumn. Now it's spring again. And I'm going out with D. this morning and afternoon.

Re Je me souviens, a few pages of which I'm revising before going out. Yesterday a passage struck me and worried me as I was going to sleep. I speak somewhere of the country house, a sort of grandmotherly house, which "we" established so that Marc could have a childhood in it like the one "we" had dreamed of having, far from town and artificiality.

I wrote "we" because this text was meant for Marc, who, I believed then, would grow up having hardly known me, since a stupid or malicious doctor had told me I was doomed, so that I expected him to be raised by his mother.

But in reality, she never cared for the country, at least not as long as I was living with her. Her dream was to have a studio in Montparnasse (she is a painter) and her ideal of marriage was to live in a different house from her husband.

Nothing existed for her outside Paris, and she often reproached me for our travels, which kept her from painting, for our moves to La Richardière and elsewhere, although the largest and best-lit room was always reserved for her use.

Isn't it ironic that she now lives in that house in Nieul that I gave her at the time of the divorce? I haven't set foot in it since I left it shortly after the arrival of the Germans. I lived there only about a year, the time it took to get settled. Marc lived there no longer than that, and recently he spent a few days there but didn't like it; he thought La Rochelle "a hole."

Another memory comes back to me, equally ironic. When we first came to Paris, my first wife and I, we quickly became aware that from a practical point of view we couldn't both of us embark simultaneously on careers of "serious art" since neither of us had any money and it would take a long time—if ever—before we could make it pay.

We discussed it calmly. We weighed the chances each of us

had of "making it." And decided, with utmost gravity, that for three years I was not to write seriously but keep the pot boiling (with short stories, popular novels) while she would try her luck at painting. If she got somewhere, I was to efface myself. If not, it would be my turn to try.

So she had canvases, easels, paints, models. We rented a room at Bernheim's for a show, then for another. . . .

My self-effacement went beyond the three years, up to the start of the Maigret series, and even, you might say, until the end of the Maigrets, since I consider these as semi-potboilers.

If she had achieved success at that time, what would have happened? I wonder and tremble. I am scrupulous by nature, and I think I might have kept to our agreement and effaced myself.

I never talked about it. Nor about Nieul. Or about the fact that it was for her sake that I settled in Paris in 1935 or 1936, Boulevard Richard-Wallace, in an apartment that I considered hers, and where I always felt like a visitor.

This makes me realize even more the near impossibility of being entirely sincere in writing notebooks like these. I'm not distorting anything. I'm not inventing anything. But sometimes I'm insincere by omission, for fear of the consequences.

Often I feel I would like to write:

"Today I made love to So-and-So. . . ."

Because it would set the tone of the day. Because these acts are part of the whole. But even if I left out names, abbreviations would make it possible for someone to guess who was meant. These women will have children someday, perhaps. Some of them already have. Or else they will fall in love. Have I the right to upset someone just to indicate the tone of a day?

Others don't have such scruples, neither Gide nor Jouhandeau, for example, and I am tempted to envy them. At the same time, it seems to me that they are the ones whose sincerity is most suspect, because they give in to the temptation of playing a part and making others play parts.

In preparing this new edition of *Je me souviens* I could re-establish the truth by putting "I" in place of "we." But would this be the decent thing to do? And wouldn't people believe it was done out of shabby revenge or resentment?

Tonight, Russian ultimatum to the Americans on Cuba.

America's reply. Cessation of peace talks in Laos. It's too much. Personally, I no longer react, I can no longer get excited, even feel interested. Doesn't the public feel the same? I hope so. It would contradict what I wrote yesterday on this subject, but so much the better.

Only in that case, if I were in the place of those who govern, I would begin to fear that after long apathy there might be danger of a terrible reaction.

Aren't there signs of this in France, where de Gaulle has put public opinion to sleep, hypnotized the Parliament?

We speak of millionaires, billionaires. The papers like to cite figures. And they mean nothing.

At one time, a man owned large flocks or small ones, or such-and-so many women, such-and-so many palaces, or even reigned over a huge or not so huge country. Or so much land, so many farms, so many slaves, so many serfs (so many souls, as they said in Russia).

Then he received so much income.

It's only in the past century, quite recently, that we've talked in millions, only since most of the world's currencies have become stable.

What is a millionaire today? In what? In old francs? In new francs? In marks? In dollars? In pounds sterling? It ranges all the way from poverty to real riches. So-and-So earns so much per film. Before or after taxes? There too the amount can range from one to several digits. How many servants has he? But real dollar millionaires in the United States have only a housekeeper, while lira millionaires in Italy have a dozen and live in historic palaces.

We go on talking about money out of habit, tradition, when money no longer represents anything real, much less anything stable. We might as well count in cowries or in beans. Yet it's in the name of these cowries that people uphold this policy or that, and incite if not massacres—for the present—at least good-sized killings.

Besides that, reading the classified advertisements in the French, American, Swiss, English, no matter what papers, is depressing:

"Discreet loans to civil servants, no formalities . . ."

"Two rooms with kitchen in a pleasant suburb . . ."

"Credit facilities . . ."

"Twenty per cent discount on all merchandise . . ."

Millions and hundreds of millions of people for whom "every penny counts," each franc or each cent, are looking for lodgings, food, clothing, with incomes that won't cover all these needs at once. . . .

"Mamma, my shoes leak. . . ."

I knew how that was in my childhood.

"I'll buy you new ones next month. This month your father needs trousers. . . ."

There aren't enough cowries.

Today, civil servants are protest-marching in the streets of Paris. For two weeks the teachers were on strike. They threaten to go out again.

There aren't enough cowries for everybody.

Besides, when people have them they buy what they need. When they buy, prices go up. When prices go up . . .

And then, who would be rich if there were no poor people?

/April 24th

Since Friday, more "historic" days and nights, not only in Cuba, Laos, the Congo, or Angola, but in France and Algeria. Uprisings. Even the word "revolution" is spoken. And last night, while tanks patrolled Paris, arms were distributed to the populace.

I listen to the radio hourly, as everybody does. My reaction? I admit to a certain satisfaction because events prove I wasn't mistaken in what I foresaw, so my judgment isn't so far wrong.

We were going to spend ten days in Paris after the revision of my last novel. Our suite was reserved at the Georges V and engagements were made with friends. We hesitated, gave up the trip at the last minute, and are glad of it. Not because of personal danger, but rather for fear of being separated from our children, knowing they would be worried here with us there.

One sometimes wonders what So-and-So was doing during the Three Glorious Days or the Commune. . . .

As for us, Friday evening we had some friends in, people who on the face of it shouldn't have been very entertaining, two professors from the Faculty of Medicine and two psychiatrists. We spent one of the pleasantest evenings we've had at Echandens.

We are often bored by people who are supposed to be bright or witty. At our house they can turn into dead weights, and we've passed tedious hours with them.

On Saturday, from seven thirty to four in the morning we had a bit of everything. Some serious discussions which I'll remember. And also, some almost childlike gaiety: one of the psychiatrists (whose life has not been an easy one) at the piano, a professor at the drums, delighted to take our Johnny's place, another, his shirt pulled out of his pants and his socks pulled up over them, did Russian dances with me, while the head of the sanatorium played the triangle. . . . A sort of gaiety that I haven't experienced in a long time. I went so far as to give a mock striptease. . . .

Then stories, not just funny ones, but all true, throwing unexpected lights on human nature.

If students had appeared that night at our house, they would have been dumbstruck, probably, because the minimum age of the men was fifty. As it happened, each of the women, whether pretty or interesting, was a true wife and lover, in love with her husband.

Generals were invading Algeria. Another general, raised to power by them, accused them of treason. . . .

We were having a jolly time putting everything in perspective, which is not necessarily the one History will choose for it.

We found this morning that for the first time, yesterday, French television broadcast all night, appeals from de Gaulle, Debré, Malraux, etc., who all look like very small men to me.

Will History think otherwise? Will they be turned into heroes? It's possible. In that case, all of History will have to be revised.

As for us, we went to bed early, D. and I, stiff and exhausted by our unaccustomed frolics.

And this evening we're going to play bridge at another medic's house.

Unawareness? Lack of sense of proportion?

In my opinion, it's the opposite.

Generals explain themselves, posing as heroes. One and all, one against all, they try to rouse the rabble. Suddenly they appeal to the very people they usually despise and consider inconsequential.

My impression as a distant but contemporary witness? Of being present not at a tragedy, nor even at a comedy of character, but at a vaudeville skit.

Too bad men have to die, for whom these gentlemen don't care a shit.

I'm going to try to telephone Marc, who is there. That's my only worry. Let's hope he isn't "dope" enough, as D. says, to get involved.

I'd rather know that, like us, he did a striptease and danced Cossack dances between two discussions of biology.

/*Wednesday, April 26, 1961*

Last night, in the course of two or three hours—in one hour, in fact—the famous revolt of the generals, which we have been told of in dramatic tones for the past four days, collapsed with only a few shots fired: three policemen wounded, we're told. But, we had been told previously, the "criminal" generals were the leading lights of the army, specialists in psychological warfare, whom de Gaulle, at one time, chose for his most delicate missions.

So for three or four days airfields were closed, the people were told to be ready to intervene. Volunteers were given uniforms and arms, specialists called up. Paris was overrun by armored units recalled from Germany. Last night I heard from Paris that a pass was required for traveling the roads of France.

Finally de Gaulle assumed complete control.

In an hour . . . With no real fighting!

I would do better to write nothing about it, not to be like the armchair strategists or prophets of the Café du Commerce, when actually I know nothing. Do contemporaries ever know the truth about what is happening? No more than judges or the public know of a court trial. Each has his small piece of the truth.

Later, memoirs will be published, white papers. Even in these there is only fragmentary or distorted truth, so that History is scarcely better served.

But quite possibly I'm wrong. This morning my feeling is still that of a great fraud. I know some of the protagonists. Was it a matter of inflating a harmless uprising so as to seize the powers de Gaulle has always dreamed of? Of putting an end to the protests of government employees and workers who were marching in the streets and threatening the government last week?

When the danger is past, will de Gaulle keep these emergency powers and use them against nonrebels?

This morning we are told it is all over. I wonder if it isn't just beginning. And if the people aren't going to question many things, if they won't suspect many mysteries in this event, as I do.

The reaction may be long-lasting. The cry "Down with Fascism!" has been heard.

Do people realize that it is the Debrés, the Freys, etc., with their idea of a "single" party, of a "great traditional party," who are the Fascists in this affair?

Up to a certain point the deception is a common one in times like these, and that's why I do not hope for a return to normal in the near future. Nevertheless it seems to me that all this false glory, all this strictly verbal grandeur is doomed and will be swept away.

I even wonder if there isn't real revolution in the air, just the thing they wanted to suppress or avoid.

Tomorrow there will be an appeal for calm in the name of the negotiations at Evian or elsewhere. Then it will be another pretext, the prestige of France, the arrival of the Kennedys, the difficulties in Otan, what have you.

In the meantime, I am returning to my revision of *Je me souviens*, which I hope to finish today; regret time spent listening to this rather distorted news, trying to understand, to come to a conclusion.

Once more, it's not my department. I hate politics, but, like Romain Rolland's Clérambault, an antimilitarist who surprised himself by falling into step with a military band in August 1914, I respond in spite of myself because I always have a confused hope that the politicians are going to bite the dust, that the people will finally see the light and sweep them out.

To be replaced by what? By others, to be sure. History shows us that. So? What good is it to rejoice or mope?

Be satisfied with plying your trade and telling stories, with busying yourself with man, not men.

/April 27, 1961

I know I'm wrong, my children, that later, when you come across the word "politics" on these pages, you'll smile indulgently:

"There goes Daddy, off the track again."

But now Johnny, at least, who follows the news on television with me, has the same reactions. On certain evenings I can feel him boiling with rage, and on certain others, like yesterday and the day before, the enormity of what he hears plunges him into a sort of discouraged dejection.

Isn't there anyone in France to write a new *J'accuse*? I admit I've wondered if I could resist the temptation, if I were French.

All politics irritate me, certainly, since a just and satisfying system has yet to be found.

But in the circumstances, it is no longer simply a matter of politics. It is a matter of a man who sets himself up, and whom others set up as an example and who strikes me as a real Tartuffe. I would like to have the time, the patience, the inclination to compare his contradictions listed in facing columns.

He was the one who once upon a time proclaimed the right to rebellion, the right to individual action, to the use of plastic bombs, to gunfire or knife fighting in the Métro, and it was he again who spoke of the Algerian rebellion with complete scorn for three years.

And when I say complete . . . He has just faced a *coup d'état* himself—a rather modest, desperate one—and already he is announcing a merciless purge, recalling another purge to us, over which he presided and which must have caused nearly as many deaths in France as the German repression during the war if not more.

Now, on the pretext of these days in Algiers (the third or fourth time, if you count the one that put him in power, with the same men acting *for* him this time), now, I repeat, that he has complete authority, he has no intention of giving it up and announces that freedom cannot be defended in a modern country . . . except by the restriction of freedom.

This is not what horrifies me most. It is the man himself, his attitude, his insolent pride, his contempt for man and man's efforts, for everything that man has done over the centuries that he isn't ashamed of or that makes him think there may be some hope for the future of the species.

The *Grandeur* which he talks about so much is the narrowest nationalism, the most inflated and the most aggressive, it is the pomp, the costumes, the uniforms, the parades, the stage sets, and a protocol that totally amazes me: unknown in the most royalist countries, it should make the world laugh.

He backs and fills. He makes the country wait until the day when he solemnly decides to pronounce an oracle. And the words change meaning each time.

Deep contempt for all men, including those who surround him. It is true that he chooses these from among the least interesting.

Yet he is held up as an example. A whole generation hears of his glory, his intelligence, his force of character, his historic consciousness.

He has done none of what he said he would. He has disappointed all expectations and no one calls him to account for it.

There he is, a living anachronism, pretending to know everything and manage everything himself, according to his own lights.

He refuses to receive professors, unions, but he surrounds himself with bank presidents and presidents of big companies, who have never had it so good.

He speaks "to the French" but the French he speaks to are not the people, whom he looks down on from a great height: they are the representatives of great private interests, the religious orders, the young people who have been behind every thrust of extreme nationalism from the days of Balzac and even since . . . why not say forever?

La Frrrance . . . which the world needs, which, with its forty million inhabitants, is once more going to restore order to a mad world . . .

La Frrrance . . . which is to say de Gaulle, who tosses off advice to other nations, and sometimes deigns to receive heads of states with two or three hundred million souls from the top of the staircase of the Elysée Palace.

He lies, he contradicts himself, he beats about the bush, he glowers or blesses with the face of a sad clown, and there is no one who dares burst out laughing or write a *J'accuse*.

How long will this go on? I don't know. I think of the real men, the ones who work in silence and who do not believe themselves infallible, who doubt, who go forward one step at a time and help mankind advance in every area of knowledge.

His presence is an insult to them.

Surely I am not the only one who thinks so. I wonder if, in the light of recent events, of which we are given only a distorted and rather mysterious version, we shall not see popular uprisings as they have happened time and again in the course of History.

I am not hoping for trouble. I am a man of peace. For the sake of man's dignity, however, I would welcome a popular movement that would put both this madman with his arms raised in a V and the little band of ambitious idiots who surround him and are trying to drag us back a century back in their proper places.

Smile if you like, children. You will see that in every man there is an ancient spring of idealism—even political idealism—which sometimes breaks through his calm.

But I am a man of serenity. And I have rarely felt so much a man of the people as I do today.

5 o'clock in the afternoon

Henry Miller spent the day at my house. He's in Lausanne looking for a home, a "place to live." He vacillated between Switzerland, Portugal, Italy, the Bahamas, etc. He had to take into account, as I do, schools for his children and those of his companion. That reminds me of when D. and I were undecided in the same way.

Miller is seventy years old. I hope that when I'm his age I'll still want to move, with the same problems and the same pleasure as ever.

Sent *Je me souviens* off to the publisher. Tomorrow, photographer. Some other obligations in the next few days, then go somewhere, doesn't matter where, with D. Maybe to Berne?

We needn't go far. On occasion we've quite happily gone to spend no more than forty-eight hours alone together . . . in Lausanne.

The sun is shining. The grass in the garden is being cut; the last rains have made it as tufted as Johnny's mop, which I love to tousle. Pierre is learning new words every day. He juggles with life. He tries everything. Why do we lose this faculty? When there is always something new to learn, to feel? There must be a reason, which isn't aging, and which we haven't yet found.

A rather intriguing idea of Teilhard de Chardin's, which I condense and simplify: Humanity is only just beginning its youth.

Aging is slowing of the rhythm of life, of activity, shrinking. . . .

But humanity is multiplying at an accelerated rhythm, same for discoveries. So humanity is still emerging from childhood.

Even stranger that, though man grows old and dies, humanity should follow the opposite course.

I think I understand, however, another idea of Teilhard de Chardin's which attracts me less: the real function of man is not to be an individual, but little by little to become integrated into a new field of action, a great body into which each would melt and which would itself have its own personality.

What astonishes me is that today one reads discussions of this kind not just in specialized reviews, but in the big-circulation weeklies, the same ones that now deal mainly with literature, painting, music, or avant-garde cinema, as if there were no general public any more, only intellectuals.

In my youth I had a certain number of friends who became "intellectualized" this way. Without exception, all of them were failures later. As if this "intellectualization" were an incapacity to adapt to life.

They thought about life instead of living it.

Among stripteasers there are a fair number, not only of women with bachelor's degrees, but of women who have gone on to postgraduate study. Are they most themselves at their studies (for their pleasure, so called) or when they undress in public?

Many books are published currently, especially in Italy, which consist largely of photographs. The Bible in particular. The fashion began in France. But it was one of my books, published about 1931, that was used for the first experiment. The idea wasn't mine but that of a young man named Jacques Haumont who, I think, invested his inheritance in the venture.

The series was called *Phototext*. The first and only volume was a long novella of mine, *La Folle d'Itteville,* and the photographs by Germaine Krull were as important as my words.

I wrote four or five others at Morsang on board the *Ostrogoth* after I came back from Holland, while waiting for the publication of the first Maigrets. In one morning, I wrote the forty-five typed pages. Haumont came to lunch at noon. I read him the novella as I corrected it. No other revision.

Haumont went into bankruptcy and, with my consent, gave the unpublished novellas to Gallimard, who published them in a collection edited by Paul Morand, *Les Chefs-d'Oeuvre de la Nouvelle.*

No one gives credit to Haumont, who invented too soon a form that is flourishing today. As Balzac initiated the formula of *La Pléiade* and broke his back doing it.

I wouldn't dare reread those novellas I wrote in three hours on the deck of my boat and revised in haste while having an apéritif in the sun. How little awareness I must have had! Or how little faith in and respect for "Literature"?

/Sunday, April 30, 1961

Back with "the papers." Stormy, unpleasant weather. Showers.

When we settled at Echandens, we did what we had done in Lakeville: had swings and gymnasium gear set up for the children at the back of the garden. All last summer, Pierre (he will be two years old in three weeks) would see his brothers, his sister, and their friends use them. But he used to circle them at a distance, he never came closer.

A month ago, at the beginning of spring, I had a swing with a back and a belt put up for him, but he only looked at it, shaking his head in refusal. For four weeks he looked at this apparatus distrustfully.

Not until day before yesterday did he decide to sit in it, though refusing to be swung. Yesterday, he could be gently pushed.

It was almost the same thing with his rocking horse. He loved it from the first day—wanted to have it in bed with him—but it took almost a month for him to get on it.

Since he has been eating things other than milk, he has had the habit of smelling each new food with the same distrust, of turning it over and over for a long time, examining it before putting it in his mouth.

This reminds me that my three other children were no different. Children are said to be reckless because they play with matches, touch electric outlets, etc. But these objects look passive and harmless.

On the contrary, if I can judge by my own, the child is as careful, as distrustful as an animal. I would even say fearful. His attachment to his parents has a good deal of fear in it, fear of being left by himself.

Why does he become reckless at a certain age? (Not always!) I think it is because he wants to impress other children, or grownups, or even himself. I should not be surprised if he became aggressive in proportion to his fear. I could swear, for example, that Marc was always afraid of his big motorcycle, as I always felt a bit afraid with automobiles.

Physical courage, when it isn't a matter of fighting for one's skin, may very well be an artificial sentiment that animals don't know, since they never run unnecessary risks.

All the same, isn't there another kind of courage, moral bravery? After the security furnished by its parents, doesn't the child or the adolescent seek the same thing in groups?

So without really wanting to I come back to a subject that I've sniffed around several times, and I don't like the conclusion I'm tempted to come to, because it is the negation of the individualism I care so much about.

Essentially, then, is man gregarious out of fear?

How many people live alone, are able to live alone, by inclination, by destiny? Isn't love most often a way of escaping solitude and its terrors?

Strong men, paratroopers, for instance, act as a group; one could even say a group that draws closer together as its members become more aggressive and more brutal.

The war hero is a group hero. And knowing this, the philosopher who moves against the current of his times or ahead of it, the avant-garde artist, almost always keeps in touch with several of his own kind.

The truly isolated man, the hermit by nature, is very rare, and psychiatrists consider him a pathological case.

If this is true, if man instinctively moves towards the herd, towards rule, towards obedience . . . These past days I've been irritated by propaganda, which begins pouring in on us in the morning and goes on all day in all forms. But the propaganda of the past in the form of daily masses, which even kings could not escape, the sermons, the *confessions* . . .

From this point of view, why such horror at the thought of the world of today and tomorrow in so many informed minds who panic at the thought of mass civilization, mechanization, standardization, which is actually hardly more advanced than it was in the life of the Middle Ages? Didn't serfs, peasants, take comfort from living more or less peacefully in the shadow of the castle, which offered them a refuge in time of danger?

If the child is naturally fearful . . .

Are there any real exceptions? Yet I see men who mouth the word "liberty" accepting posts, honors, ridiculous titles, gilded medals, cattle-show ribbons.

A Blaise Cendrars . . . A Henry Miller . . . Other people I know who have had the reputation of being real wild men, wholly pure, spend a good part of their lives seeking each other out for reassurance. Blaise Cendrars accepted a most belated medal on his deathbed. Miller wears the rosette of the American Academy on his sports jackets.

Isn't it pitiful how, beginning with nothing but a swing, a simple parental observation, in spite of myself I come back to one of the three or four ideas I'm always circling around like a circus horse?

Aren't our little habits, our manias, also a way of reassuring ourselves?

We speak of man as if he existed in the individual state. What if there were only men, a mixture of men, much more like each other than they first seem to us, a sort of human caviar which . . .

Come on! I'm off again. And living, then? What do these ratiocinations have to do with life? And the papers I'm going to read? And the television I'll be watching tonight? And the rage that comes over me as I listen. . . .

In ten minutes we'll sit down to our meal and Pierre will watch the door until every one of the family is in his place in the dining room.

For him, the unit now is the family, until it becomes the school, the regiment, the office, the political party, the country, Europe.

How I wish the unit were man!

/*May 3rd*

Day before yesterday morning in my study, a bumblebee flew in clumsily, beating against the three windows, passing close to my head each time. I know they don't sting. But was it a hornet? Still, I know the difference. But I kept dreading some unpleasant contact and suddenly I decided to kill it. Because I wasn't sure. And because I wasn't used to it.

For similar reasons people have slaughtered snakes that are useful and harmless, other animals, screech owls, bats, etc., which are now greatly missed, according to zoologists.

Gide used to say to me, speaking of my son, that I should be sure to teach him natural sciences, especially about plant life, the study of which had always delighted him.

Alas, I never studied botany, because in my time it was largely a science of nomenclature. I've studied very little zoology. Johnny isn't studying it at all in school—at least up to now.

I feel remorseful at having killed this bumblebee, which had only a few days or hours to live.

The same evening, on television, *Night and Fog*, a documentary on Nazi concentration camps, crematory furnaces, and gas chambers, piles of naked corpses, etc.

Doesn't the one explain the other? The same fear, the same ignorance, the same disgust.

Yesterday, in a rage, Johnny called me a bastard. As I promised myself I would, I have taught him not to "respect" me as my mother insisted on my respecting her, on my respecting my uncles and aunts, grownups, institutions. An hour later, poor Johnny was very sad. I was too. I still am, a bit. However, for him the word means nothing. It is an outlet for righteous wrath. I had been fooled by his sister's air of innocence and had scolded him unfairly. Today we both wanted to ask each other's forgiveness.

A holiday. Going to Geneva, D. and I. Lunch alone together somewhere. Ouf!

/*Wednesday, May 3, 1961*

Yesterday was a better day than I expected. Not only did D. and I enjoy it, but everything fell into place for us, everything went well, it was as if we were juggling life and dropping nothing.

Found the English desk I've been looking for for six months in an antique shop, even more perfect than I'd dreamed, also a unique armchair, and the English dining set that we'd given up on into the bargain.

Scarcely back at the house, two phone calls for D., both on business, both successful. A day that will figure in our intangible album of memories. And for me, another opportunity to appreciate, vividly and in depth, D.'s maternal quality, her amazing patience. In a single day, she was companion, businesswoman, buddy, mistress, mother, I don't know what not.

In the evening, alone with Johnny, tender and troubled.

"Did I hurt your feelings yesterday?"

I admitted he had.

"Mostly because I understood that you couldn't help it, and I was afraid for you. . . ."

He understood. It was the "bastard" that most perturbed him. Like his mother, he needs to explain, not to leave anything in the dark.

"You know in school we don't mean anything by that, it's a word we use all the time. It's not even as strong as 'idiot' or 'imbecile.' . . ."

Dear Johnny, who forgets that in all of his rages he calls me an idiot or an imbecile!

As for Pierre, here he is in his turn, in love with his mother, unwilling to let go of her in the evening, inventing pretexts as cleverly as Marie-Jo. He doesn't go to sleep before nine thirty, after exhausting all the resources of his imagination.

I'm already beginning to feel the itch to write a new novel. A party at the school in the course of which Johnny is to play the part of a Chinese and be carried on a shield by his schoolmates.

D.'s birthday the 14th. The 23rd or 24th—I never remember my children's birthdays—Pierre's second birthday. Life is lovely and good.

/Friday, May 5, 1961

All right—let's try to talk about this damned question of money. Each time I begin to write in this notebook my dream is to do it lazily, sometimes elaborating a detail, following the course of my thoughts without haste. I never manage it. I always "work small."

I don't think it's laziness, although I can't stand sitting too long at my desk. It's more a sort of reticence that keeps me from giving too much importance to a reflection, a detail. It's the same for my books, whose brevity is the despair of my English and American publishers (they often have to publish two novels in one volume). I condense in spite of myself and I am reinforced in it by my apprenticeship in the popular novel, in which there must always be movement, where it is forbidden to leave the slightest space for boredom.

The question of money has occupied, and occupies, very little place in my life, although it had such a great one in Balzac's or Dostoevsky's, to whom I should never think of comparing myself.

From the beginning, I've wanted it, so as to be free of certain worries, and especially not to have to count it. To buy without asking the price. To live without knowing what life costs. It was already a dream in my childhood, in a house where calculations went on from morning to night.

But I don't keep it. I don't hoard it. I have always said that money is only stored-up man, since a given sum represents so many hours of labor, thus so many hours, so many days, so many months, of human lives.

From there to keeping these symbols of life in a safe . . . It horrifies me. To such a point that I have often made enough crazy purchases to find myself broke again and forced to work.

I have a horror of capitalism. It seems revolting to me that money should earn money.

That's all. It seems to me that I had a lot to say on this subject, and I see I've already exhausted it. For today, anyway.

I'm not afraid of going back to a way of life I knew in my childhood, of living in a small apartment or in a little house in the country and, if no one wants to read me any more, of working at a publisher's, at no matter what, like so many former colleagues.

However, I should not like to have my children suddenly in straitened circumstances, having to account for francs and centimes.

"No, Pierre, that's too expensive. . . ."

Or: "We can't afford that."

Which doesn't mean it couldn't happen, since life has rarely been so fluctuating and unpredictable as it is today.

I shall have done what I could.

4 P.M.

Having a half-siesta just now on the drawing-room sofa and allowing my thoughts to wander in the gray of a rainy day, I arrived not so much at ideas as at preoccupations that I don't like very much.

Did it begin with the question of Algeria? There is a lot of talk about specific mentalities, the mentality of the French colonials in Algeria, the "officer mentality," or the "unit mentality," etc. . . . and among so many people who don't understand each other there no doubt are a majority of men who honestly believe in their cause.

In the United States I knew the "McCarthy mentality" and the "egghead mentality" and now there is that of the new establishment as opposed to the old, the Pentagon, the CIA, and so forth.

In *Je me souviens* I tried to give an idea of the Brüll clan and the Simenon clan. Though I revolted against both, there is no doubt that I remain marked by them, that I sometimes, as today, react as a function of my education.

In the same way I rebelled against the Christian Brothers whose pupil I was, less against the Jesuits, and this rebellion left its mark. I have often said that the cult of the Virgin changed the behavior of men towards women.

In this way I could go back to a number of themes which recur in my mind and, in spite of myself, rule my actions or my thought: "Laziness is the mother of . . ." "Man must earn his bread by the sweat of his brow. . . ." "Only the bread one has earned tastes good. . . ."

The words "idle hour" . . . as if there were anything more beautiful than an idle hour!

Thus we more or less submit to the imperatives of the clan, the race, the family, education, the environment.

I was a jingoist in 1914–1918, a pseudo-anarchist in the following years, though these were spent at the very Catholic *Gazette de Liège*. I took on the style of life of postwar Montparnasse (1921–1930) and of the painters who peopled that section.

I saw life as a sailor when I lived aboard my boats, as a Parisian in Paris, a Southerner in the Midi.

In the United States I judged the political life and customs from the point of view of Americans, and I scarcely recognized France when I came back.

Just now, on my sofa, I began to smile at my cult of personality, of the individual. What individual, if a trifle can change him? "Conditioning"—Pavlov's, and that of the present-day Russians —is it as theoretical as we would like to believe?

I've seen my wife give birth "painlessly" thanks to conditioning, and today in Moscow major operations are performed without anesthesia.

What individual? If what I do is the sum of my acquired reflexes, plus what has influenced me plus what has stuck to me and sometimes reappears unconsciously, what is left of me?

I observe my children. At the moment, they seem original to me. But when I see an old photo of them a few years back, they look to me still unformed, and I have the feeling that their personalities only came to them later.

What is left of me, of others?

Tonight we are dining at the house of some friends, medics, as usual. Monday, three days of holiday together. End of the month, end of various engagements, and, I hope, a novel.

Between the last one and the one to come I will have had three days of vacation alone with D.

Dined at our friends', yesterday, with a physicist (should I say atomicist?) professor at the C.E.R.N. [European Council for Nuclear Research] in Geneva, world-famous, it seems, who wanted to meet me. I understood at once why. He is crazy about detective novels and . . . science fiction. He devours them. Very proud of having his friends call him Nero Wolfe, the hero of my colleague Rex Stout.

(He is only fifty-four but seemed to me older than I am. This now happens frequently. I meet people who appear heavier, more serious, more established, more mature, and I am surprised that they are younger. Is it possible that I'm mistaken and that they, from their point of view, have the same impression?)

He is from the Baltic region, like Keyserling, whom he reminded me of a little, like him speaks several languages perfectly, has lived in Germany, in the United States, in Paris, now for seven years in Geneva. Often goes to M.I.T. His wife, German, twenty years younger than he, has lived in Paris too, then was seven or eight years with the Mayo brothers in Minnesota. This kind of couple turns up more and more frequently.

He confirmed certain impressions I had which were based on nothing definite. Oppenheimer: he tended to play Mahatma Gandhi more and more; a scientific romantic. Braun: a scientist with a flair for publicity.

In scientific circles, he told me, each one knows his precise niche in the hierarchy. No argument possible, for this niche is decided by precisely measurable works. Art and medicine are debatable, have an area of imprecision.

He found my first book on a bench on the Champs-Elysées when he was fifteen, and since then has read all of them. I feel it was true. But I found no echo in his conversation as I do with doctors and psychiatrists. It is Maigret who mainly interests him.

He is the sort of man who speaks with apparent abandon, with a certain humor, and who is then suddenly silent for a long moment, as if the conversation were no concern of his.

He wanted to have me meet other scientists in Geneva, where they are coming in growing numbers, either as residents or passing through. I don't yet know if these circles will interest me. I don't feel comfortable in them.

We talked about the mean age at which man gives the best of himself in art or sciences, and also in politics. According to statistics, this age is much later than one would think (reassuring!). I've already mentioned this. But, according to him, and he should know, this is not true for the sciences. It is considered the rule that a physicist or mathematician who hasn't made any discovery by thirty will never make any.

Which brings science closer to poetry.

"In some respects we are poets," he told me.

No interest in the influence of scientific discoveries on philosophy, on the history of human thought.

"That doesn't concern us. Up to others to draw conclusions."

Which must give a certain serenity.

This morning, a gay, clear sun.

/*Sunday, May 14th*

Yesterday D.'s birthday. A perfect day for me and the children. About D., I'm not so sure. She is much more sensitive than I to the least shadow, to a trifle, which can easily spoil her pleasure. Our three days in Berne were so good that I dream about them. Nothing out of the ordinary. Just being alone together, with no cares, without interruptions every moment. Walks in streets that can hardly be called picturesque; that was enough for us, as was a lazy visit to the museum of natural history. Yesterday delivery of the elegant English desk (late eighteenth century) that I finally found for my study, which is not complete and of uniform style. I am writing on it for the first time, a little intimidated by it. It faces two ways, has fifteen drawers, and, like a child, I'm putting off until tomorrow—or until this afternoon—the pleasure of stowing my things away in them.

New dining-room furniture too, in the same style.

Yesterday, "punishment day" as the Americans say. In bed until noon, headache. However, I hadn't overdone it much. Almost nothing is now too much for me. Was it in the United States that I learned the shame that weighs me down the day after? A painful day. Total discouragement. Not in front of the children!

Today I returned to my normal activities, I am busy with Friday's dinner, with Pierre's birthday; tried on two sports coats.

The papers have me being considered for the Nobel again. This is beginning to exasperate me. One year I'm called the favorite, another, an outside chance. And this has gone on for more than six years. I've asked nothing. I don't ask for anything. Let them f . . . off and leave me in peace. The Nobel would have given me pleasure a few years ago. Now I'm not sure I would accept it.

Hope to write a novel in the first days of June but haven't the least idea of the subject, or even the tone. However, I'd better write it. I feel the need. We'll see if between now and then I'll have an inspiration. (That's the wrong word, of course. But what other can I use?)

I would like a quiet story, almost serene, with lots of sun, little touches of color, a waxed staircase, patches of shade, and reflections.

Yesterday, Johnny gave me his latest French composition to read. There were odors in it, sounds, little joys, as in my novels. He isn't imitating me. He hasn't read me enough for that. Say rather that he is attracted by the same things that I am, by the savory, incidental aspects of life. For example, he sees a grocer in front of his iron blind, smells the odor of the bakery. . . .

To please his teacher, he added one or two conventional pieces of "fine writing," but in his revision he cut them out. He's a good cub.

I would like to say many things about my four children. But it will be long. I'll wait for another day.

As for D., two nights ago I saw her as she was in 1945, with her face so puzzled and touching, especially her eyes. I must always remember to see her this way, which is her real self. I know it. I'm sure of it.

Sometimes I forget, I doubt—but never for long. She is a real woman, and I think back to the two of us, naked, walking in the moonlight at Tumacacori, after crossing a flooded arroyo. We undressed to ford the water. (There were no bridges.) Why get dressed again when there wasn't another human being for miles around? That was the nearest we came to nature. We were like a pair of coyotes, and real coyotes must have been watching us.

Too bad one can't more often . . . Too many obligations, bondages, though this is neither by desire nor by·ambition, but because these obligations pile up, because one doesn't want to cause trouble, fear that . . .

The main thing is never to lose sight of the fact that all that counts for nothing, to remember the naked couple in the desert, to know that it is still the same couple, plus the little ones—one of whom has already left the nest.

/Sunday, May 21, 1961

The papers are full of articles on the responsibility of parents in the education of children. And the State, which has become almost all-powerful and substitutes itself for the individual in most realms, insists on this responsibility too.

By temperament, by taste, I am a "child lover," if I can put it that way, meaning that I devote a good part of my time and attention to them. Not only with the passion of a father but with that of a collector (I envy my neighbor Charles Chaplin's collection!).

However, while I do my utmost for mine, I still haven't that sense of responsibility. Still less am I tempted to follow the rules and theories of education which are adopted in rapid succession.

Friday we had twenty doctors here, several of whom were quite famous professors at the medical school, and a number of whom were pediatricians. I was comforted to see that most of them, and especially the best, those who have remained most simply human, rejected this sense of responsibility as I do—which did not prevent them, again like me, from feeling anxious and often tormented.

(Just interrupted by D. Don't hold it against her, on the contrary. But am going to have trouble returning to my train of thought, if thought there was!)

They think that no one can foretell what will have influence in the life of a child. Each is a different being, and what will mark one will leave another indifferent. All the rules of psychology are false. I have seen Marc, Johnny, Marie-Jo successively at the age Pierre is now, and not one has reacted in the same way as the others.

Marc, for example, who seemed the most attached to me, almost alarmingly so, who never raised his voice, never protested, never stood up to anyone, is without question the one of the four who is least influenced by me. I could be wrong, since at twenty-one, twenty-two, his development is not complete, and the others' has barely begun.

Johnny has sudden gusts of rebellion, stands up to me as an enemy for a few minutes or a few hours, but I have an impression that it's more a rebellion against himself, that he is too much identified with me.

As for Marie-Jo, I hardly know her, for, since her birth, I have felt the presence of a woman, a different being. Does she resemble her mother? That's a game I refuse to play, which in most families becomes the bane of children's existence. Of course, they have something in them of their parents and their grandparents and their great-grandparents. But first of all, they are a unique combination.

Why wish to assimilate them to one of two clans? For that is what happens. In each couple—the most loving—a struggle, the struggle of the clans, goes on, like social or tribal struggles. And each one, the father and the mother, once in possession of a child, tries to turn it into an ally, to assimilate it to his clan.

"He has eyes like . . ."

"And as for his personality . . ."

Documents, family photos, old stories, more or less exaggerated, are used in evidence. In spite of himself, each of the parents treats the child according to whether he belongs to (or resembles) this or that clan.[1]

The other day it seemed to me that I had a great deal to say on this subject. But I'm already finished. It's unclear. No idea emerges.

A quiet Pentecost, gray, with an occasional ray of sun. The children are playing in the garden. Downstairs, D. is receiving an English publisher who came to see her between two planes.

While reading papers and magazines I am thinking of my next book.

/*Monday, May 22nd*

What a queer profession ours is! Can it be called a profession? There are moments when it is more like a vice, for which one has a bad conscience and wants to excuse oneself.

During the writing days it's all right. Even strangers realize you're working and respect your solitude. But between novels? Those who are amazed by my writing three to six novels a year are also astonished when I'm not always available, like a worker on holiday.

It's true for those near me, too, almost true, sometimes true, and I understand it. They are so much in the habit of seeing me

[1] This is obviously because each one is trying, unconsciously, to survive himself. . . .

lead a life like everyone else's that though they know I "also" work, when I am not in the middle of a book, they forget it.

But I shouldn't just have said "also," but rather "especially," for with a novel, aside from the anguish over the first chapters, the actual writing is a deliverance, while the gestation is invariably painful. No one, myself included, knows when this gestation begins. And I'm the first not to want the whole family to walk on tiptoe because Daddy is "thinking." Like Maigret, I don't think. But good God, how laborious it sometimes is!

If I happen to need a lesson in humility, I have only to think of my first wife's grandfather. I didn't know him. I never exactly knew if he was a workman or a foreman in the big foundry at Seraing. He must have been quite a character, because at a certain point in his life he left for Valenciennes with his wife and half a dozen children to become a lay clerk in a church.

One day, if my understanding is correct, he invented a process for scaling boilers. The patent earned him a certain amount of money.

From that time to his death—he died quite old—he spent his life sitting in an armchair, *thinking,* demanding silence around him.

Since he had become an inventor, he was inventing. And, as I said earlier speaking of myself, isn't the essential moment in invention as in literature that of conception?

He invented nothing else. Forty years of thinking . . . of nothing. With his family walking respectfully on tiptoe in the fear of spoiling a miracle!

/Tuesday, 23rd

People—including the most serious sociologists and, for different reasons, psychoanalysts—talk a lot about woman's increasingly important place in society, and of the tendency of man, in leading countries like the U.S.A. more than others, to a sort of resignation, of self-effacement of the male.

Certainly the suffragettes of day before yesterday, who can still be seen in old newsreels, looking ridiculous, could never have dreamed of a more rapid transformation of customs and laws.

Is it chance that this is the time when science is succeeding in artificial insemination, that it is on the point of being able to preserve sperm indefinitely, and that we are in sight of the "test-tube baby"?

It is not *because* of the new emergence (or aggressiveness) of the female element that scientists are carrying on research in this direction. It is the result of other research of a purely biological order. Chance, then, in that area.

But don't things happen as if . . .

As if humanity, foreseeing the more or less imminent reign of the female, is arranging things in such a way as to make this reign possible and absolute?

Wouldn't that be funny?

Some tribes in the distant past of the world, and even some today in a few remote places, have known such a state. Who knows whether at the beginning of human life . . .

But why, suddenly, has man, in two or three decades, abandoned the prerogatives that he formerly held so fiercely?

For it seems to me not only that he has abandoned them, but that it is he who cedes ground before being attacked.

To put it another way, woman isn't taking over occupied territory but is simply occupying a place that has been vacated.

Curious and amusing.

Especially since this development runs parallel to what is happening among the races: some, all-powerful yesterday, are inviting those who were then considered inferior to pick up the torch.

All this is very good, since it *is*. And it is, perhaps more than the atomic bomb and flights into space, the major characteristic of our era.

Re—for I have the impression that I've already set down similar re-flections once or twice. Yesterday went to Béthusy School, where Johnny was in a play with his schoolmates, both boys and girls.

Found there some of the same atmosphere as in schools in the United States where the child feels completely at home, where constraint is at a minimum. What struck me was the freedom in relationships between boys and girls.

When I was in school, the idea of coeducation was thought monstrous. To such an extent that our relations with little girls were very distant. Only country children and what were then called children of the people, the "street kids" as my mother used to say, had easy access to precocious sexual relationships.

Johnny, who makes no secret of it, has already had some super-ficial experiences. Marc, whose puberty was later, nevertheless began at around fourteen. And from sixteen on, he lived in a world in which sexual acts were not taken too seriously.

What strikes me is that in spite of that, young people, those young girls who know neither continence nor the mystery of sex-uality, are scarcely less sentimental than we were.

People talk about their cynicism, their disenchantment, when this last word in particular would better suit the snobbism of the end of the last century and the beginning of this one. Couples form . . . and break up. They know passion, jealousy, tender-ness. . . .

In short, I don't see anything basically different, and this amazes me, for doesn't it prove that love is probably rooted in our nature? They get married so young. They set up housekeep-ing. They live the best they can, side by side.

Raised in another period, I have a deep innate need for "exclu-sivity," not just in the present but in the past of the woman. This need, in man, existed for centuries if not thousands of years, and feminine virginity was almost an institution.

Today it has no more importance. It does not seem that men suffer from it. And woman?

Never mind. This is another subject that I don't want to get into, noting only that so-called modern life, sexual familiarity, has changed nothing in love, and that the couple, up to the present, anyway, remains the basic cell.

This seems to contradict what I wrote yesterday, but I can't help it.

I'd like very much to go back to school! . . .

/*Thursday, 25th*

I'm often reproached for my pessimism about human nature and its limitations. God knows, however, that I always give a man a chance, that I always see him first with sympathy, even enthusiasm.

I've spoken here of a doctor, a professor on the Faculty, whom I had alone here in my study, of our exchange of looks, of a sort of immediate and almost accomplicelike understanding.

He came yesterday. He is writing a book of memoirs. I soon saw that beneath the surface he harbored certain resentments he wanted to air, certain more or less conscious selfish motives and small vanities which I would have preferred not to know about. The man is no less sympathetic to me. I am tempted to add: on the contrary. However, someday I would wish not to be disappointed, to like and admire one hundred per cent! . . .

Have I spoken of those other doctors, mostly pediatricians, at our last party? One of them struck me by the intensity of his curiosity about human nature, by the enthusiasm he brought to understanding it. I see him again, going from group to group, listening avidly, and from the little he said I understood that of all of them, he was the most up-to-date on all the latest works in the medical field, including those only remotely connected with his specialty.

Why did I have the impression that he had some secret which gave him a tragic look?

Yesterday I learned that, while still a student, he was caught stealing—small thefts—sometimes bars of chocolate from newspaper kiosks. He is a true kleptomaniac, a clinical case.

He was treated as such. All the same, after a few years, he had to move to another city. And in the one where he presently lives, he has relapsed. He does not steal valuable objects. It is the act that is important. He knows it, and cannot cure himself.

For two years, though, he has not been caught. Has he got control of himself? If so, is he like a reformed alcoholic who knows that a single drink could plunge him back into disaster?

Now I understand better why his look struck me, and his bashful allusions to certain of my characters.

I'll probably see him again. Will I be disappointed again? Or must I repeat to myself—only theoretically!—that it's wrong of me to give every man, each man, the advantage of a prejudice in his favor?

Good day, aside from that. Especially with D. "It is not good that the man should be alone." And I never feel that I am alone for an instant.

Tomorrow, Pierre's second birthday. He is waiting for his cake with two candles with smiling and slightly greedy impatience.

/Saturday, June 3rd
10:30 in the morning

Terrible panic. I would like to begin a novel this afternoon. I've been getting ready for it for two weeks. The last ten days I've lived with my characters, in their ambiance. I've just sharpened my four dozen new pencils and my hand is trembling so that I've taken a half-tablet of belladénal.

Will I make it? I'll know this afternoon. For the moment I'm in a panic, and as usual I am tempted to put it off until later, or else not to write it at all, or make do with a restful Maigret.

I'm going out for my traditional walk, and when I get back I'll know a little more. It's a gray day, almost cold. Kennedy is going

to Vienna, where he is to meet Khrushchev. It's very important to
world peace, but I say f . . . it!

Novel finished.
I re-enter life.

Saturday, celebrated the end of the novel with D. with loving
and passionate fireworks. It is marvelous to find the wife and the
female in the same woman. And the pal, because, as usual, in the
night club where we went I took the telephone numbers of three
performers. Four, to be exact. Which embarrasses me.

Because I don't really want them that much. I shall go to see
them to set my mind at rest, so as not to be left with the itch of
desire. I shall enjoy it much less than with my wife. Still, a necessary hygienic measure. In this way dreams and vague urges are
purged which I believe poison most marriages. Perhaps I shall
telephone No. 1 soon. I have to push myself to do it.

I am being given, I am obliged to accept, a literary award, at
fifty-eight! And I can't refuse. It carries no prestige, since it is unknown, and no doubt it was specially created for me. This one is
given septennially by the province of Liège, which has had many
interesting or illustrious (?) men, but never a novelist. I am
obliged to accept. As I was obliged to accept a seat in the Academy of Languages, etc., etc. And the decorations that have twice
unexpectedly been bestowed on me.

So, later, they will be able to say—they will say—that I was a
worthy citizen who . . . and that . . .

What to do? Refuse? So lend importance to what has none?

More touching is the idea of the city of Liège giving my name to the public library in my neighborhood. I shall attend the opening ceremony. Until the age of eighteen, all my reading was in public libraries, and I feel great gratitude to them.

If someday my name should be given to a street in my native city, let it not be the Rue Pasteur where I spent my childhood years, but the Place du Congrès nearby, where I played my first games. It is a square where modest people live, far from the center of town, and I spent wonderful hours there. I do not wish for it.

6 o'clock in the afternoon

Went. Didn't enjoy it. Odd idea to inoculate myself in this way against future urges!

Last Saturday at this time I was triumphant over finishing my book. I've had a happy week.

Today, battered, discouraged. We had a fierce fight over nothing, over a misunderstanding, D. and I. She too is miserable and I can do nothing but be quiet and wait. It is one thing to understand mankind and another to understand those near to one. It seems that at some point I failed miserably. On only one point, it is true, as if there always had to be a spot of shadow in the picture, no matter what. Poor us!

/June 20, 1961

Calm, sweet, reassuring day yesterday, in perfect harmony with D. This afternoon I hope to begin the revision of *La Porte,* but so far this morning I feel quite lazy. Weather beautiful and warm.

Last night, going off to sleep, a rather absurd idea came to me. It is quite unlikely that I shall be remembered in the future as what is called a great writer. I know the value of my contribution, my limits, which are of the modest sort. However, anything is possible. It is just this possibility that troubles me.

I remembered a sentence of Talleyrand's, I believe, but which I'm not going to take the trouble to look up. In substance: "Nations would be terrified if they knew by what small men they are ruled. . . ."

Isn't what is true in politics also true in other areas? Suppose that I should be classed among the great writers someday: would they realize what a small man I am, with all the weaknesses, all the temptations, all the ridiculousness of which those who make up the crowd, the common man, imagine that others are exempt from?

Happily, the prospect is improbable. I should have the feeling of a hoax.

I have known two men who believed themselves or knew themselves to be great men, behaved as such, without shame: Anatole France and André Gide.

What struck me about them was the care they exerted to appear as they were thought to be. They lived for their image—and not their own lives. This greatly disillusioned me at the time, and I wasn't surprised to see their stature diminish later.

/June 23rd

Revision of *La Porte* finished in four days. I go from the heights to the depths. Finally I no longer know. I'll begin at once to live in the next novel, in the hope of succeeding at something, of attaining I don't know what.

In the meantime, I'm going to pick up D. and buy some kitchen chairs.

304

Sunday! A real one, as in a picture book. The first of the summer. Warm, bright, rumbling with the departure of the *Tour de France* for Rouen. I feel calm, relaxed, breathing in the small joys of a family Sunday, and I feel very close to everyone, understand everyone.

Have no desire to write in this notebook. I do it as a duty. It would be unfair not to put down anything but troubled or anxious days.

But I'm afraid I see a certain tendency in myself to note these moments especially. Happy hours, hours of complete harmony, it seems enough to live them and there is no temptation to set them down in a notebook. With the ultimate result that this would be a very unfaithful mirror, showing nothing but shadows.

Many tender thoughts of D. I marvel at this conscientiousness that keeps her going from the time she gets up, this need for perfection which sometimes irritates me but at other times, like today, I understand better.

Tonight she got up to write down things to be done in the house during our vacation. As for me, sometimes, in an otherwise empty day, the fact of being obliged to do an errand in town is enough to darken my mood.

She has neither idle days nor idle hours. She is like the spring in a mechanism that becomes more and more complicated and eats away at her from morning to night.

It is easy to tell oneself that this is her own need. How much effort, great and small, humanity patiently expends, knowing that in the end . . . And not only man, but all of nature, everything that lives; no doubt some time or other science will tell us that · this is what we owe our life to.

An immense and marvelous machine that has run this way since . . . must one count by billions of years? . . . Or even more? . . .

To go where?

I don't find that an anguishing question—not today—and I am

content to marvel, to be. I and mine. This little cell among all the other little cells that gravitate like ours in the infinity of time and space.

At noon, Sunday dinner. Roast beef, as in that other little cell where I spent my childhood, as in the cell in Ottawa, with other parents, other brothers and sisters, where D. spent hers.

A new whole, made with pieces of other wholes, which in turn . . .

This could be entitled "You can't have everything."

When I was very young, like my son Johnny, I had a passion for beautiful paper, beautiful printing, handsome layouts, editions that were not vulgarly elaborate but of a simple and noble design. (From the time I was fifteen to nineteen the greater part of my pocket money went to booksellers, and later, at about twenty-one or twenty-two, in Paris, I sold my first editions of Balzac, Hugo, Bourdaloue, etc., bought during my adolescence and lived off the proceeds. . . .)

Having become a novelist, one might think I could have had the pleasure of seeing my own works well printed. Isn't it paradoxical that for the launching of Maigret, I initiated the six-franc book (the usual book was then sold for twelve francs), badly printed, on bad paper that yellowed in a year?

The public I then reached, the public I wanted to reach, the largest possible, I've since kept, so that I am doomed to see my books come out in rather cheap form.

Yesterday I was brought two beautiful works, handsomely designed and produced. But they are printed in editions of one or two thousand which won't be read, but will stay on library shelves. I'm not complaining. I've had what I wanted. But all the same, sometimes I'd like . . .

But I certainly would have been indignant if at sixteen someone had told me on what paper and how I would be printed.

The children are playing in the garden. Birds are flying through the fountain to cool off. Below me, I hear D. dictating.[1]

I'm going to read one of these books in the coolness of my study, books so carefully designed as to make me feel ashamed.

/*June 28th*

Strange! I've never written about the war of 1939 (except *Le Clan des Ostendais*, which is rather special). Now, just two months ago, I wrote *Le Train*, which plunged me back into the atmosphere of the exodus. The novel is still being serialized and isn't even in the bookstores yet when here we are, storing provisions again as we did in 1914 and 1939. This time on the advice of the Swiss government, which wants to avoid panic buying.

Same lists as before: noodles, oil, sugar, tea, coffee, soap. . . . I'm adding razor blades and nails because I remember the difficulty in finding the smallest nail around 1942! And thread! This afternoon I went to buy tin boxes, like biscuit boxes. They are already hard to find.

So history repeats itself. Not to the end, I hope. Next week we leave for the mountains, and for the first time we shall take Pierre, who has never spent a night away from home. So he's going to rub elbows with the outside world, experience the comings and goings of a big hotel.

Preparing for our departure, D. is juggling with the household, furnace men, painters, carpet layers, cleaners. I don't understand how she keeps it all in her head. Not to mention the fact that the whole family needs summer clothing, staff vacations must be arranged, etc.

And here's the nuisance of supplies on top of all the rest! Which makes the other worries a little less urgent, a little less real. Suddenly we remember the basic needs, and the gasoline,

[1] Into a dictaphone, as she always does in the absence of secretaries.

the candles that must be thought of take on more importance than the refrigerator and our many conveniences.

In about 1944 I bought very dearly a cask of carbide that came in most handy when the electricity was cut off in the Vendée.

A story comes back to me which I've never told. Right from the beginning of the war I dreamed of getting back to the free zone. Not out of patriotism. More because the atmosphere of occupation was stifling to me. Because Marc was then a baby, and because of my duties at the reception center, I could not leave at once, and later it became very difficult.

One day I met a friend whose activities I had never exactly known. Married to an Englishwoman, he went back and forth between Berlin and Madrid by car, provided with all the passes in the world, and I was told that he had as easy access to Hitler as to the English and American ambassadors in Spain. I don't know what became of him.

So I mentioned to him my wish to go to the free zone and he promised me a pass for my car. I laid in supplies of gasoline, liter by liter, in exchange for butter. As there were no shortages in the Vendée, I laid in a ham, butter in jars, rice, etc., etc. My car not being large enough to hold all this, from a garage owner in Fontenay-le-Comte I rented—I swear this is true—the truck used to carry the dead from one city to another.

Weeks later, my friend, unable to obtain my pass, lent me the license plate of his own car for a week, and I had it affixed on mine.

We disinfected the truck-hearse. We spent the night loading it. We decided to leave at six in the morning.

At six o'clock I started the engine, and while awaiting the others I turned on the radio.

It was to learn that the Germans had just entered the free zone that very night. There was no longer any reason for leaving.

I emptied the truck, the car . . . and, of course, returned to my friend his magic plate, which had been of no use to me.

This sounds like fiction, or edited fact. All the details are true, however.

The people of Fontenay wondered why I hadn't left. To exchange occupation for occupation . . .

Later, after the Liberation, I left for the United States, where I stayed more than ten years, and where I was to meet my wife.

/*June 30, 1961*

I have so much hatred—or rather distrust—for the word "author," for the telling phrase, for slowly simmered ideas that have to be phrased "just right," that for a full week I've been ashamed of myself.

For the first time in one of my novels I used a phrase of this kind, not a very original one, and I haven't had the courage to cut it. I hesitated. I thought of it in bed.

While the manuscript was being photostated, I very nearly went down in order to cut the precious phrase. Now the text has gone to the publisher and I'm still bothered. What is it? A small thing, really. In an argument between a husband and wife, a half-sentence saying approximately: working people rarely worry beyond their immediate chores.

That's all. I left it. I hold it against myself, because it is an intervention by the author, it's intruding an idea that isn't worth expressing. I promise myself to cut it when I receive the proofs for the last corrections. I would have made a terrible playwright.

So I'm not exempt, as I'd like to be, from a certain smugness, and in a short text that I wrote for a radio broadcast, for I don't know which friend's anniversary, I put down a sentence that I had the weakness to believe important:

"The only thing that life has taught me, as it has taught so many others, is that man is worth much more than he thinks, whether of others or of himself."

That doesn't amount to much, one way or the other! But it's better to write a novel without gems from the author or pseudo-philosophical thoughts!

A beautiful day, luminous and warm. Last night, a fairy-tale hour. We are getting ready for the holiday. D. is on edge. In a month all this will have disappeared into the past.

One might say we use our time to manufacture memories as if only the present didn't count. Always horrified by the importance we attach to the past and the future and the slight importance we give the present.

Wonder if it exists. I don't believe I'm far off in saying that scientifically, biologically, the answer is no.

An hour later—went to play with Pierre and Marie-Jo in the garden. And suddenly, because of what I wrote just now, something struck me. I don't know yet if there's truth in it or not. In my popular novels, then in the first Maigrets, and even in my first nondetective novels, I almost always wrote in the present.

Little by little I began to use the past (for which I have been much reproached) and only later was it called flashback.

But it wasn't planned on my part. It didn't help the story, which was only further complicated by it, quite the contrary. What I suddenly ask myself is if I didn't use this device almost instinctively, out of intuition, feeling that the only way to give weight to an hour or an event was to give it through a memory, that is to say by means of the past.

In the present, it remained insubstantial, incomplete. Each thing takes on its real life only with recall, the unconscious filter of memory.

In any case, it never was a device on my part, a method. This is the first time I've thought about it this way and that I've found a justification for what was purely instinctive.

/July 3rd

A *Tour de France* Sunday. Yesterday read a book by Astier de la Vigerie: *Sept Fois Sept Jours*. Glad it didn't come out before I wrote *Le Train*. However, it isn't a novel. Astier is more preoccupied with politics.

But, as in *Le Train*, I find in it a sort of relief at the moment of downfall, as if in losing a life that weighed on him, or for which he no longer had any taste, he discovered a new reality, his own, at the same time as objective reality.

Like my character in *Le Train*, like everybody, no doubt, his receptivity to the external world is much greater in difficult or tragic moments.

Out of this very simple and rather trite idea, what is called my atmosphere was born. What is true in time of war, in mass catastrophe, is true at a personal level, of drama which does not affect millions of men.

I liked the book very much. I shall see d'Astier, who wants to see me too. We have certain positions in common, including our reaction when the war was over and we hoped things would change, were sure of it, and then we saw the world go back to its egoistic concerns.

In any case this book once again showed me the dangers of reading for the novelist. If I had read this book six months earlier, I might not have written *Le Train*, or I would have written it differently, afraid to follow another's path.

The two books are as different as possible, one about an ordinary, mediocre man to whom almost nothing happens and who allows himself to be carried along by the current, the other about a man of action who is one of the people who started the Resistance.

Curious how, in the end, they aren't so far from each other.

And now, the papers.

D. has to clear away her mail before beginning the packing and she dictates ceaselessly. I'm doing nothing.

I enjoy playing golf and I've already got out my clubs and have been trying them out in the garden.

Hemingway died yesterday. I suppose he committed suicide because he was ill. I feel upset by it. I never met him. I read little of him. Nevertheless he was one of those with whom I felt a bond.

I keep a rather curious material memory of him. When I moved to Lakeville, my lawyer was also the lawyer of the first or second Mrs. Hemingway. He gave me one of my novels bearing the date 1934, on the first page of which Hemingway had written his name and address. And it was at about that period that I was reading him.

D. finished her work last night, or rather tonight, and this morning she is already in town doing errands. I'm hanging around the house waiting to leave. It's very hot. This morning Pierre has his first girl friend, his own age or a little younger, the daughter of a temporary housekeeper.

Since she is Italian, he uses the few Spanish words he has learned at meals, where we are waited on by a Spanish maid. He is already putting on protective airs. To see them, one would call them a couple, a little female and a young male.

This morning at eight o'clock it was announced again that Louis-Ferdinand Céline was gravely ill. The same radio station announced at eight thirty that he died on Sunday and that he was buried this morning.

One might say that his career ran in every way counter to that of Hemingway. I wonder which of the two will endure—unless both of them do. I never met Céline either. I know very few of my colleagues, and those I do know I know by chance rather than by choice.

But chance has it that the ones who become more or less

friends aren't always the ones I admire most. I say more or less because I have no real friends. I have a wife. I think you have to choose. Or rather that one is a friend type or a couple type. One can also, like Céline, be a solitary type, I think.

Can't these be recognized by a certain tone in their work? Don't they give themselves to it more than the others, more obstinately, in any case? Always, it seems to me, with a note of bitterness, which hurts me. If I often happen to admire the works of these solitaries—in all the arts, past as well as present—still I never feel on equal footing with them.

/*Same day, 3* A.M.

Among the stupid things the papers publish on the (probable) suicide of Hemingway there is one that strikes me. Almost everybody considers this end as almost predestined. Given the writer's temperament, he must have reacted this way to a threat of slow death, progressive decline.

But less than a year ago, another writer, Blaise Cendrars, died, whose character and myth rather resembled Hemingway's. Cendrars too traveled all over the world looking·for adventure, he too celebrated the brutal joys and fearless male nobility in his books.

However, he chose an opposite solution. Far from committing suicide, he lived for several years, ill, paralyzed, struggling against his disease with tenacity, and they say (?) that he refused all medications which could have lessened his suffering in order to remain lucid in spite of everything. I believe it. It would be like him. For I knew him well.

Today I'm thinking a good deal about those two men with parallel lives and different ends.

It's a lesson for the psychologist. A given man, with a given character, in given circumstances, does not necessarily react according to a given logic.

Unless there is a Hemingway logic and a Cendrars logic applying to each in the same circumstances.

As to knowing which of them chose the easier solution . . .

Bürgenstock. So this is holiday homework, almost in mid-holiday. We have been here ten days with the three children (first time Pierre has been away from home). From the first day, as we did last year in Venice, we adopted a routine nearly as rigid as the one at home.

Wherever we are, D. and I, we keep to a schedule, even for three days, as recently in Berne; we establish habits that we follow almost religiously. I think it originates with me. However, I've always envied people who live impulsively.

Swimming pool in the morning (except for the past three days. It rained too much and the water was cold). A few games of ping-pong with the children and golf in the afternoon. Two tea dances. At nine in the evening we are in our suite.

Relaxed. Real holiday mood. We haven't spoken to anyone, made any acquaintances.

The formal atmosphere of a big hotel in the mountains doesn't bother me. I don't feel any need to chat with people. On the contrary. It may be laziness.

At twenty, I went to night clubs, and all the places where people play, to observe them. I was looking for what I called the "common denominator." I pretended that men could be known better by seeing them at play than at their everyday occupations.

I still think so. My neighbors here, as in Venice and elsewhere, are almost all important people in one field or another, and their employees must tremble before them. Here, they play with a little ball, stammer in front of their tennis, or golf, or swimming teachers.

I've always believed, too, that one knows someone only after

314

seeing him naked. I have gone to bed with women not because I desired them but so as to see them naked, with the little flaws in their skins, their cracks, their bulges, their faces bare of make-up.

It isn't a need to debase, to depoeticize. On the contrary! A need for the real, a contact with the real person. One knows a man better after having seen him make love.

It's not so much a matter of taste that we stay in these "palaces," and I often envy those who go to the more simple inns. I'd prefer to meet ordinary people without fuss, and that's why I like bistrots so much.

But I confess my hatred for the WC at the end of the hall, the bathroom on the landing, etc. And the telephone facilities, the mail, the service, are indispensable to us.

I regret it for my children, who consider it quite natural to have service at their disposal whether at home or traveling, and I must bite my tongue not to make the ridiculous remark:

"When I was your age . . ."

It isn't their fault, but mine. Here we are together with them from morning to night, and I am discovering many things. I would like to be perfect and never irritated, and above all not to go against my own principles, as happens to me all the time.

Because of the framework of conventions, I've turned out little conformists in spite of myself. Out of fear of annoying the neighbors, shocking them, etc.

The Americans have found a solution to this problem. The richest of them take their vacations in what they call camps, log cabins out in the wilds, far from any facilities, where they do their own cooking and housework.

This is the greatest luxury to them, to be without telephones, without mail, and the *ne plus ultra* is to find a spot by one of the Canadian lakes which can be reached only by helicopter.

Impossible here. It is true that there are bathrooms and every comfort in these camps. In New England, however, a few miles from Boston, some of them spend their summers in bungalows with neither running water nor electricity. Would I be able to do it? Or my children?

Another of my ideas that have never changed, that I've had since adolescence: A man can be content with the necessary, with the indispensable, and be almost happy. But when one gets into the realm of the superfluous, luxury or near luxury, there are no limits, therefore no satiety, no satisfaction.

And we are in a period when the superfluous has become necessary to everyone, or almost. Doesn't this explain many of the anxieties that we hear so much about, especially in the most highly developed countries, and even certain illnesses—not just mental ones?

Enough! We were to spend the day on the lake but the rain stopped us, and as in Lausanne or elsewhere I drove D. to the hairdresser. Just now it's Johnny's turn. Waiting for him, ping-pong. I too play with little balls, and it relaxes me, like playing with a new pair of breasts.

/July 18th

A significant detail comes back to me as I look through press clippings, which I always find more or less irritating. Someone who saw these notebooks (didn't read them—*saw* them—and only because he wanted to know my handwriting) wrote in effect:

"Simenon only writes on one side of the page in the notebooks he keeps, which is revealing."

Revealing of what? Does he see in it an intention of publication, texts to be sent for composition being written only on one side of the page? It's much simpler than that. If I only write on the recto, it's because in a notebook it is uncomfortable to write on the verso because of the bulge it forms, and besides it is unpleasant to see the writing through the transparency of the preceding page. What use is there in explaining such natural things to a journalist?

End of vacation tomorrow. For three weeks we have lived the formal life of big hotels. Bath. Luncheon. Golf, sometimes ping-pong with the children. Bowling. In the evening, half an hour of dancing with Marie-Jo; one evening, hours of dancing with D. as if we were alone in the world.

After a week, decided to take golf lessons again. For two weeks I was the middle-aged gentleman whom a pro tried in vain to teach the natural movements of childhood, and whom he encouraged with positive tenderness.

There must have been several millions of us in the world at the same moment, people of my age or older, who were thus relearning some game with humility: golf, tennis, swimming, riding (under the interested eye of a "monitor").

Some of these pupils are famous or important people feared by thousands of clerks and workers. Others have risked ruin in the casinos, or have been ruined, by watching a little ball seeking its hole. 7? 21? 8? Good luck or bad.

A whole industry, perhaps the most important in the world, has been built on this need for *play* in every sense: need to recover the movements of the child or the African native's faith in luck. No doubt it's a good thing, a real need.

Friday I shall be at home in my study. I promise myself to continue to play golf. That was good for me. I have never felt so well. I know that it will take a lot of will power for me to continue, to believe in it, to make it the important hour of my day. However . . .

/Sunday, July 30th

Home! Since Friday. For the first time a bit awkward around the house. Pulling the wrong drawer, for instance. And not knowing just how to fill time. Realize that basically the schedule was and is going to be as artificial here as there, with the difference that here it is considered important, as "work." Believe I found a subject for a novel yesterday, a Maigret, but don't want to hurry myself and first want to play a few games of golf, for discipline and health. Almost to prolong my holiday. This morning haven't followed the Sunday schedule but walked in the Morges park where at one end campers are crammed together, more crowded on top of each other than in Paris apartments. And since they all have radios, and some television . . . But didn't we do the same?

/*Thursday, August 3, 1961*

For several weeks little desire—and again today—to write in this notebook. I don't think this has only to do with the holiday mood which I've been in for the first time in years.

For about two years, if my health hasn't been really bad, I've often felt tired and especially dizzy, more exactly, I've had dizzy spells (Ménière) for which I was treated. These discomforts suddenly disappeared almost at the moment when I was writing *Le Train*. All at once I recovered a taste for physical life, for exercise, and my study stopped being a sort of refuge.

What connection with these notebooks? Did I write here only when I felt under par, threatened? I don't know. Diagnosis is delicate. On the other hand, I have never had such an urge to work, to write. Three novels by the first of July, and I itch to get into another.

So there is a marked difference between my need to write my books and the need to write in these notebooks. On the one hand, better health makes me write more. On the other, this improvement almost takes away the need to write.

This is the truth today, but what will be the truth tomorrow?

Golf yesterday. Golf the day before. Golf this afternoon with D. I'm enjoying it. Even if I play badly.

I have the impression that we're very much on the wrong track in our explanations of bacteria, microbes, viruses, etc. (including the latest theories on interferon) and that someday quite soon all this rubbish will seem ridiculous.

On that day, will cancer seem no more frightening than tuberculosis and syphilis have become?

Day before yesterday my wife cleaned my pipes; yesterday, my typewriter. In the evening I carefully arranged my accessories in my study, as a circus acrobat takes care of his gear and checks it, as a magician fills the pockets of his suit.

This morning at six o'clock, for the hundred and eightieth time approximately—people find this figure enormous; it seems ridiculous to me when I think that I am fifty-eight and have done nothing else in my life!—this morning, I repeat, I went down to do my number.

Coffee. "Do not disturb" on both doors, etc. An hour afterwards, with five pages written, I stepped off the runway. It's by design I've used these circus and music-hall terms. I was wrong, it would seem, in wanting to write this novel somewhat as a performance.

I've already written three this year. I dreamed of writing five or six, as I used to, and, in my mind, it was a way of proclaiming that I'm not getting old, that I'm still in good form. (At the same age that I am today, Chevalier, as if in defiance, gave a solo performance for an hour and a half.) I had all the best reasons for not beginning this novel. Holidays, first of all, the children's, everybody's, the atmosphere of vacation to which I am not immune, telephone calls, unexpected visits from friends. Then, perhaps above all, a mad desire to play golf until I'm sick of it, to spend myself physically, since this was so good for me in Bürgenstock. I wanted to write in spite of everything, to get five or six done by the end of the year, and it's too bad about me.

I forgot Berlin, the Berlin crisis as they say, and the threats of international conflict. I admit that after two wars, two occupations, twenty threats of universal explosion, this reason was not uppermost in my mind, though to listen to the radio and television one necessarily has a doomed feeling of uneasiness and unimportance.

Still, I wrote *Il Pleut, Bergère* just as war was declared in 1939 to prove to myself that life goes on. It went on. Not for everyone, alas!

Basically, threats of catastrophe rather stimulate me to write—as bombardments help me sleep—as a way of detachment, because personal life must go on.

Strange that I could detach myself from catastrophe but vacation should affect me.

It was a Maigret, but a Maigret that could have been a very short novel. I'll probably return to the subject when it has cooled off.

I think I know the truth of this failure. D. recently turned up some stories written some twenty years ago, and God knows why, probably because I forgot them, they had remained unpublished. I had the bad idea of rereading them, since people are always asking me for stories and novellas for newspapers and magazines and I can no longer write them. Question of wavelengths, as they say today. And for once the expression is right. I think too novelistically to write short stories any more.

Whatever it is, this reading disturbed me. I suddenly realized that like a painter I've had my "periods." And the period of these stories corresponds to the Fauve period of the painters I've known, Vlaminck, Derain, etc. I found an Impressionism, or more exactly an Expressionism, of which I'm no longer capable, a jumble in words, in sentences, in images, which suddenly discouraged me.

Do my painter friends, when they approach sixty, have the

same feeling as they arrive at a period which people call neoclassical? Did they take it for a weakness, a possible impotence, a lack of daring, a lack, certainly, of youth? I have Derain in particular in mind. Picasso is the only one of the group to have followed the opposite course, and I wonder if it isn't out of cleverness.

Anyway, my Maigret of this morning—*Maigret et l'Honnête Homme,* which I almost called *Maigret et l'Assassin Consciencieux*—suddenly seemed flat, heavy and slow, without sparkle.

I wasn't too upset, contrary to what usually happens in these cases. We went to play golf. I played badly. This afternoon I went to see some girls, without enjoyment. On the other hand, I had the pleasure of finding an Egyptian scarab that was missing from D.'s necklace, and I was happy about that.

So here I am at leisure for a time. Golf? I hope so. And above all, nothing intellectual. I have a bellyful of the intellectuality into which people—or the emptiness of life in my study—plunge me in spite of myself.

Do anything at all, but do something, and be done with this need to analyze once and for all.

Live quite simply. Like someone who isn't a novelist. Even, if possible, like an imbecile.

/Friday, August 25th

Golf every morning. Then more holidays until the children's are ended. Although D. and I scarcely speak on the links, each of us pursuing his little white ball, there are few places where I feel so close to her.

On this subject, a small—very small!—idea is going around in my head. It isn't the key to any serious problems, but I wonder if it wouldn't open certain doors.

Like everybody else, I've had successive, changing opinions about love, not only the love of the couple, but the love of children, friendship, even the kind of love that some devote to a collective or an idea, to the fatherland, for example, or a party, or a regiment.

I devoured Freud in 1923 or 1924, then his disciples, and I continue to read with great interest the works of Jung, who extended this notion of love to the tribe, even to the species.

And now I end by wondering if all that, romantic love, passionate love, sexual love, love of the child or of the mother, patriotism, etc., can't be traced back to one elementary idea, to a minute common denominator that could be expressed as follows: the essential, vital need of every human being, strong or weak, to rely on someone or something, to have confidence in a single being.

A single being! With certainty. Whom one doesn't doubt. And one is saved.

Mother, fiancée, lover, bride . . . For some the friend . . . And finally, if there is no person, a group or an idea: the regiment, the party, the fatherland.

Give me a place to stand and . . .

If it is true in physics, why shouldn't it be true in psychology?

What strikes me is that the deceived child and the deceived patriot, the duped lover and the duped partisan react in the same way, use the same terms to express their resentment, sometimes commit the same spectacular desperate acts.

. . . *on whom one can count* . . . a person or idea. I prefer the person to the idea and I prefer the female for the male, and for the female her male.

Happy is he . . . Happy is she . . .

Happy am I!

/Saturday, September 2nd

End of holiday. Two months of golf, with gritted teeth, as if my life depended on it and sometimes with the same panicky fear as when I start a novel. I went back to it passionately and this morning, having a last round before taking up again our usual life, I felt a kind of nostalgia.

I rarely give myself to any activity other than my literary activity in this way. On the one hand, it was a question of health. I rediscovered a physical life that I haven't enjoyed for a long time. On the other hand, and above all, I feel wonderfully happy with D. in a place where no one disturbs us and we stroll along side by side.

Now I go back to my study, where I have only been a visitor recently. I wonder if I'm going to be able to write again. For weeks, I've felt guilty. Feeling of *playing* instead of doing my work.

Surely and always this has to do with the fact that I was born among the common people and I learned that one must earn one's bread by the sweat of one's brow. However, if I were a civil servant, if I were Maigret, I would be retired.

Now I'm in a rush to reassure myself, to prove to myself that I can still write. I'm going to spend laborious hours and days until one or two chapters are written. There is rattling around in my head a Maigret that I tried to get on paper before, when I came back from Bürgenstock. Sometimes I'm tempted to choose another subject, sometimes it comes back to me insistently. I don't know yet what I'll do. First, it's important to put myself in a state of grace.

In any case, two good months, in spite of guilt. Weren't they, D.? Monday the children will be in school, the factory will be working full tilt on the ground floor, and I'll be doing my best here to go back to being a novelist. As if, really, that were any more important than hitting a little white ball and walking over the grass.

/Monday, September 11, 1961

Novel finished at nine forty-five. Unable to say if it's good or bad. In a hurry to reread it. Going to play golf first.

/Saturday, September 23, 1961

Suddenly an urge to speak of a lot of things here, to write at great length of things good and bad. Sweet and a little bitter. It will come tonight or tomorrow. I don't know.

Ten minutes later

Is it laziness or reticence? Each time I open this notebook I feel overcome with something like dizziness, and instead of writing quietly what I meant to write, I hedge, I leave it in a sort of shorthand.

For example, I wanted to tell in detail what has just happened to D. For more than two weeks, while I was writing my novel, then when we had our friend Sigaux here for three days, then during my revision, she was living a life that was removed from —though so close to!—mine.

I found her nervous, absent-minded. At a certain point I seriously thought that she found my novel bad (a simple Maigret) and didn't dare let me know. I kept telling myself that one day it would happen, that the spring would snap, that my sentences would no longer make any sound. In short, I was spying on her and I was worried. I even wondered if she wasn't beginning another depression like last year's.

Evening before last, she went down to put her office in order before we went to bed. She knew I was in a hurry to go to sleep.

But I heard her call on the extension, then, for more than twenty minutes, the green light on the telephone was lit.

I came close to feeling resentment. I remembered the telephone calls to our friends the Martinons when she was at her worst. I looked into my own heart. . . . Suddenly she signaled me to pick up the receiver. . . .

"I have just got *the best news of my life.* . . . Do come downstairs a moment."

I had guessed nothing. And suddenly I learned that for more than two weeks she had been keeping it from me that a doctor believed that Marc had pericarditis; all that time, unknown to me, deceiving me in order to make long-distance calls, she had had him get tests by professors and doctors in Paris, then in Cannes. Her last call, in response to a letter in code, was to a cardiologist in Cannes, who entirely reassured her.

Two years ago both of us lived through the same story with Pierre when his life was in danger. We almost sneaked him to Lyons, like thieves. We waited day after day. But there were two of us then, and we didn't have to hide anything from each other. But I was scarred by it for more than a year.

I have been the center of a conspiracy of silence, so much so that I speak of it now with a sort of detached stupor. I lived through a drama without knowing it. I didn't learn of it until the moment of the happy ending.

I knew that D. considered Marc as her son. I just now *felt* it. It has been her turn to be thoroughly shaken, and for two days now she has had a hard time recovering from the shock.

As for me, outside of a warm wave of tenderness, a curious sense of having remained offstage this way, of having known nothing, of having behaved the same as usual, of having suspected D. of heaven knows what when this conspiracy had only my peace of mind in view.

All that over a Maigret which, after all, may be no good. For I begin to have doubts. Or rather . . . But we are going out tonight, D. and I, and the rest will follow another time, if I can screw up the courage or if I still remember it—it concerns the "bitter" part announced in the inventory. I'm going upstairs to dress and we are going to a fashion show at the Hôtel Beau-Rivage, which may be fun.

Yesterday morning I promised: some sweet and a little bitter. I've written the sweet, though perhaps unable to express all the tenderness I feel.

The rest is still more hazardous, for if I don't give each word its exact weight, if I don't encompass my thought with precision, I risk falling into the grotesque or the melodramatic.

Also, this is not a matter of thoughts, properly speaking, but of vague ideas, barely formed sentiments which come to me from time to time—quite often in these last months—and if I finally speak of them here, it's so that the children—my own, of course —will one day learn why I am occasionally more irritable with them than I would like.

In a few months I shall be fifty-nine, nearly sixty. I feel in good physical form, especially since I've taken up golf again—and intellectually, too, insofar as I've ever been in any intellectual form at all.

Always when Maigret announces his retirement for three years hence—because he is fifty-two and retirement age for a police chief is fifty-five—I myself feel that I also want to retire.

Not to stop working, though. Not to stop writing. I have written for more than forty years. At the beginning, when I wrote popular novels for money, I turned out eighty pages a day. Then I wrote both as a job and for pleasure. Then, finally, for myself, out of personal necessity. I've often said so.

Only my novels are not all there is. Little by little, something more and more important, something almost obsessive, has been

326

engrafted onto these, which is a full-time occupation for my wife and two secretaries. At Echandens we have a whole floor of offices, and that's not too much.

D. takes care of all this, of course, but this business still dominates our life, our schedule, our comings and goings, etc. I sometimes say to myself that I have reached the age when a man who has worked hard finally has the right to live for himself, in his own way, according to his own tastes. . . .

Then, really, I have a more or less vague wish to retire. For example, I should like to live in the real country, grow apples, plums, tend espaliers, have chickens, etc. I've had them before. I quickly had enough of them. It is probable that I'd have enough of them as quickly again. . . . I should like . . . to get away from the Simenon business, from the mail, from all the exploitation of my work. And it's impossible.

We've worked a lot. First I, then my wife, especially she, to escape from the author's being exploited by publishers. Result: everything is negotiated from here, translations, radio, movie rights, serial rights, television . . . We are constantly answering letters. And the work cannot be done from some other place. It would be giving up a struggle when we have won it, for the only way would be either to take on an agent, who would spoil everything, or to sell rights to publishers. . . .

I'm trying to follow my thought, and I see that it is twofold, that what I have just said is true, but that perhaps it begs the question. When I speak—smiling, I assure you, children—of retiring from business, I also have in mind another aspect of my professional life. To speak frankly, I am not only a writer—I am not so much a writer, perhaps—as a kind of star.

It is the star that the magazines and papers talk about most, and not about the content of my books. If I hadn't written nearly two hundred, if there were no star performance, no doubt I would be left in obscurity.

Is that what I'm tired of? Certainly, in part. And of writing at my determined, obsessive pace, which is, however, my very own.

I should like: in a simple house, after cultivating my garden, to write, by hand, a few pages now and then without worrying about whether they would become a novel.

Or rather, for some years I have wanted to write a long novel with no beginning or end. . . . I'll never do it. If I were in the house of which I've just written, I'd soon hire a gardener, enlarge the premises, and soon we would have a staff of ten and four cars again. . . .

There is nothing serious in all that, a dream that everyone has, I think, when turning sixty?

Playing golf almost every day, I realize one of these dreams. I do it guiltily, to be sure, as if I were stealing time. I should like . . . everything and nothing!

At bottom, at the very bottom, I wonder if the truth isn't that I really don't much believe in my work any more. But it isn't a question of pride. If it isn't important, if it isn't worth the trouble, what's the point of having adapted my whole life to it, and continuing to do so?

For the rhythm of the house, the life of my children, everything around us depends on my work. It produces articles—mostly about our life, even more than about my books—some sympathizing books, letters from readers, above all from spongers.

It furnishes us with a great deal of comfort, but with a little flair the same amount of industry in any other business or enterprise would have made us richer still. If my work doesn't exist, I have created a market of fools. And it is just this question that I ask myself more and more often.

For a year, when I had the dizzy spells, I thought about stopping working, writing, because of my health, and this wasn't too tragic because I considered myself something of an invalid.

Today, when I feel in good shape, I sometimes say to myself that if I were to stop writing, except for myself . . .

For myself! An expression I was already using at sixteen, when I was a young reporter. To write for myself, that is to say regardless of all the rules, all the forms, all idea of publication. Would I really write? Without wanting to, without knowing it, wouldn't I come back to the same old treadmill on which, in spite of myself,

I grind out my works, like a craftsman who repeats the same movement over and over?

Discouragement? No. Disappointment? Perhaps a little. Much has been given me, but little of what I hoped for. Next month I shall write another novel along the same lines, mine, always trying to push on a littler further.

I'm the one who chose this way, because I believed in it. Basically I still do. But this simplicity, this starkness, this willful absence of originality, of brio, of obvious "art," how can I expect people to understand it?

Perhaps someday I'll tear up these two pages. I should like to have my children read them, however, for they will then forgive me certain moments of ill-temper that are not characteristic of me, certain impatient reactions that make me ashamed. Isn't it ridiculous at my age, when I'm supposed to be a man, to play the frustrated writer and threaten to give it all up?

Retire! I know I never will, or rather I hope not, for a grave threat to my health is the only thing that could force me. Accepting this, from time to time, alone in my corner, I grumble, like Maigret, and I dream of his little house in Meung-sur-Loire, of his strawberry plants, his espaliered apples, his chickens on the manure heap, and his fishing pole.

Forgive me, D., you who carry the weight of the "Simenon business" on your shoulders (plus the "Simenon family"!), this moment of defeat or of romantic reverie. Do you remember? At Bradenton Beach there was no office. We went fishing together, any time, and we went swimming naked at midnight in the Gulf of Mexico. . . . No office? I forget the telephone calls to London, Paris, the money worries. . . . Come on! I'm going down to see you and we'll play Bradenton Beach in the garden. With three children around us, who give me so much joy.

And too bad if in twenty years, in thirty, my novels are moldering in attics. Too bad if people are beginning to consider me a phenomenon from the era between the two wars, a sort of freakish excrescence of literature.

Let's go on! Tomorrow, in two weeks or a month, I won't think about it any more. Above all, when you read these pages, understand the meaning of the words, try to grasp the nuances, say to yourself that all this is insubstantial, fleeting, and that I'm already looking back at it with a smile. Besides, I never have stopped smiling, for, as you know, I never take myself too seriously.

Courage!

5 o'clock

I just took a walk in the garden with D. and hit a few golf balls. Actually, this week I've revised my last Maigret in three days. Is that what depressed me? No, it goes back further. But it's true that I didn't feel the spark in revising.

It seemed pallid to me, a little flat. The next day I wrote a song in one morning, a bit as at Cannes, where, in an hour, I wrote a ballet, *La Chambre,* for Roland Petit.

This time it was putting words to the music the B.B.C. is using as a theme for the Maigret series. It was great fun doing it. I'm waiting impatiently to know if it's all right, for I'm quite ignorant about such things.

At any rate, I spent an enjoyable morning. Maybe I'm wrong to keep away from everything that isn't my own work, meaning my novels, with the result that I feed too much on myself. Is this true? I no longer know, for I'm less and less interested in anything that isn't that work, and above all in anything that isn't *us*. Shall I end up by living only for us? It's not impossible. For my next novel I'll try to break the pattern, writing by hand, regardless of the time, letting D. type my text instead of doing it myself.

This was done for *Le Fils* because I was convalescent. It's a bit as if I were trying to escape, without knowing precisely from what: from rules I set myself, or rather habits which have almost unconsciously become rules, and which sometimes make me fearful or obsess me.

Oh, to hell with it!

Fortunately, I don't reread myself, I have a horror of rereading myself, even more so this notebook. With what joy would I tear out the two pages from yesterday! Words give not just undue importance but *duration* to vague passing thoughts.

I wonder if my discontent with myself doesn't proceed, at least in part, from the fact that I had to reread myself last week. Not just to myself, but spoken aloud, alone in front of a microphone in a glass cage, with technicians who nodded their heads from the other side of the enclosure.

It was for a record. Passages were chosen for me, one from *Pedigree*, the other from "Roman de l'Homme," and while I was reading I was seized with the urge to change everything, to cross it all out, I was ashamed of the imperfections in my text.

And to think that those who will listen to the record will believe that I revel in my prose! I left furious with myself. Why did I accept this chore ? First, because I didn't realize. Then because it belongs with the rest. As it is, I accept only the minimum of outside demands on the writer. How do those others, who are continually pushed before the public eye, manage to keep it up? I wonder.

Last night, in bed, thought of that famous rambling novel . . . which I'll never write. Against my wishes! Because, once for all, I've chosen a way which keeps me going in the same direction, leaving no room for fantasy. I'm wrong to persist in revolting against this discipline, though only occasionally. I don't know where I'm heading, but I follow the thread. Too bad if others get tired of it, if it seems monotonous or facile. I was going to write that it's none of my doing. Anyway, it's too late to change.

Still in a period of sulks. It makes me think how often we judge someone after a single meeting, without asking ourselves whether this person isn't going through a more or less exceptional phase. My present mood, for instance, is not my habitual mood. I know that in a few days, perhaps in twenty-four hours, it will have changed.

There are other cycles. For example, for three months I have lived a largely physical existence, amazed to be rid of my dizzy spells (which I rediscovered, or rather which rediscovered me today) and playing golf as if my life depended on it.

In these three months I haven't read one of the medical reviews which I habitually devour the moment they arrive, and which are piling up on their shelves.

Yesterday, for the first time, and because of what Sigaux said to me about it last week, I opened the definitive edition of the *Goncourt Journals,* the earlier edition of which disappointed me. Will this one also be disappointing? I read avidly, but also with irritation. Faced with all those stories about men of letters I feel so little the man of letters. Why not consider myself as a craftsman and be satisfied? It's so much more in character. And wasn't the craftsman's life what I dreamed of from twelve to sixteen?

I'm beginning, very vaguely, to feel the next novel sprouting— I hope to write it when I get back from Belgium—this too has something to do with my mood. Poor D. watches me out of the corner of her eye in these moments and doesn't know what to say, she's so afraid of irritating me. It's true that this morning I lost my temper over nothing, because I was clumsy at golf.

I hope my next novel, still so nebulous I hardly know anything about it, takes shape quickly!

/September 29, 1961

Johnny's birthday. He is extraordinary. He is the only one to understand my depression—which, really, is only physical, in spite of appearances. Just now I told him the story of the man sitting on the sidewalk at night howling like a dog at the moon. Questioned by a passerby, he only howled:

"I'm fed up with myself."

That didn't surprise Johnny, who admitted to me that this happens to him too, but that it would be hard to make his mother understand.

As if women didn't have their bad times too!

Their advantage is that it happens on a fixed date so that it's anticipated. Each month they have this safety valve!

/*October 4th*

Returned to the somewhat withdrawn but soft and almost voluptuous life in my study where everything will be perfect when it is time to light the fires. Attempt to get to the end of the *Goncourt Journals*. Have finished only the first volume and am as nauseated as when I read the first version twenty or thirty years ago.

It is one of the most depressing works I know, and in spite of that, once into it one goes on with simultaneous guilty conscience and pleasure. These malicious bits of gossip about personalities of the period, famous or not, remind one of today's reporting, and paradoxically, Goncourt was already complaining of this sort of low journalism, as he calls it.

He reports, probably with exactitude, sentences picked up at dinner tables, and pretends this is the way to depict a man. Other people's mediocrity, ill health, decline are what attract him.

Yes, everything is paradoxical, the ridiculous pretension to aristocracy, to artistic writing, to sophisticated taste in painting . . . not to mention the knickknacks, all that chinoiserie he delights in. . . . He thought he was creating a movement and he was only following the fashions of his times. He knew Manet, Degas, etc. But his gods in painting were the worst painters of the period. He denied the talent of Ingres, Delacroix, Courbet, etc. He saw nothing at all in Impressionism, which was emerging around him.

Only Savarin is great! . . . Maupassant is nothing but a little monster and a charlatan. . . . One could add examples *ad infinitum*.

Still, one reads on with curiosity because we learn of certain eccentricities, certain bedside secrets of great men of the period as today we learn about ours in the weeklies.

Two passages struck me. Berthelot announcing, around 1865, that within a century science would unriddle the atom. Claude Bernard making the same prediction about the living cell. They weren't far wrong.

Would like to get this over with. It's somewhat like an enema and may help my health.

Next week Liège. What I look forward to most is to show D. the chapel in the Bavière hospital where I served at Mass. Provided I won't feel disappointed.

No golf these days. No desire for physical life.

/Sunday, October 8th

Bad cold or slight grippe which I'm trying to get rid of before the trip to Liège and Germany, Wednesday. Living in my study and still immersed in the four fat volumes of the *Goncourt Journals*, which irritate me and which I want to be done with.

I'm in the middle of the third volume. More than a volume and a half to go, but it becomes more and more unpleasant. At sixty-five, with his friends old, sick, or dying, he no longer talks about anything but decrepitude and death.

At times I wonder if I'm the one who is abnormal. For after all, his portrait of literary society is pretty much the same as today's. My author or playwright friends meet each other at all the gatherings, the suppers, the receptions. I only see them by chance every other year or so, and have less and less desire to talk things over.

There was a time when I had an overwhelming need to be in contact with people, to go out, to talk, but I've always preferred people of other professions or even the man in the street. More and more I get a feeling of laziness at the thought of what is called conversation, perhaps because I know in advance what is going to be said to me, and that I am going to repeat myself with more or less smugness and be ashamed of it afterwards.

What's the use? It isn't a question of age, or else I was old at forty. I prefer to live with my own family, and a few contacts at long intervals are amply sufficient for me.

Is that good? Is it bad? I don't know. In any case, I can't seem to understand how people could meet for years—intelligent people, some truly superior—every week in the same setting to exchange the words one finds precisely noted in the *Journals* and which were selected as most interesting.

My God, what were the rest like? Last year, the year before, I lived a week in Paris in this milieu. Every day, lunch, dinner, or supper with people the papers talk about. How much a stranger, how ill at ease I felt! I learn more about men observing my children for an hour than in listening to those people for three or four evenings. And how much better I feel spending my evenings with D., even when we say nothing! Or when we go for our ride in the car in the afternoon!

Why did a Flaubert, a Zola, a Daudet, loaded with work—and, in Daudet's case, happy with his family—feel the need to rush together at each other's houses, or at the house of some princess, banker, whoever, as if they needed to reassure themselves of their importance or fame?

. . . .

In 1885 they were already talking about—not the *Nouveau Roman*, as today, but, in the same sense, the *Roman Nouveau*. Rosny discussed concrete and abstract art (in literature, not painting).

Then, in 1889, Goncourt, having stopped writing himself, announced that the novel was dead, that the form was definitely exhausted, that something else must be found! How difficult it is to grow old!

Remarks made in 1890 that could no doubt be heard in 1820, 1760, etc., etc.:

"Respectable women today look like . . ."

or: "behave like . . ."

"Youth no longer knows how to laugh . . ." ". . . no longer respects anything . . ." "youth today is made up of old men. . . ."

"The decadence of the press, the vulgarity, the dishonesties of journalists . . ." (in the seventeenth century, of gazetteers).

"The noise, the hurry, the hectic atmosphere of Paris . . ." "the exhausting pace of modern life . . ."

We go on repeating! And our sons and grandsons will go on repeating!

/October 19, 1961

Came back evening before last two days ahead of schedule. Do I get tired of traveling? I was happy to be home again, especially to be with the children. Now I'm anxious to write, in a couple of weeks probably, the novel that came to me in the car between Aix-la-Chapelle and Cologne.

In Liège, at night, a curious feeling seeing the same windows I used to look at at fifteen or sixteen, with their faintly lit shades permitting one to guess at the intimacy of family life within—and which used to fill me with a panicky urge to escape.

Finding them again, unchanged, I was almost afraid of becoming caught in a trap. Why there and not somewhere else? Then, however, Liège gratified all my wishes. One might say I've always run away from my youth. This time I went on purpose, to find it again at the chapel of the Bavière hospital where I served at Mass, in the Ursuline convent where we used to go Sundays to visit an aunt who was a nun, in certain streets where I used to walk, dreaming ambitiously of the future. But this pilgrimage was less for myself than to give D. a sense of my childhood.

My novel is coming closer. These last weeks no wish to write in this journal (?), which suddenly seems vain and pretentious to me. Yesterday, sixteenth anniversary of our meeting, of our life together, D.'s and mine. That is so much more important! Delighted that the children took part in this celebration, that they understand the importance of it for our little human group—and that for two or three years now we have replaced our individual birthdays with this anniversary as a couple.

Odd that I, furious individualist that I am, have not only accepted but passionately desired this cell, further enlarged by children—so long as these children need us; oughtn't I to understand, by this fact, that others accept—need—those larger cells that have always horrified me: the village, the province, the country, or a religion or party?

I realize quite well that I am stubborn on this point, that I will be to the end a man for the couple, the male and female in the jungle.

/*Sunday, November 18, 1961*

One more! Finished a new novel on Friday, *Les Autres*, which I haven't had the courage to type each morning as I usually do. Two sessions a day, writing by hand. D. is going to type it.

/*Sunday, December 17, 1961*

I would like to note—as on a calendar—next to the past days:
        nothing
        nothing
        nothing

nothing
nothing

Isn't this a good sign? I think so. No desire to write. Everyday life. D. and I spent a few days in Milan, so as to sleep in peace. Now she is typing my novel. I will revise it between holidays. Christmas soon. Spent much time agreeably, getting ready for it. A little room downstairs is full of packages.

The publication of *Betty*, coincidental with the end-of-the-year prizes, passed unnoticed. That hurts me a little, not for me but, I was about to write, for her.

It's a little as if she had not been given the chance to begin her independent existence. I don't attach too much importance to it. A twinge only because this novel marked a convalescence that was both physical and to some extent moral (end of discouragement, anxiety).

What was the point of all that?

December 17th: nothing.

It's simpler. And it means, all in all, happy days without history.

(Does that mean that I was less happy or more tormented or . . . etc., etc., when I wrote in these notebooks almost every day? I don't think so.)

/Monday, January 22, 1962

These past few days I've come very near to destroying these notebooks. I'm a bit ashamed of them. I wonder what forced me to write them.

Did it correspond to a period of rather poor health? The fact is that for almost two years I haven't felt at home in my skin, to use an expression I've often applied to my characters, with frequent dizzy spells at certain times of the day. If I haven't entirely got rid of them, I feel better, no longer worried. Have I simply passed through a sort of change of life?

Whatever it was, I think with a certain embarrassment of these notebooks whose pages I've been pleased to blacken. What have I really said? I don't know and I don't want to know.

What would humiliate me most would be to have unconsciously wound up taking myself seriously. Is this the case? Have I fallen into the trap of so many of my colleagues whom I see pontificating on television and in the columns of the newspapers, on literary juries, and elsewhere?

If so, I hope it's over and over for good now that I've regained my balance.

As for not destroying these pages . . . I'm certain it's not because I attach importance to whatever comes from my pen.

But primarily, someday this may show my children that I've had my weaknesses like everybody else; then who knows if, tempted to fall into the same pit again, it won't be enough to cast my eyes over a few of these pages to cure myself?

I'm not sure of anything, but if I had to make a quasi-medical diagnosis I would say that for about a year and a half I haven't been altogether myself, that I allowed myself to be troubled by various questions—aging, for example—to which there is no answer, and that finally, instead of keeping to my profession of novelist, I have not always avoided the temptation to philosophize.

This love for the four walls of my study, for long solitudes with my books, is not like me, and I am almost certain that it had a basis of anxiety.

Grippe—a very slight grippe, almost a voluptuous one—has kept me from writing my first novel of the year in January. In contrast to what happened last year, or what might have happened, this didn't bother me. I'll begin at the end of the month.

To give each thing its due importance. Have I, at long last, got there? I hope so, and if I don't write "The End" here it's more because of superstition, because I believe I really am cured.

Living without notebooks and without mirrors, except for shaving!

So long as I haven't made my family suffer during this time. And if I've upset them, ask their pardon!

P.S. If someday I add something to these notes, I promise to put it in context, to write at the top: "Second Crisis"—or "Relapse."

/*Saturday, February 10th*

Oh no! I'll write neither "Second Crisis" nor "Relapse." I even wonder if I ought not to write "End of Crisis" or, in case I should go on with these notebooks, "Family Chronicle."

Events that are important only to us but that are of the first order have just come to a head in the last three days, and I'm not sure if the preceding year wasn't disturbed for me by unconscious anticipation of them.

We just decided, suddenly, in a few hours, D. and I, not only to leave Echandens but to build—an idea that has often tempted me in the course of my life. The next day, we had already chosen land, an architect, and we go to the notary on Monday the 12th, the day of my official birthday, my fifty-ninth.

A new house, from top to bottom, made for us, conceived for us, for our life and our children's.

I'm very excited about it, too much so to talk about it now. But, once more, if I had to make a diagnosis, I wouldn't discard the idea that all the fermentation of the past twelve to eighteen months reflected in these notebooks had this unconscious need for renewal as its deepest source.

We'll see if I've succeeded.

/*Friday, March 16, 1962*

La Belle Epoque! That's an irrelevant aside. No doubt it's been said a hundred times. I just felt it very strongly, which is not the same thing. Just now, putting Johnny to bed, I was looking at the Canal Saint-Martin by Bernard Buffet in his room.

Today it gives the impression of a venerable old Paris, sentimental, picturesque. But in fact it is the picture of an iron footbridge across the hard metallic gates of a lock, a canal in straight lines. Six-story houses. Two with eight stories. A century ago, this was still countryside. Footbridge, lock, eight-story buildings must then have passed for the height of modernism, of the "life of tomorrow."

When I was a child, what was called "la Belle Epoque" was the Second Empire. When I was twenty, it was the period of 1900 to 1914. "Before the war" they said, too.

Now, "la Belle Epoque" is the one I lived as a young man, 1925–1930.

It has even begun to extend to 1939. And young people who say "before the war" mean the Second World War.

And people talk about the cruelty, the inhumanity, the implacability of "the machine" as once they talked about the first trains, the first cars, the first airplanes, which we feel so sentimental about today.

As the "terrible" skyscrapers in New York will make us sentimental in a few years, will appear as gently, humanly picturesque to us as the iron footbridge and the six- or eight-story houses on the Canal Saint-Martin.

This for my children, who will one day smile at our aerolites and the little metal spheres we send into space—which to them will be the suburbs of the earth.

Odd that officials, chiefs of state, continue to live and to receive one another in the palaces of another era, the Kremlin, Versailles, the Elysée, the White House, Buckingham Palace . . . as if they wanted to escape into the picturesque, however provisional, preferring the very old which, by virtue of its antiquity, has become "noble."

There are always people around us who live in "la Belle Epoque."

A week of television. Saw part of a Buñuel film, among others. Marvelous images. Thought of Gerelhrode (?), who just died. There are two kinds of artists. Total rebels, the irrational ones, who are against everything without distinction, and others who arrive at a certain acceptance without being duped. Curious that *all* those in the first category whom I've met are psychiatric cases. So? Where does that put acceptance?

/Friday, February 15, 1963
9:30 in the morning
32nd day

A whole month, my darling. Thirty-one days we have been apart. And I, from the first heart-rending day, I've had the temptation to take this notebook up again and write in it every morning and night.

If I haven't done so, it's because it would have been too sad, and these sadnesses must leave no traces behind them, no scars. No, later I only want to remember your courage, and also the re-discovery I have made of you, which may fill this emptiness I struggle against.

Not a true void, since I feel myself nearer to you than ever. It is rather a physical emptiness I strive to fill by occupying myself with the children and, on a more modest scale, with the house, waiting for the time to hurry to Prangins. Now I can tell you—for when you read this short note you will be well again—it has often been difficult for me to keep up a show

(First interrupted by your telephone call, then by a journalist. I'm beginning again at eleven fifteen.)

. . . of good humor. I haven't even the right to talk to you about your return, for I feel that you exert all your strength not to precipitate it, and I don't want to make your task even more difficult.

Actually this note is useless. I am sure you are going through the same trials that I am, that you too, at certain hours, have to make an effort not to weep and that you can't always keep your voice steady, even on the telephone—and you have to force yourself to smile when we leave each other at five o'clock.

This separation wasn't necessary to prove to us that we need to be together. For a month I have lived in a world that seems artificial to me. I know that it's the end.

Another few days, a week or ten days, perhaps, if not less. I won't ask you again if the doctor has been to see you, because you would come to share my impatience and would lose the benefit of the enforced rest.

You have been good, my D. Courageous.

And never for a moment have you lost your sweetness. I've seen adorable, touching sides of your nature that I don't believe I've appreciated before.

It's not a new life we're about to begin, of course, since all that has gone before has been good too, seventeen years, almost eighteen of happiness.

But we'll fit together better than ever, more warmly, in every curve and corner! Come quickly! I am greedy for you, in every sense. You caught me off guard this morning on the telephone, and I told you the truth about what I was doing, but I won't show you these lines until you return.

It has been hard, very hard, the hardest test of my life. But I know it was worth it, that it is worth it, and that our life together will be fuller than ever.

Soon, then, my D. Soon, dear girl whom I love and whom I keep lovingly and passionately within me.

End of the Third Notebook